Contents

T5-AFC-744

Quick Find Distance Chart

(Inside back cover)

Legend

Freeway / Divided Highway – sealed
Autobahn / Autostrasse
Autoroute / route rapide à chaussées séparées
Autostrada / superstrada

Freeway – future
Autobahn – im Bau
Autoroute – en construction
Autostrada – in costruzione

Major Highway – sealed / unsealed
Durchgangsstrasse – befestigt / unbefestigt
Route principale – revêtue / non revêtue
Strada di grande comunicazione – pavimentata /
    non pavimentata

Metroad
Metroad

Main Road – sealed / unsealed
Hauptstrasse – befestigt / unbefestigt
Route de communication – revêtue / non revêtue
Strada principale – pavimentata / non pavimentata

Minor Road – sealed / unsealed
Sonstige Strasse – befestigt / unbefestigt
Autre route revêtue / non revêtue
Altra strada – pavimentata / non pavimentata

Track, four-wheel drive only
Piste, nur mit 4-Rad-Antrieb befahrbar
Piste, utilisable pour véhicule à 4 roues motrices
Pista, praticabile solo con trazione integrale

Walking Track / Trail
Fussweg / Pfad
Sentier
Sentiero / viottolo

Total Kilometres
Totaldistanz in km
Distance totale en km
Distanza totale in km

★ 44 ★

Intermediate Kilometres
Teildistanz
Distance partielle
Distanza parziale

⸝ 20 ⸝ 24 ⸝

National Route Number / National Highway Number
Nationale Strassennummer / Nationale
    Durchgangsstrassen-Nummer
Numéro de route nationale / de route rapide
Numero della strada nazionale / Numero della
    strada di grande comunicazione

State Route Number
Staats–Strassennummer
Numéro de route d'Etat
Nùmero della strada dello stato

Railway – in use / disused
Eisenbahn – in Betrieb / stillgelegt
Chemin de fer – en service / abandonné
Ferrovia – in esercizio / interrotto

Lake or Reservoir
See oder Reservoir
Lac ou réservoir
Lago o lago artificiale

Intermittent or Salt Lake
Periodischer oder Salzwassersee
Lac périodique ou d'eau salée
Lago periodico o salato

National Park, Reserve
Nationalpark, Reservat
Parc national, réserve
Parco nazionale, riserva

Regional Reserve
Regionalreservat
Réserve régionale
Riserva regionale

Conservation, Protected Area
Schutzgebiet
Zone protégée
Regione protetta

Aboriginal Land
Aborigines–Gebiet
Région d'aborigènes
Regione d'aborigeni

City or Major Town
Gross–oder wichtige Stadt
Ville importante
Città grande o importante

Gawler ●

Town / Community / Locality
Stadt oder Gemeinde
Ville ou commune
Città o comunità

Skipton ●

Homestead
Gehöft
Ferme
Masseria

'Plumbago' ■

Tourist Point of Interest
Touristische Sehenswürdigkeit
Curiosité touristique
Curiosità turistica

Lookout ●

Rest Area with Toilet / Water Tank ... and with Overnight Camping
Rastplatz mit Toilette/Wassertank
    ... und Camping (nur 1 Nacht)
Aire de repos avec toilettes/citerne d'eau
    ... et camping (seulement 1 nuit)
Area di riposo con gabinetto/serbatoio d'acqua
    ... e campeggio (solo 1 notte)

Outback Roadhouse
Rasthaus im Hinterland (Outback)
Auberge dans l'arriere-pays (Outback)
Posto di ristoro nel retroterra (Outback)

Tourist Route
Touristenstrasse
Route touristique
Strada turistica

204

Airport
Flughafen
Aéroport
Aeroporto

✈

Mountain / hill
Berg / Hügel
Montagne / colline
Monte / colle

+ Mt Brown

State border
Staatsgrenze
Frontière d'Etat
Confine dello stato

Queensland

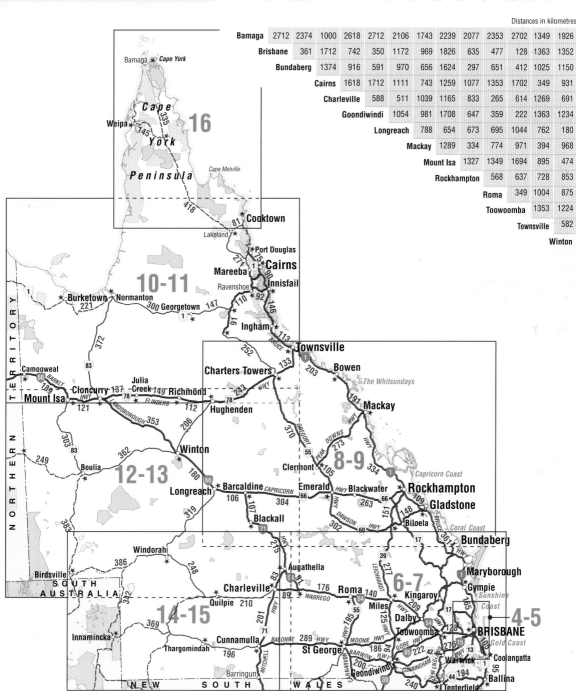

Distances in kilometres

Bamaga	2712	2374	1000	2618	2712	2106	1743	2239	2077	2353	2702	1349	1926
Brisbane		361	1712	742	350	1172	969	1826	635	477	128	1363	1352
Bundaberg			1374	916	591	970	656	1624	297	651	412	1025	1150
Cairns				1618	1712	1111	743	1259	1077	1353	1702	349	931
Charleville					588	511	1039	1165	833	265	614	1269	691
Goondiwindi						1054	981	1708	647	359	222	1363	1234
Longreach							788	654	673	695	1044	762	180
Mackay								1289	334	774	971	394	968
Mount Isa									1327	1349	1694	895	474
Rockhampton										568	637	728	853
Roma											349	1004	875
Toowoomba												1353	1224
Townsville													582
Winton													

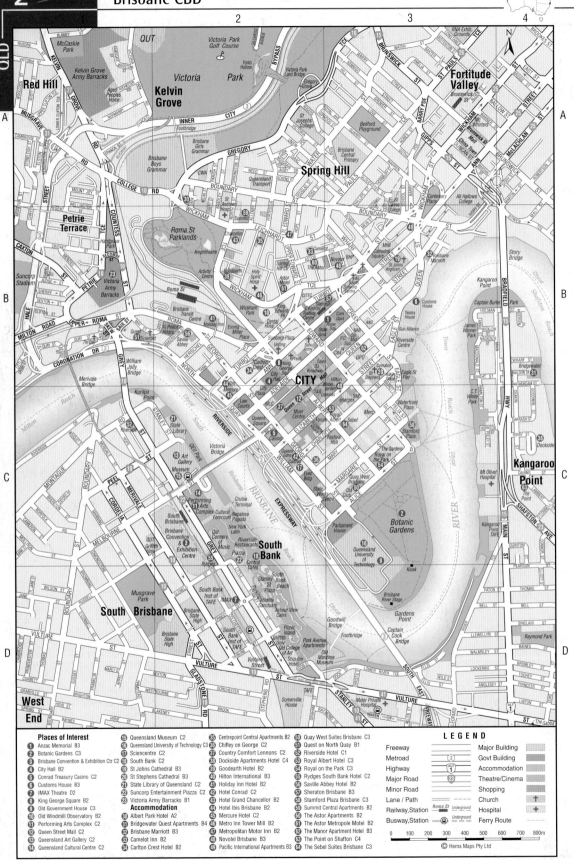

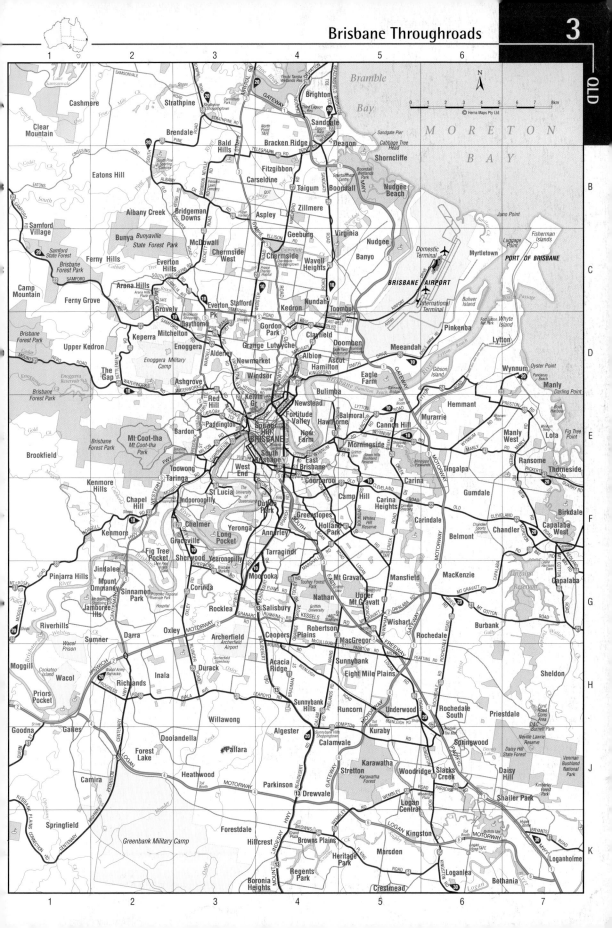

1 2 3 4 5 6 7

27°00'

153°30'

PACIFIC OCEAN

SOUTH

SOUTH PACIFIC OCEAN

15 km

© Hema Maps Pty Ltd

N

Cape Moreton
North Pt
Moreton Island National Park
Moreton Island
Comboyuro Pt
Bulwer
Cowan Cowan
Tangalooma
Tangalooma Pt
Kooringal
Campbell Pt
Reeders Pt
Amity Pt
Amity

MORETON BAY

Mud Island
St Helena Island
St Helena Island Nat Park
Fisherman Islands
White Patch
Juno Point

Sunshine Coast
For more detail on this area, see Hema's Sunshine Coast Map

Maroochydore
Alexandra Headland
Mooloolaba
Buddina
Warana
Bokarina
Wurtulla
Kawana Waters
Currimundi
Dicky Beach
Shelley Beach
Caloundra
Golden Beach
Pelican Waters
Sunshine Coast Turf Club

Bribie Island
Woorim
Skirmish Pt
Bongaree
South Pt
Bald Pt
Banksia Beach
Bellara
White Patch
Welsby
Godwin Beach
Sandstone Point
Ningi
Redcliffe
Scarborough
Margate
Woody Point
Clontarf

Pumicestone Channel
Bribie Island National Park
Toorbul
Meldale
Donnybrook
Beachmere
Deception Bay
Rothwell
Brighton
Sandgate
Shorncliffe
Nudgee Beach
BRISBANE AIRPORT

Buderim
SUNSHINE MWY
Mountain Creek
Tanawha
Forest Glen
Palmview
Eudlo
Mooloolah
Landsborough
Beerwah
Campbellville
Coochin Creek
Loralls Is
Thoorbos Is

Woombye
Palmwoods
Flaxton
Montville
Maleny
Witta
Wootha
Bald Knob
Cedarton
Peachester
Glass House Mountains
Beerburrum
Elimbah
Caboolture
Morayfield
Burpengary
Narangba
Deception Bay
Griffin
Bracken Ridge
Bald Hills
Aspley
Kallangur
Petrie
Lawnton
Strathpine
Albany Creek
Cashmere
Ferny Grove
Samford Valley
Camp Mountain

CONONDALE
Kondalilla Nat Park
Donovans Knob
Mt Cabinet
Conondale Nat Park
Mt Langley
Mt Raheighen
Borobin
Stanmore
Woodford
D'Aguilar
Delaneys Creek
Neurum
Mt McLean
Mt Mellum
Wamuran
Wamuran Basin
Bracalba
Upper Caboolture
Moodlu
Bellmere
Kurwongbah

RANGE
D'AGUILAR
Durundur
Pleurun
Mount Mee
Mt Mee
Ocean View
Mt Pleasant
Dayboro
Kurwongbah
Samsonvale
Mount Samson
Mt Kobble
Mt Samson
Cedar Creek
Mt Nebo
D'Aguilar Nat Park
Brisbane Forest Park
Mt England

Summer Mtn
Mt Cooke
Mt Kilcoy
Villeneuve
Glenfern
Winya
Mt Ann
Mt Archer
Mt Byron
Bulls Knob
Dundas
Wivenhoe Dam

Cononsale
Kilcoy
Lake Somerset
Mt Brisbane
Crossdale
Bryden
Wivenhoe

Yednia
Gregors Creek
Hazeldean Vale
Lower Cressbrook
Fulham Vale
Mt Beppo
Caboonbah
Moombra
Coominya
VALLEY

152°30'
Jimna
Monsildale
Mt Moore
27°00'
Mt Goomburgerung
Mt Brisbane
BRISBANE
Esk
Mt Hallen
Mt Esk
Split Yard Creek Dam
Coolana

Somerset Dam

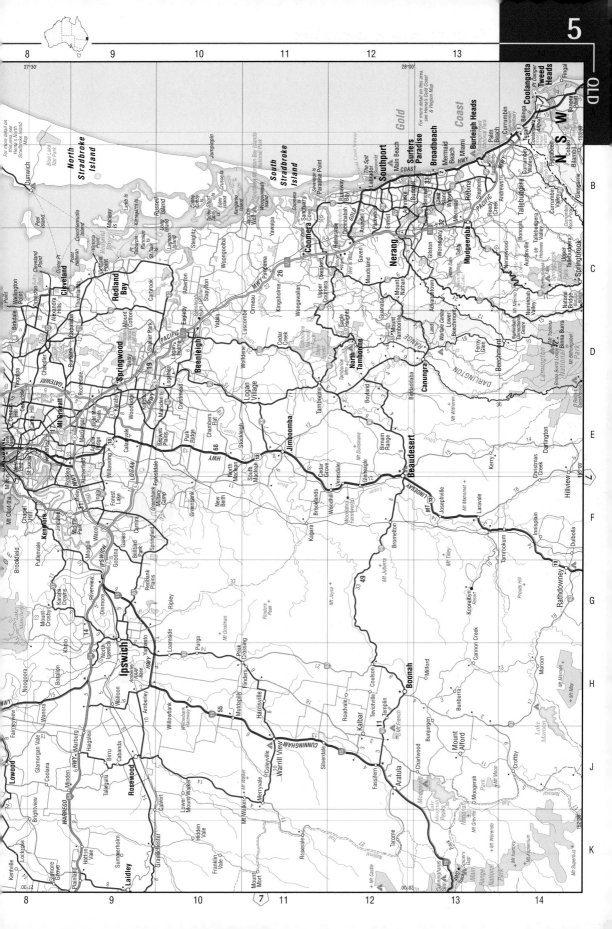

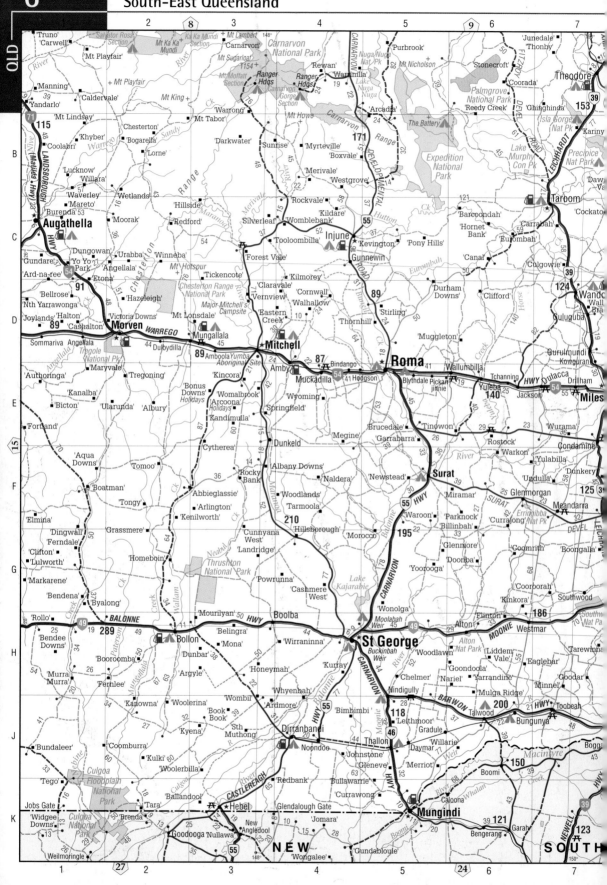

N

0   50km

© Hema Maps Pty Ltd

8   9   10   9   11   12   13

Kurrajong   Cania Gorge NP   Kalpowar   Kolan   Yandaran   Miara   Moore Park

Moonford   Mungungo   Bancroft   Monduran Dam   Avondale   Burnett Heads   Coral

landore   Three Moon   **Monto**   Mulgildie   Bargara   **Bundaberg**

Camboon   Rawbelle   South Kolan   Bullyard   Rum Distillery   Elliott Heads   HERVEY BAY   Rooney Pt   Sandy Cape

'Barram'   Abercorn   Gin Gin   Elliott   Burrum Coast   MARINE PARK   Platypus   Maroo Bay

'Glencoe'   Tireen   Cynthia   **113**   Wallaville   Woodgate   Hervey Bay   Whale Watching   Orchid Beach   Waddy Point

racow   Wuruma Dam   'Rosslyn'   Mount Perry   Cordalba   Goodwood   Burrum Heads   Great Sandy National Park

'Calrossie'   Ceratodus   **Eidsvold**   'Kerwee'   Booyal   Isis Junction   **Hervey Bay**   Cathedral Beach

'Redbank'   'Widbury'   Binjour   Byrnestown   Dallarnil   **Childers**   **118**   Howard   Torbanlea   Woody Is   Happy Is   Fraser Island

'Yerilla'   **Mundubbera**   **52**   **Biggenden**   Brooweena   Tenthills Dam   River Heads   Kingfisher Bay

'Hawkwood'   Dykehead   **Gayndah**   Coalstoun Lakes   ISIS   **86**   **Maryborough**   Eurong   SOUTH

Mt Misery   Ban Ban Springs   Mt Walsh Nat Pk   Aramara   Mungar   Maaroom   Boonooroo

'Auburn'   Mt Saul   **147**   Teebar   Poona   Poona   Hook Point   Inskip Point

Monogorilby   Brovinia   **75**   Boogooramunya   Mt Bauple Nat Pk   Tiaro   Tuan   Wide Bay

'Pinedale'   Lake Boondooma   Boondooma Dam   Windera   **17**   Tansey   Kilkivan   Woolooga   Bauple   Military Training Area   Tin Can Bay   Rainbow Beach   Double Island Point

enrowan'   Allies Creek   Proston   Theebine   **81**   Glenwood   Gunalda   Cherry Venture

Barakula   'Durah'   Hivesville   Byee   Goomeri   WIDE   BAY   **75**   Wolvi   Great Sandy National Park

'Fairyland'   **Murgon**   Manyung   Glastonbury   **Gympie**   Kin Kin   Lake Cootharaba   PACIFIC

lumboola   Baking Board   Wondai   Cherbourg   Manumbar   Amamoor   Cooran   Boreen Pt   Laguna Bay

Goombi   Canaga   Tingoora   Wooroolin   **82**   Elgin Vale   Kandanga   Pomona   Tewantin   Noosa Nat Pk

ndamine   Boonarga   **Kingaroy**   Memerambi   Lake Barambah   Imbil   Cooroy   **Noosa Heads**

Chinchilla   WARREGO   **Jandowae**   Kumbia   **173**   Goodger   Lake Borumba   Brooloo   **122**   Euchindi   Coolum Beach

Brigalow   Cootanga North   **Nanango**   Jimna   Kenilworth   Yandina   **Nambour**   **Maroochydore**   Sunshine

Warra   **82**   Bunya Mtns Nat Pk   Yarraman   D'AGUILAR   Yednia   Conondale NP   Mapleton   Alexandra Headland   Mooloolaba   Coast

Kogan   **126**   **54**   Bell   Cooyar   Conondale   Montville   Buderim   OCEAN

Macalister   Jimbour   Pirrinuan   Blackbutt   Kilcoy   Maleny   **Caloundra**

Daandine   Kaimkillenbun   Wutul   Blackbutt   Moore   **85**   Beerwah   Bribie Is Nat Park

th Tara   Goranba   Weranga   Gulera   **Dalby**   Quinalow   Harlin   Somerset Dam   Glass Hs Mts   Beerburrum   Bribie Island   Cape Moreton

awin'   Kumbarilla   Peranga   Kulpi   Haden   **118**   Toogoolawah   L. Somerset   Woodford   Bongaree   Moreton Island Nat Park

Tulagarie   Bowenville   Jondaryan   Acland   Crows Nest   Esk   Wamuran   **43**   Moreton Island   Tangalooma

'Halliford'   **83**   Goombungee   Crows Nest Nat Pk   **Caboolture**   Deception Bay

112   Oakey   Merengandan   Hampton   Cooinya   Dayboro   Deception Bay   For more detail on this area, see Hema's South East Queensland Map

Cecil Plains   Aubigny   Murphys Ck   Helidon   Lowood   Petrie   **Redcliffe**

'Waar Waar'   **49**   **TOOWOOMBA**   **54**   Gatton   Marburg   Strathpine   Samford   Amity   Point Lookout

Moonie   Brookstead   Cambooya   Laidley   **IPSWICH**   **BRISBANE**   Bay   Blue Lake Nat Pk

'New Dunmore'   Pittsworth   Greenmount   Rosewood   **128**   Capalaba   Dunwich   North Stradbroke Island

River   **222**   Nobby   Clifton   **42**   **Logan**   Redland Bay

Millmerran   **84**   **162**   **15**   Jimboomba   **Beenleigh**   South Stradbroke Island

'Allawah'   Leyburn   Allora   Aratula   Kalbar   Tamborine   **105**   Coomera

'Trevanna Downs'   **85**   GORE   Karara   Hendon   Boonah   **13**   **Southport**   Gold

'Wyaga'   Leslie Dam   **Warwick**   **283**   **Nerang**   **Surfers Paradise**

Bendidee Nat Pk   CUNNINGHAM   Mt Barney   Beaudesert   **Broadbeach**

oondiwindi   Inglewood   **200**   Cobba-da-mana   Killarney   Rathdowney   Canungra   Mudgeeraba   Burleigh Heads   Coast

Whetstone   **42**   Coolmunda Dam   **15**   Woodenbong   Binna Burra   Springbrook   **Coolangatta**   **Tweed Heads**

Gilbell   Yelarbon   Pikedale   **114**   MT LINDESAY   Urbenville   Tyalgum   Kingscliff

Kurumbul   Limevale   Kunghur   Uki   Pottsville

aroi   North Star   **Stanthorpe**   Sundown Nat Park   Wiangaree   Mullumbimby   **Murwillumbah**   Ooonabah   **95**   **Brunswick Heads**

Texas   Wallangarra   Nimbin   Cape Byron   **Byron Bay**

240   **44**   Silver Spur   Mole River   **127**   **44**   **Casino**   **Lismore**   Lennox Head

Bonshaw   Glenlyon Dam   BRUXNER   Alice   Mt Pikapene Nat Pk   Coraki   Broadwater   **Ballina**

WALES   **Tenterfield**   Woodburn   **Evans Head**

For more detail on this area, see Hema's Fraser Island and Wide Bay - Burnett Maps

For more detail on this area, see Hema's Sunshine Coast Map

Major towns: Townsville, Ayr, Home Hill, Bowen, Proserpine, Charters Towers, Hughenden, Pentland, Collinsville, Moranbah, Clermont, Capella, Emerald, Dysart, Longreach, Barcaldine, Aramac, Muttaburra, Isisford, Blackall, Tambo, Springsure, Alpha, Rolleston

Grid columns: 1 · 2 · 11 · 3 · 4 · 5 · 6 · 7

Grid rows: A · B · C · D · E · F · G · H · J · K

Route/distance markers: 252, 244, 53, 78, 133, 115, 88, 38, 32, 46, 191, 257, 273, 203, 55, 243, 205, 124, 150, 183, 167, 105, 66, 168, 136, 107, 163, 100, 246, 248, 70, 106, 246

Selected place names:
Lyndhurst, 'Clarke River', Bluewater, Pallarenda, Yabulu, Deeragun, Cape Cleveland, Cape Bowling Green, Darley Reef, Kangaroo Reef, 'Oak Park', 'Werrington', 'Oak Valley', 'Star', Niall', Spring Creek, Bluewater Springs Roadhouse, Thuringowa, Nome, Antill Plains, Mt Stuart, Toonpan, Mt Elliot, Alva Beach, Old Reef, 'Craigie', 'Maryvale', 'Allensleigh', Dotswood, Woodstock, Calcium, Reid River, Giru, Barratta, Brandon, Rita Island, Peters Is, Cape Upstart, 'Cuba Plains', 'Felspar', 'Southwick', 'Toomba', 'Burdekin Downs', Macrossan, Millaroo, Clare, Woodhouse, Inkerman, Gumlu, Abbot Point, Gloucester Island, 'Maiden Springs', 'Reedy Springs', 'Myrrlumbing', 'Fern Spring', Sellheim, Millchester, Sherri Cross, 'Cardigan', Ravenswood, 'Strathalbyn', 'Strathbogie', Merinda, Bowen, George, 'Mount Sturgeon', 'Mt Emu Plains', Killarney, Powlathanga, Balfe's Creek, Mt Leyson Mine, 'Brittania', Dalbeg, 'Mt Abbott', Mt Aberdeen National Park, Mt Dangar, Jaragal, Briaba, Almoola, Proserpine, 'Boonderoo', 'Mt Emu Plains', Goldsborough, 'Oak Vale', Homestead, Cornella, Kimburra, 'Bracebrough', Mt Windsor, 'Bletchington Park', Merricourt, 'Pallamana', 'Mt Cooper', 'Saint Pauls', Strathmore, Scottville, Collinsville, Bloomsbury, Mt Crompton, Yalboroo, 'Torver Valley', Pentland, Warrigal, Cape River, 'Wambiana', 'New Victoria Downs', 'Corea Plains', Victoria Downs, 'Harvest Home', Lake Dalrymple, Burdekin Falls Dam, 'Glendon', Heidelberg, 'Havilah', Birralee, Hughenden, 'Blantyre', Torrens Creek, Burra, 'Lauderdale', 'Milray', Pajingo, Broadleigh Downs, Egera, 'Mt Elsie', 'Lornesleigh', 'Ukalunda', Pyramid, 'Conway', 'Mt McConnell', 'Hidden Valley', Mt Leslie, 'Afton Downs', Jardine Valley, Tindo, 'Oakley', 'Oxenhope O.S.', 'Natal Downs', 'Mirtna', Dawson Vale, Mt Bingeringo, 'Plain Creek', 'St Anns', Ibis Creek, Mount Coolon, 'Mt Lookout', 'Glen Eva', 'Whynot', 'Weetalaba', 'Byerwen', 'Redcliffe Vale', Newlands Mine, 'Newlands', Glenden, Eungella, 'Nettledale Vale', Homevale Resources Res, 'Exevale', 'Arrara', Cheltenham, 'Wowra Park', 'Koburra', 'Tarella', 'Cranford', Ulva', 'Yarrowmere', Blackwood Nat Park, Belyando Crossing, 'Bulliwallah', 'Wilandspey', Glen Park, 'Disney', 'Avon Downs', 'Warrego', 'Gunjula', 'Suttor Downs', Elphinstone, Mt Britton, 'Catumnal', 'Dunrossie', Thornton', 'Caledonia', Forest Den Nat Park, 'Bowie', 'Kyong', 'Labona', 'Doongmabulla', 'Elgin Downs', 'Wyena', Moranbah, 'Diamond Downs', 'Nungaroo', Coppabella, 'Levuka', Bangall, 'Potosi', Thistlebank, Lake Galilee, 'Jochimus', 'Bimbah East', Epping Forest Nat Park, 'Epping Forest', Frankfield, 'Kilcummin', 'Solferino', Peak Downs Mine, Saraji Mine, 'Bombandy', Cumberland Downs, 'Niagara', Peak Range Nat Park, 'Cotherstone', Dysart, 'Kensington Downs', 'Bungoona', Muttaburra, 'Bowen Downs', 'Tyrone', 'Ranken', 'Coorabah', Eastmere, Maynard, 'Laglan', Mt Donnybrook, 'Clonmell', 'Cairo', 'Beresford', 'Kalang', 'Monteagle', Blair Athol, Clermont, Copperfield, German Creek Mine, Tieri, 'Norwich Park', Middlemount, 'Lillianfels', 'Kingsborough', 'Highbury', 'The Lake', Widgeman', Chunie Vale', Dunrobin', 'Albro', 'Recruit', Springvale, 'Retro', Capella, Oaky Creek Mine, Gregory Mine, 'Dalmore', 'Payne', 'Dilulla', 'Rodney Downs', 'Auteuil', Taree', 'Politic', 'Rangers Valley', 'Boongoondoo', 'Cremorne', 'Old Banchory', 'Kingston', Carmmoor Resources Res, 'Forrester', 'Retro', 'Kabelbara', Jurema, Langley Downs, 'Darr River Downs', 'Darriveen', 'Westbury', Aramac, 'Crossmoor', 'Glenample', 'Ravenswood', Lennox', 'Degulla', Surbiton, 'Islay Plains', 'Craven', Burtle, Sapphire, Rubyvale, Anakie, Taroborah, Fairbairn Dam, 'Yamala', Comet, 'Gindie', Gadwell', 'Melton', Pine Hill, Bogantungan, Withersfield, 'Kelbar', 'Tango', Emerald, Longreach, Ilfracombe, Barcaldine, Jericho, 'Eureka', 'Oakleigh', Alpha, Willows, Willows Gemfield, 'Ducabrook', 'Minerva', Rutland', 'Bonnie Doon', Turkey Creek, 'Fernlees', Springsure, Devonshire', 'Dandaraga', 'Clover Hills', 'Stratford', Lancevale, Joycedale, Sedgeford, Avonmore, Avoca, 'Urambie', Home Creek, 'Evora', 'Mena Park', Yalleroi, 'Durrandella', 'Marston', Blacks Palace, 'Alpha', Glen Avon, Joe Joe', 'Echo Hills', Snake Range Nat Pk, Vandyke, Minerva Hills Nat Pk, 'Orion Downs', Isisford, 'Oma', 'Rutland Park', 'Bilbah Downs', Springfield, Thornleigh, Glenstuart, Blackall, 'Champion', 'Cheshire', 'Fairview', 'Mantuan Downs', 'Nandowrie', 'Riverside', Heathwood, Meteor Downs, Albinia Downs, Rolleston, 'Glen Alton', 'Springleigh', Benlidi, Malverton, 'Bloomfield', The Springs', Windeyer', 'Killarney Park', 'Kelpum', 'Truno', 'Carwell', Castlevale, 'Kia Ota', 'Kareela', Lake Salvator, Savador Rosa Section, Carnarvon National Park, Mt Lord, Tanderra, 'Emmet', 'Albilbah', 'Ungo', Konupa, 'Milton Downs', 'Carlow', 'Bonnie Doon', 'Brides Creek', Tambo, Jabinda', 'Ivanhoe', 'Manning', 'Caldervale', Mt Playfair, Peawaddy', Consuelo', Rewan', 'Wardinilla', Yaraka, 'Highlands', Idalia National Park, 'Koondoo', 'Minnie Downs', 'Forest Hill', Lansdowne', Mt King, Ranger Hqds, 'Mt Sugarloaf', 'Mt Moffatt Section', 'Nuga Nuga'

State/developmental roads labeled: GREGORY DEVELOPMENTAL ROAD, FLINDERS HWY, BRUCE HWY, LANDSBOROUGH HWY, CAPRICORN HWY, DAWSON DEVELOPMENTAL ROAD, GREGORY HWY, CARNARVON DEVELOPMENTAL ROAD, KENNEDY DEVELOPMENTAL ROAD, MATILDA HWY

© Hema Maps Pty Ltd

0   50   100km

N

SOUTH

CORAL

Barrier

Reef

PACIFIC

SEA

OCEAN

GREAT BARRIER REEF MARINE PARK

Mackay / Capricorn Section

TROPIC OF CAPRICORN

Marion
Reef

Hardy
Reef

Black Reef East

Hook Reef

Hayman Island
Hook Island
WHITSUNDAY GROUP
Border Island
Whitsunday Island
Whitsunday Islands Nat Park
Hazelwood Island
Hamilton Island
Lindeman Island
Lindeman Islands Nat Park
Shaw Island
The
Whitsundays

Long
Island

Blacksmith Is
Smith Islands Nat Park
Goldsmith Is   Linne Island

Rabbit Is   Carlisle Is
Newry Is NP
Brampton Is
Hillsborough NP

Cockermouth
Is
Wigton Island
Scawfell Is
Sth Cumberland Islands Nat Park
Calder Is

St Bees Is

Bucasia
Slade Point

Mackay
Bakers Creek
Hay Point

Prudhoe Is

Knight Is
Digby Is
Hotspur Island
NORTHUMBERLAND
ISLANDS Nat Park

POMPEY

COMPLEX

Ripetide
Cay

Elusive
Reef

Campwin Beach

Sarina
Llewellyn Bay

Cape Palmerston
Koumala
Greenhill
Temple Is
Cape Palmerston Nat Park
Curlew Is

Pine Peak Island

Middle
Island   Percy Isles NP
North East Island
PERCY ISLES
South Island

Thomas
Cay

Koumala
South
Iibilbie

Yarrawonga Point
West Hill Is
Poynter
Island

West Hill
Orabie
West Hill

SWAIN REEFS
National Park

Carmila
Carmila Beach
Flaggy Rock
Bamborough
Is
Aquila Is Wild Duck Is
DUKE ISLANDS

Gannet
Cay

'Collaroy'
Blaie
North Pt
Marble Is   Hexham Is

High Peak Island

Cheviot Island

Clairview
Clairview Bluff
Kalarka
Stanage
229
Long
Island

Broad
Sound

Arthur Pt
Quail Is

Shoalwater Broad
Con Is Bay

Cape Townshend

St Lawrence
Rosewood Is
Torilla

Leicester Is
Collins Is
Townshend Island
Reef Point

'Croydon'
Wumalgi

Warginburra
Peninsula
Peninsula

Perforated Point

Peninsula
Double Mtn

Cape Manifold

Ogmore
Bowman
Kooltandra

SHOALWATER BAY
MILITARY TRAINING AREA

Cape Clinton
Freshwater Bay
Cliff Point

Tooloombah
Marlborough
Princhester

Byfield
Stockyard Point
Byfield National Park
Water Park Point

For more detail on this area, see
Hema's Central Queensland Map

'Apis Creek'
Kunawarara
'Eden Garry'

Capricorn

Capricorn
Resort

Channel

105
Kaiuroo
'Burkan'

Yaamba
The Caves
Mt Etna Caves
Nat Park

North Keppel Island

North Reef

Ridgelands
Parkhurst
Yeppoon
Roslyn
Bay
Great Keppel Island

Dalma
Gracemere
Kabra
Cawarral
Emu Park

North West Is
Tryon Is
Wilson Is
Wreck Island

'Melmoth'
Foleyvale
Rockhampton

Keppel Sands

North West Is

CAPRICORN
Heron Island
Scientific

Capricornia Cays

Blackwater
Bluff
Dingo
Duaringa

Stanwell
Wycarbah
Bouldercombe

Mount
Morgan
17

Broadmount

Cape Keppel

Erskine Is
Masthead Is

One Tree Island
National Park

Parnabal
Gogango

Bajool
Marmor

Port Alma

Curtis Island
Black Head

GROUP

'Eastbrook'
Dululu
145

109

Raglan
Ambrose
Southend
Yarwun

Fitzroy Reef

Llewellyn Reef

'Wooronah'
Wowan
Mt Alma
Mount Larcom

Facing Island

Hoskyn Islands
Scientific

Woorabinda

Dawes

Bedford
39
17
Rannes

Calliope
Taragoola
Barmundu

Gladstone
Boyne Island
Tannum Sands

BUNKER GROUP
Fairfax Islands
Lady Musgrave
Island

Baralaba
Mimosa Park

Jambin
60
102

Callide
'Bindawalla'
Boynedale

Rodds
Bay

Richards Point

Bustard Point

Round Hill Head Joseph Banks (Round Hill Head) Lady Elliot Island

'Barranga'

Gbovigen
Weitalaba
Nagoorin

Castle
Tower
Nat Park

Iveragh
Bororen

Euripibica
Nat Park

Seventeen Seventy
Agnes Water

Con Ford

Goomally

46
Banana

Callide
Coalfields

Biloela
Thangool

Callide Dam

Ubobo

Mirriam Vale

Deepwater Nat Park

Bauhinia
166
Moura

60
54
'Junedale'

Dawes
Range

Many Peaks
Builyan

162

Makowata

Rules Beach
Lowmead
Wartburg

Littlemore
Lake
Cania

Kroombit Tops
National Park

Mt Molangul

Rosedale

Littabella
Winfield
Norval Park

Bauhinia
Downs'
Thonby

Glandore

97

Gania Gorge
Monfort
Mungungo
Bancroft

Kalpowar

Yandaran
Avondale
Moore Park

Monduran
Dam

Bargara
South Kolan
Bundaberg

HERVEY BAY
Coral
MARINE PARK

Sandy Cape

'Stonecroft'
'Coorada'
Palmgrove
National Park

Theodore

Monto
Mulgildie

Three Moon
17

Bullyard

Bundaberg
Rum Distillery

Marloo
Bay

Orchid
Bay

Coast
Platypus Bay
Waddy Point

Nicholson'
Rawbelle
Camboon
Gin Gin
Elliott

Elliott Heads

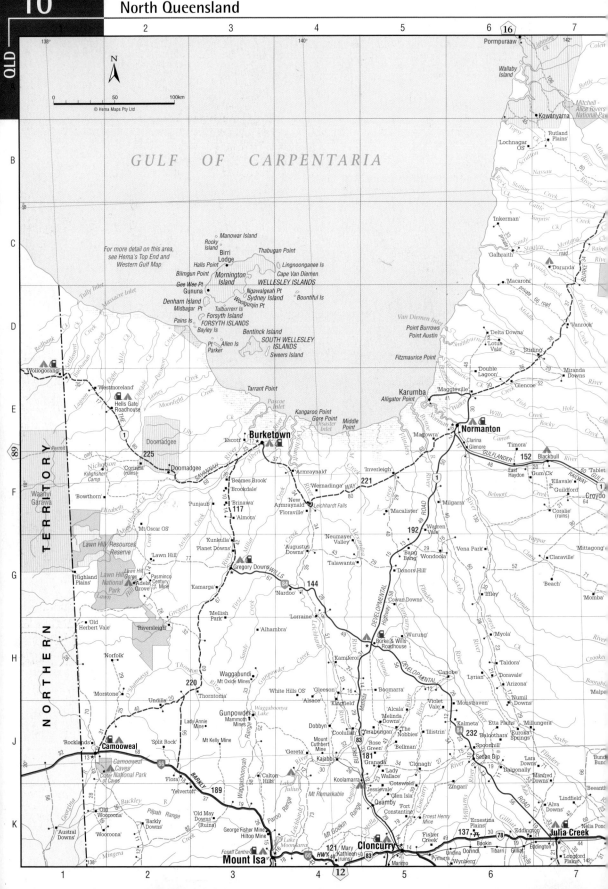

GULF OF CARPENTARIA

For more detail on this area,
see Hema's Top End and
Western Gulf Map

© Hema Maps Pty Ltd

N

0   50   100km

138°   140°   142°

Pormpuraaw

Wallaby
Island

Kowanyama

'Lochnagar
OS'

Rutland
Plains'

'Inkerman'

'Galbraith'

Manowar Island
Rocky
Island
Birri
Lodge
Halls Point
Thabugan Point
Bilmgun Point
Lingnoonganee Is
Cape Van Diemen
Gee Wee Pt
Mornington
Island
WELLESLEY ISLANDS
Gununa
Ngawalgeah Pt
Sydney Island
Woolgunjin Pt
Denham Island
Bountiful Is
Midbagar Pt
Tulburrer Is
Forsyth Island
Pains Is
FORSYTH ISLANDS
Bayley Is
Bentinck Island
Pt
Allen Is
SOUTH WELLESLEY
Parker
ISLANDS
Sweers Island

'Macaroni'

'Dorunda'

'Vanrook'

'Delta Downs'
'Lotus
Vale'
Stirling
Point Burrows
Point Austin
Van Diemen Inlet
'Double
Lagoon'
Fitzmaurice Point
'Miranda
Downs'
'Maggieville'
Karumba
Alligator Point
'Magowra'
Normanton
Clarina
Glenore
'Glencoe'
Timora'
GULFLANDER
152
Blackbull
East
Haydon
'Gum' Ck'
Ellavale'
Guildford
Croydo
'Coralie
(ruins)
Van Diemen Inlet

Tarrant Point

Kangaroo Point
Gore Point
Middle
Point
Pascoe
Inlet
Disaster
Inlet

Wollogorang

'Westmoreland'

Hells Gate
Roadhouse

Doomadgee

225

Escott'
Burketown

'Beames Brook'
'Brookdale'
'Brinawa'
'Almora'

Armraynald'

'Inverleigh'

'Wernadinga'
'New
Armraynald'
'Floraville'
Leichhardt Falls

'Macalister'

'Milgarra'

192

'Warren
Vale'

'Vena Park'

'Mittagong'

'Claraville'

'Beach'

'Momba'

'Iffley'

NORTHERN   TERRITORY

89

'Bowthorn'
Waanyi
Garawa
Nicholson
'Corinda
(ruins)
Doomadgee
Kingfisher
Camp
'Punjaub'
117
'Mt Oscar OS'
Lawn Hill Resources
Reserve
'Lawn Hill'
'Highland
Plains'
Lawn Hill
National
Park
Lawn Hill
Gorge
Adels
Grove
Pasminco
Century
Mine

'Kunkulla'
'Planet Downs'
Gregory Downs
'Kamarga'
'Nardoo'
144
'Augustus
Downs'
'Neumayer
Valley'
'Talawanta'
'Bang
Bang'
Wondoola
'Donors Hill'
WILLS
84

'Old
Herbert Vale'
'Riversleigh'
'Norfolk'
'Morstone'
'Mellish
Park'
'Alhambra'
Lorraine
Waggabundi
Mt Oxide Mines
220
Thorntonia
Undilla
Kamileroi'
'White Hills OS'
'Gleeson'
Alsace
'Boomarra'
'Canobe'
Burke & Wills
Roadhouse
'Wurung'
DEVELOPMENTAL
'Taldora'
'Doravale'
'Arizona'
'Myola'
'Lyrian'
'Numil
Downs'
DEVELOPMENTAL HIGHWAY
'Monstraven'

Gunpowder
Mammoth
Mines
Lady Annie
Mine
'Split Rock'
Mt Kelly Mine
Dobbyn
Coolullah
'Tarabungan'
Alcala
Melinda
Downs'
Violet
Vale'
The
Nobbies
Illistrin
232
Kalmeta
'Etta Plains'
Millungera'
'Euroka
Springs'

Camooweal
66
Camooweal
Caves
Crater National Park
of Caves
'Flora'
Yelvertoft
189
'Rocklands'
'Calton
Hills'
'Gereta'
Kajabbi
'Rose
Green'
'Bellman'
83
181
'Granada'
'Cotswold'
'Clonagh'
Lady
Wallace'
Koolamarra
Spoonhill'
Sedan Dip
'Lara
Downs'
Dalgonally'
'Manfred
Downs'
'Lindfield'
'Alva
Downs'
'Austral
Downs'
'Old
Wooroona'
'Barkly
Downs'
'Old May
Downs'
(Ruins)
George Fisher Mine
Hilton Mine
Mt Godkin
'Woolroona'
BARKLY
'Fort
Constantine'
Quamby
'Jessievale'
'Glen Isla'
Ernest Henry
Mine
'Ernestina
Plains'
137
Bookin
78
'Eddington'
Nelia Pond
Julia Creek

Mount Isa
121
66
Cloncurry
83
Mary
Kathleen
(ruins)
Fisher
Creek
Fossil Centre
Lake
Moondarra
Marimo
Wynberg'
Oorindi
Tibarri
Gilliat
Eddington
'Longford
Plains'
Beeantt

12

1   2   3   4   5   6   7

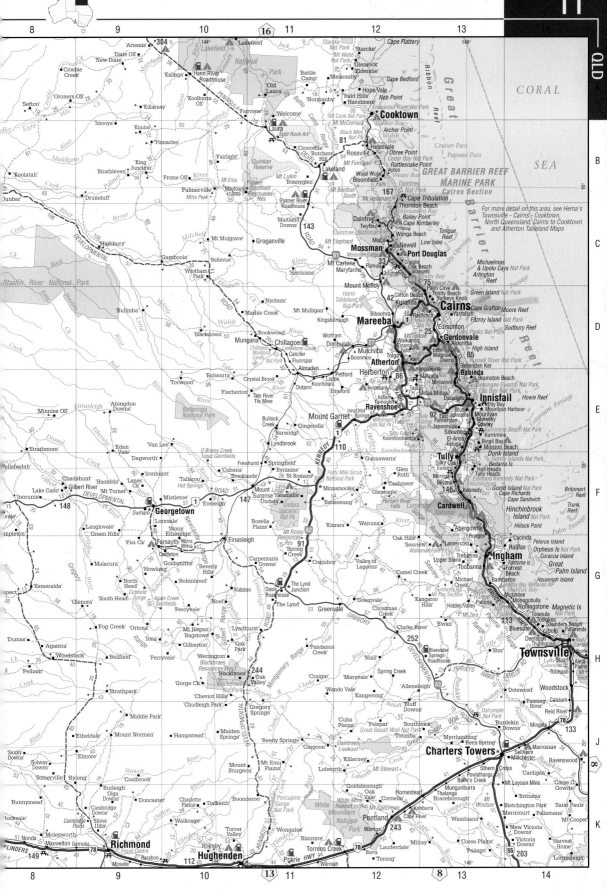

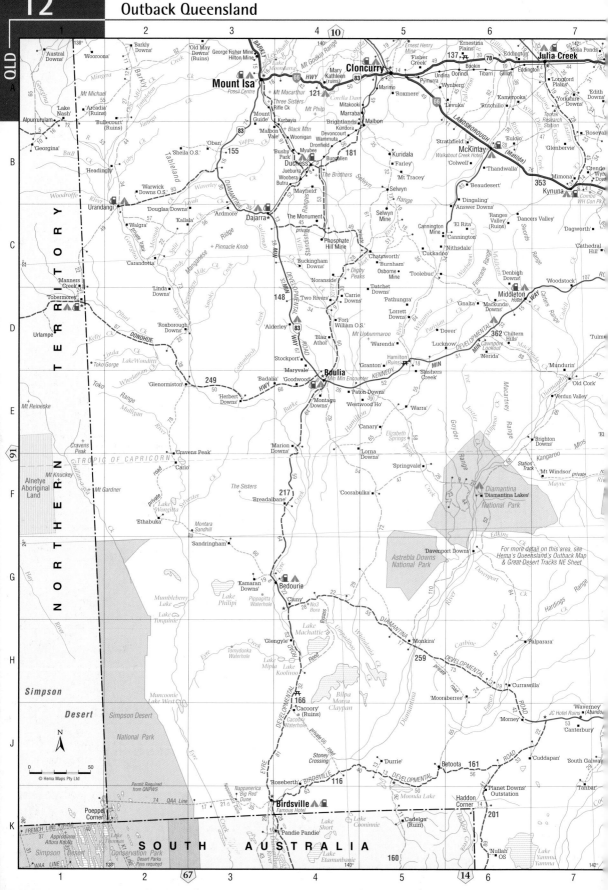

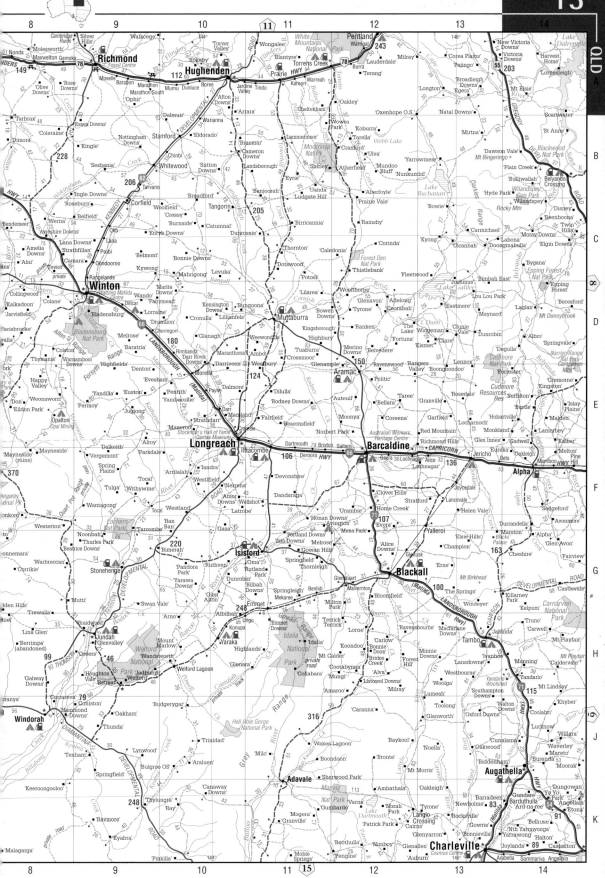

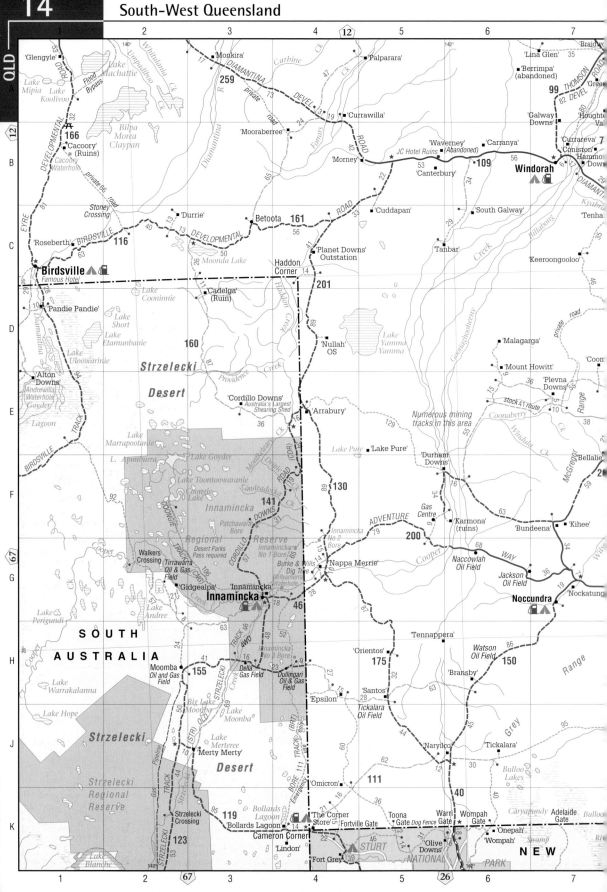

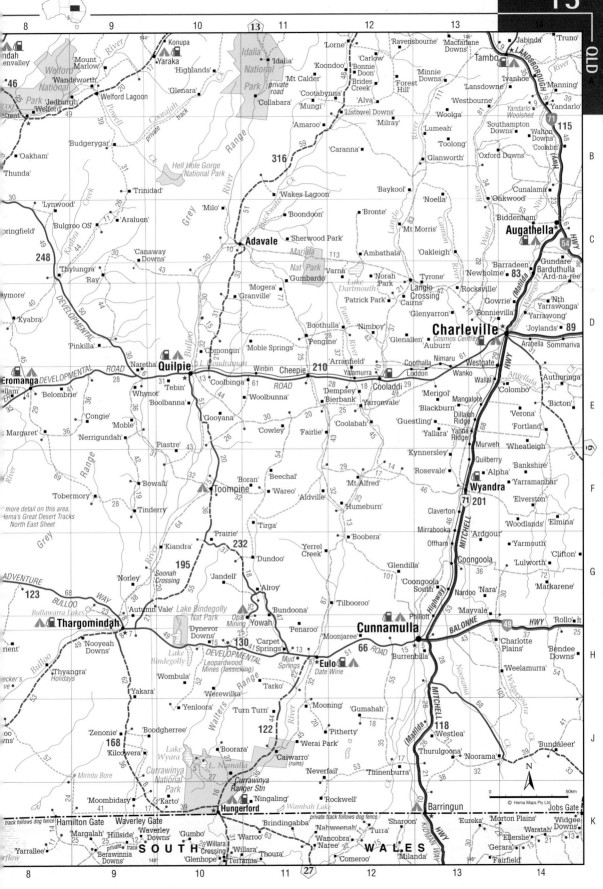

N

0   50   100km
© Hema Maps Pty Ltd

TORRES STRAIT

Orman Reef
Gabba Island
Zagai Island
Yam Island
Mabuiag Island
Sassie Island
Boot Reef
Badu Island
Moa Island
Suarji Island
Getullai Island
Mt Ernest Island
Ashmore Reefs
West Island
Hawkesbury Island
East Strait Is
Wednesday Island
Hammond Island
Goods Island
Friday Island
Thursday Island
Horn Island
Wasaga
Prince of Wales Island
Muralug
Possession Is
Cape York
Little Adolphus Island
Mount Adolphus Island
Albany Island
'Somerset' (ruins)

ARAFURA

Endeavour Strait
Seisia
Umagico
NPD
Injinoo
Bamaga
Escape River Fish Habitat Res
Van Spoult Head
Turtle Head Island
Sharp Point
Crab Island
Furze Point
Jardine River Resources Res
Ussher Point

Jardine River National Park

Orford Bay
Denham Group
Nat Park
Orford Ness
Puddingpan Hill
False Orford Ness
Vrilya Point
Helby Hill
Hunter Point
EAST ISLANDS

SEA

Donkey R
Jackson
Captain Billy Landing
Raine Is
Heathlands Resource Reserve
Heathlands
Shelburne Bay
Cockburn Reef
Great Detached Reef
Port Musgrave
Culleen Point
Mapoon
Double Pt
Round Point
Cape Grenville
Middle Peak
Conical Hill
Hicks Island
Nomad Reef
Yule Detached Reef
Single Rock Entrance
Wreck Bay
Black Rock Entrance

PACIFIC

Bramwell
335
'Agnew' (ruins)
'Old Bertiehaugh'
Bolt Head
Temple Bay
Mosquito Point
Fair Cape
Ferguson Reef
Cape
80
Bromley
Moreton Telegraph Station
'Wattle Hill'
Weymouth Bay
Iron Range Nat Park
Portland Roads
Cape Weymouth
Quoin Island Entrance
Weipa
Napranum
Mission
145
Batavia Downs
Iron Range Resources Res
Chilli Beach
Cape Griffith
Quintel Beach
Long Sandy Reef
GREAT BARRIER REEF
Providential Entrance
Duyfken Point
Mt Tozer
Iron Range
Lockhart River
MARINE PARK
Wooldrum Point
Bligh Reef
Bligh Boat Entrance
Far Northern Section
Albatross Bay
Boyd Pt
Pera Hd
Thud Pt
False Pera Head
Cape Direction
Second Three Mile Opening
Merluna
'Wolverton'
Round Point
Night Island
Bopard Point
For more detail on this area, see Hema's Cape York Map
Tijou Reef
York
114
Archer River Roadhouse
Gone Peak
Friendly Point
Worbody Pt
Wallaby Is
Aurukun
Birthday Mtn
Cape Sidmouth
Campbell Point
Ogilvie Reef
Creech Reef
First Three Mile Opening

OCEAN

Mungkan Kandju National Park
Kapdju National Park
'Rokeby'
'Merapah'
Kendall River
Quarantine Station
Mt Croll
Wilkie Is
Claremont Isles
Roberts Point National Park
Lowrie Passage
Melville Passage
Cape Keerweer
Coen
Mt White
'Silver Plains'
Corbett Reef
Peninsula
'Holroyd'
Moojeeba
Claremont Point
King Island
Pipon Island
Waterwitch Passage
Kulinchin'
Port Stewart
Evanson Point
Stanley Is
Flinders Is
Cape Melville
'Running Creek'
Bathurst Head
Princess Charlotte Bay
St Pauls Bay
Rocky Point
South Warden Reef
Barrow Point
Reef
'Ebagoola'
'Yaraden'
Jewell Reef
Mt Ryan
Lily Vale
'Marina Plains'
Aioszville
'Wakooa' (Ruins)
HOWICK GROUP
Red Point
Howick Is
HOWICK GROUP NP
'Strathburn'
Murdock Point
Lizard Island Nat Park
Strathgordon OS
'New Strathgordon'
'Glen Garland'
39
'Musgrave'
'New Bamboo'
'Violet Vale'
Cape Melville National Park
Brown Peak
TURTLE GROUP Nat Park
Lookout Point
Cape Flattery
Pormpuraaw
'Strathmay'
'Strathaven'
304
Lakefield
Kalpowar
Juck Lakes
Starcke
Nat Park
'Starcke'
Munburra Resources
Munburra
'Artemis'
'Dixie OS'
'Lakefield'
'New Dixie'
Mt Webb
Nat Park
'Glenrock'
'Elderslie'
Wallaby Island
'Crosbie Creek'
'Kalinga'
'Koolburra OS'
Hann River Roadhouse
'Old Laura'
'Battle Camp'
Melsomby
Cape Bedford
'Sefton'
Oroners OS
'Normanby'
'Bald Hills'
Hazelmere
Hope Vale
Nob Point
Mitchell - Alice Rivers National Park
'Killarney'
'Fairview'
'Welcome'
Mt Cook Nat Park
Walker Bay
Kowanyama
'Imooya'
Kimba
'Pinnacles'
Laura
Split Rock Art
Mt McCormack
Black Mtn Nat Park
Archer Point
Walsh Bay
Cooktown
81
Helenvale
Obree Point
'Lochnagar OS'
'Rutland Plains'
Quinkan Reserve
'Crocodile'

New South Wales

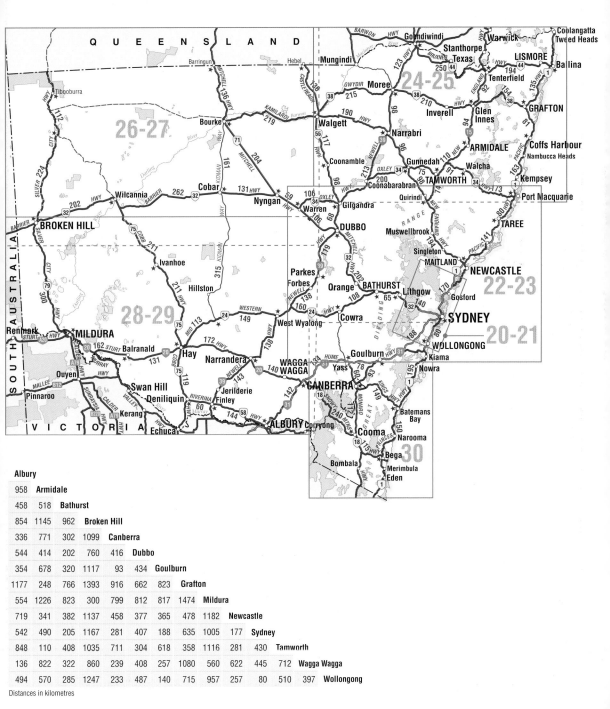

Albury												
958	Armidale											
458	518	Bathurst										
854	1145	962	Broken Hill									
336	771	302	1099	Canberra								
544	414	202	760	416	Dubbo							
354	678	320	1117	93	434	Goulburn						
1177	248	766	1393	916	662	823	Grafton					
554	1226	823	300	799	812	817	1474	Mildura				
719	341	382	1137	458	377	365	478	1182	Newcastle			
542	490	205	1167	281	407	188	635	1005	177	Sydney		
848	110	408	1035	711	304	618	358	1116	281	430	Tamworth	
136	822	322	860	239	408	257	1080	560	622	445	712	Wagga Wagga
494	570	285	1247	233	487	140	715	957	257	80	510	397	Wollongong

Distances in kilometres

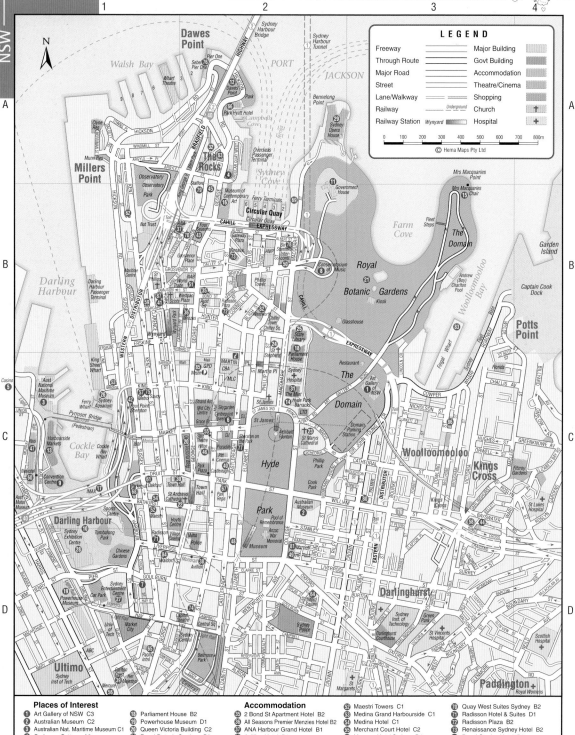

Places of Interest

1 Art Gallery of NSW C3
2 Australian Museum C2
3 Australian Nat. Maritime Museum C1
4 Cadmans Cottage A2
5 Casino C1
6 Centrepoint, Sydney Tower C2
7 Chinatown D1
8 Conservatorium of Music B2
9 Convention Centre C1
10 Darling Harbour C1
11 Government House B2
12 Harbour Bridge Arch Walk A2
13 Harbourside Marketplace C1
14 Hyde Park Barracks C2
15 Mrs Macquarie's Chair B3
16 Museum of Contemporary Art B2
17 Panasonic IMAX Theatre C1
18 Parliament House B2
19 Powerhouse Museum D1
20 Queen Victoria Building C2
21 Royal Botanic Gardens B3
22 St Andrews Cathedral C1
23 St Marys Cathedral C2
24 St Stephens Church B2
25 State Library of NSW B2
26 Sydney Aquarium C1
27 Sydney Entertainment Centre D1
28 Sydney Exhibition Centre D1
29 Sydney Opera House A3
30 Sydney Town Hall C1
31 The Mint C2
32 The Rocks A2

Accommodation

35 2 Bond St Apartment Hotel B2
36 All Seasons Premier Menzies Hotel B2
37 ANA Harbour Grand Hotel B1
38 Avillion Hotel D2
39 Carlton Crest Hotel D1
40 Castlereagh Inn C2
41 Corus Hotel Sydney B1
42 Four Point Sheraton Sydney C1
43 Four Seasons Sydney B2
44 Hampton Court Hotel C3
45 Harbour Rocks Hotel B2
46 Hilton Hotel C2
47 Hotel Ibis C1
48 Hyde Park Inn Motel D2
49 Hyde Park Plaza Hotel C2
50 Intercontinental Hotel B2
51 Le Meridian Hotel B2

52 Maestri Towers C1
53 Medina Grand Harbourside C1
54 Medina Hotel C1
55 Merchant Court Hotel C2
56 Mercure Hotel Sydney D1
57 Metro Suites on King C1
58 Millennium Hotel Sydney C3
59 Napoleon on Kent B1
60 Novotel Sydney on Darling Harbour C1
61 Oakford Darling Harbour C1
62 Observatory Hotel B1
63 Old Sydney Holiday Inn A2
64 Oxford Koala D2
65 Pacific International Inn D1
66 Park Hyatt Hotel A2
67 Park Regis Hotel C2
68 Parkroyal Darling Harbour C1
69 Quay Grand Suites B2

70 Quay West Suites Sydney B2
71 Radisson Hotel & Suites D1
72 Radisson Plaza B2
73 Renaissance Sydney Hotel B2
74 Royal Garden Hotel D2
75 Savoy Apartments C1
76 Sebel Pier One A2
77 Sheraton on the Park Hotel C2
78 Sir Stamford at Circular Quay B2
79 Stafford, The B2
80 Sydney Boulevarde Hotel C3
81 Sydney Marriott Hotel D2
82 The Wentworth Sydney B2
83 W Hotel B3
84 Waldorf Apartment Hotel D1
85 Westin Sydney C2
86 Woolloomooloo Waters Aparts C3
87 York Apartments B1

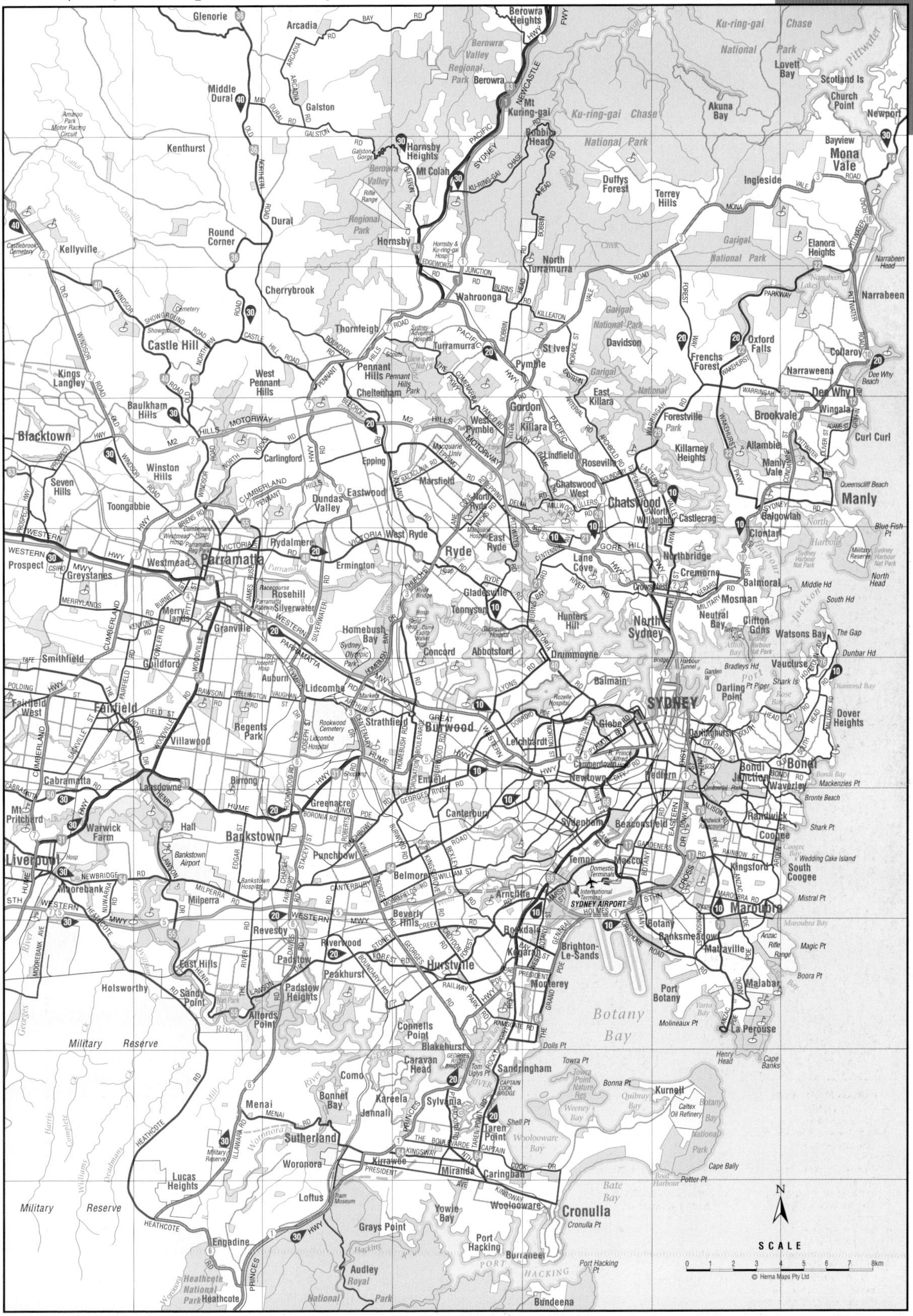

A
B
C
D
E
F
G
H
J
K

SCALE

0 1 2 3 4 5 6 7 8km

© Hema Maps Pty Ltd

N

SOUTH PACIFIC OCEAN

PACIFIC

Broken Bay

Budgewoi
Toukey
The Entrance
Terrigal
Avoca Beach
Wyong
Gosford
East Gosford
West Gosford
Woy Woy
Palm Beach
Whale Beach
Avalon
Newport
Mona Vale
Dee Why
Morisset
Hornsby
Wisemans Ferry
Windsor
Richmond
St Albans
Putty
Yengo National Park
Wollemi National Park
Dharug National Park
Marramarra National Park
Ku-ring-gai Chase National Park
Brisbane Water National Park
Popran National Park

SYDNEY NEWCASTLE

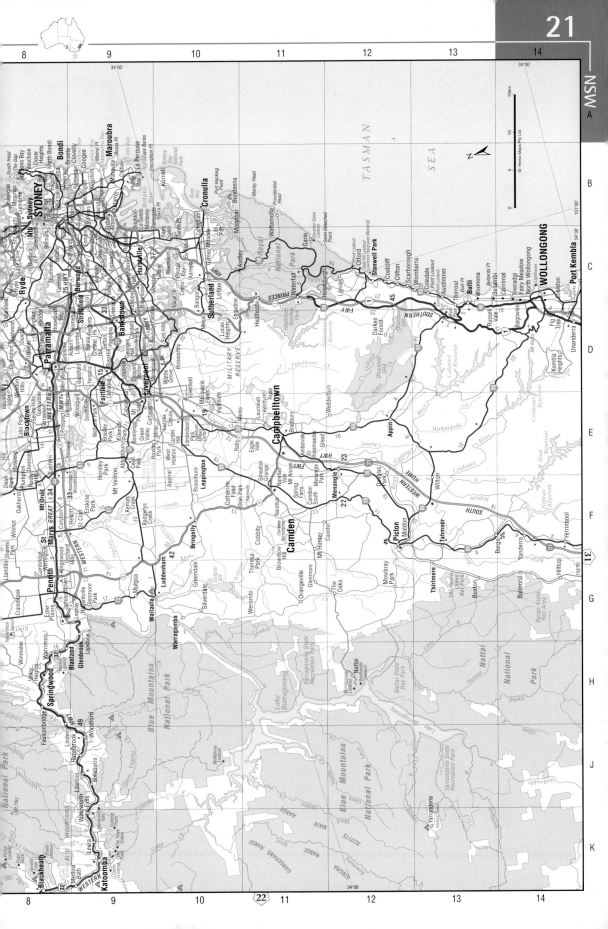

NSW

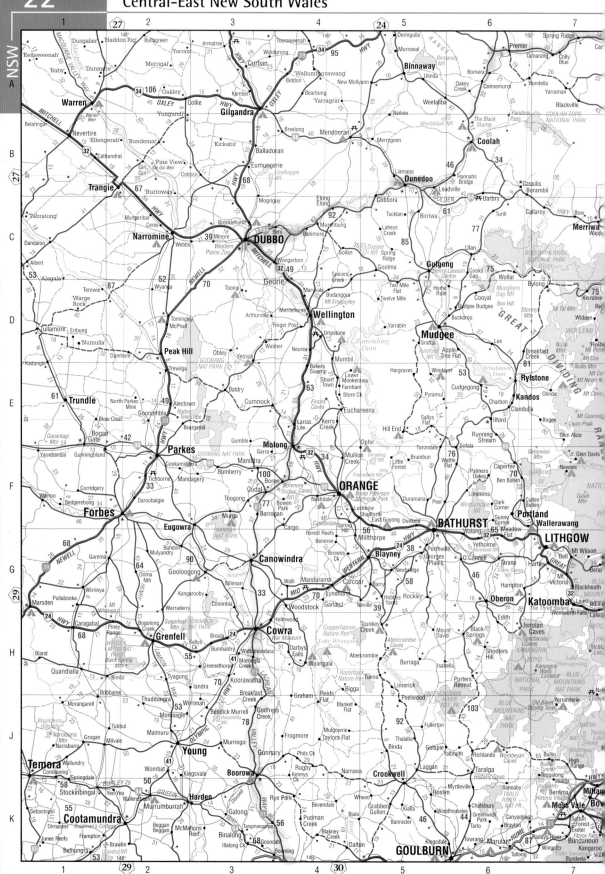

8 9 10 25 11 12 13 14

Quipolly · Bowling Alley Point · Nundle · Hanging Rock · Myrtle Scrub · Birdwood · Rollands Plains · Point Plomer · Limeburners Creek Nature Reserve · Telegraph Point

Quirindi · The Ranch · Wallabadah · Wallabadah NR · Nowendoc · Mt Seaview · Yarras · Ellenborough · Long Flat · Kindee · Pappinbarra · Pembroke · **Port Macquarie**

Ridge · Castle Mtn · Braefield · Barry · Cooplacurripa · Byabarra · **Wauchope** · Tacking Point · Lake Innes · Lake Innes Nature Res

Old Warrah · Warrah Ck · Ardglen · Willow Tree · Glenwarrin · Elands · Combyone · Heron's Ck · Kendall · North Haven · Bonny Hills · Lorne · Laurieton · Watson Taylor Lake

Murrurundi · Mt Helen · Timor · Ellerston · Tomalla · Cootera Hill · Glamis · Number One · Caparra · Bobin · Wherrol Flat · Killabakh · Johns River · Landsdowne · Coopernook · Moorland · Crowdy Head · Harrington · **CROWDY BAY NATIONAL PARK**

Blandford · Wingen · Sylphs · Gorge NR · Moonan Flat · Hunter Springs · Upper Bowman · Rookhurst · Marlee · **Wingham** · Mt George · Tinonee · **TAREE** · Purfleet · Old Bar · Farquhar Inlet

Owens Gap · **Scone** · Parkville · Gundy · Woolooma · Belltrees · Cobark · Barrington · Bundook · Kimbriki · Burrell Creek · Krambach · Khappinghat NR

Bunnan · **Aberdeen** · Glenbawn Dam · Dangarfield · **Gloucester** · Rawdon Vale · Faulkland · Belbora · Nabiac · Failford · Tuncurry · **Forster** · Cape Hawke

Castle Rock · **Muswellbrook** · McCullys Gap · Davis Ck · Mt Royal · Barrington House · Chichester · Stratford · Craven · Warranulla · Coolongolook · Upper Myall · Coomba · BOOTI BOOTI NAT PARK · Elizabeth Bay

Hollow · Denman · Hebden · St Clair · Miraннie · Salisbury · Eccleston · Wards River · Weismantels · Bunya · Wootton · Pacific Palms

Martindale · Glen Gallic · Liddell · Ravensworth · Mt Olive · Gresford · Halton · Bandon Grove · **Dungog** · Stroud Road · Stroud · Girvan · Seal Rocks · Sugarloaf Bay

Camberwell · Glendon Brook · Vacy · Paterson · Clarence Town · Allworth · Bulahdelah · Marshdale · Booral · Brookfield · Mungo Brush · Tamboy · **MYALL LAKES NATIONAL PARK** · Broughton Island

SOUTH

Howes Valley · Mt Kindarun · **Singleton** · **Branxton** · Woodville · Lochinvar · Seaham · Karuah · Hawks Nest · Tea Gardens · Port Stephens

Putty · Mt Yengo · Broke · Wineries · Hunter Valley Wineries · **MAITLAND** · **Kurri Kurri** · **Raymond Terrace** · Lemon Tree Passage · **Nelson Bay**

CESSNOCK · Bellbird · Millfield · Mulbring · Beresfield · Williamtown · Anna Bay · Morna Point

Wollombi · Freemans Waterhole · Watagans NP · Wallsend · Stockton · Port Hunter · **NEWCASTLE**

YENGO NATIONAL PARK · Bucketty · Cooranbong · **Toronto** · **Belmont** · Lake Macquarie · **Swansea**

Colo Heights · St Albans · Kulnura · **Morisset** · Wyee · MUNMORAH STATE REC AREA

PACIFIC

Mangrove Mtn · Peats Ridge · **Wyong** · Doyalson · Budgewoi · Norah Head · Lake Munmorah · Tuggerah Lake · WYRRABALONG NAT PARK

Wisemans Ferry · Old Sydney Town · Ourimbah · **The Entrance**

Kurrajong · **Gosford** · Terrigal · BOUDDI NAT PARK

Richmond · **Windsor** · KU-RING-GAI CHASE NAT PK · Kilcare · Palm Beach · Broken Bay

Ringwood · **Penrith** · **Hornsby** · Mona Vale · Long Reef · SYDNEY HARBOUR NP · Port Jackson · Manly

OCEAN

Parramatta · **Liverpool** · **SYDNEY** · Opera House, Powerhouse Museum, Sydney Aquarium, Beautiful Harbour, Taronga Zoo, Sydney Tower, The Rocks, Australia's Wonderland, Darling Harbour · Airport · Sutherland · Botany Bay · BOTANY BAY NP

Camden · Oaks · **Campbelltown** · Bundeena · ROYAL NATIONAL PARK · Port Hacking · Waterfall · Garie · Helensburgh · Stanwell Park · Scarborough · Coledale · Thirroul · Bulli

Appin · Corrimal · **WOLLONGONG**

TASMAN

Red Point · **Port Kembla** · **Shellharbour** · Bass Point Marine Res

Minnamurra · Bombo · **Kiama** · Blowhole Pt · Gerringong

SEA

N

0 10 20 30 40 50 60km

© Hema Maps Pty Ltd

GREAT DIVIDING RANGE · LIVERPOOL RANGE · BEN HALLS NAT PARK · BARRINGTON TOPS NAT PARK · WOLLEMI NATIONAL PARK

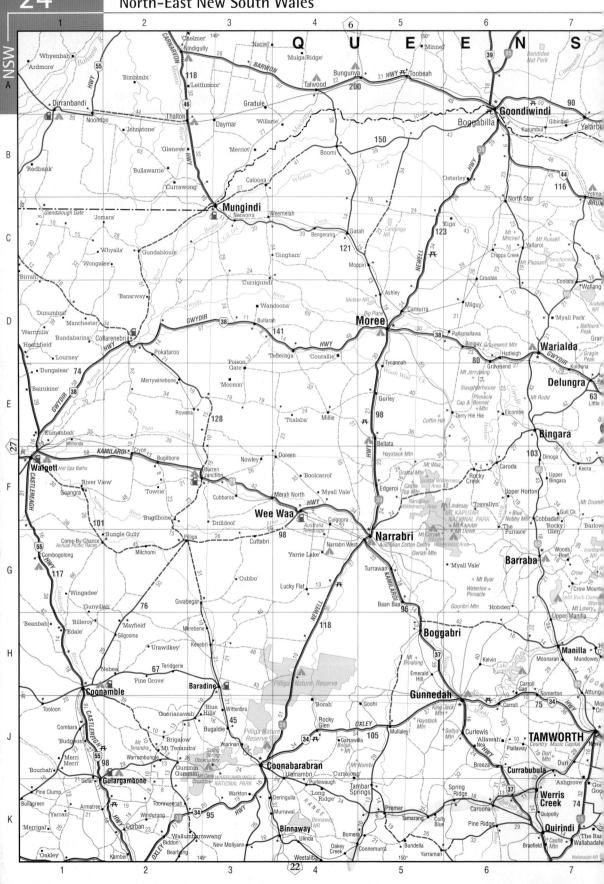

LAND

CUNNINGHAM HWY

Karara Warwick Killarney Legume Woodenbong Rathdowney Springbrook Coolangatta Tweed Heads Murwillumbah

Cobbada-mana Coolmunda Dam Hewetsons Mill Urbenville Grevillea Kyogle Mullumbimby Brunswick Heads

Whetstone Pikedale Liston Tooloom Old Bonalbo Georgica Cedar Pt Ocean Shores Byron Bay Cape Byron

Limevale Stanthorpe Amosfield Wilsons Downfall Bonalbo Ettrick Nimbin The Channon Bangalow Lennox Head

Texas Ballandean Boonoo Boonoo Pretty Gully Tabulam Mummulgum LISMORE Casino Bentley Clunes Bexhill Ballina

Silver Spur Glenlyon Dam Girraween N.P. Drake Mallanganee Yorklea Coraki Wardell Empire Vale

Bonshaw Mole River Tenterfield Black Swamp Demon Alice Wyan Rappville Woodburn Broadwater Evans Head

Ashford Torrington Bolivia Deepwater Baryulgil Camira Ck Whiporie BROADWATER NAT PARK BUNDJALUNG NATIONAL PARK

Stag Mtn Emmaville Tent Hill Dundee Glen Elgin Fine Flower Coaldale Chatsworth Harwood Iluka Yamba

Bukkulla Wellingrove Bald Knob Cangai Copmanhurst Lawrence Maclean Angourie

Cherry Tree Hill Oakwood Nullamanna Sapphire Glen Innes Red Range Jackadgery GRAFTON Ulmarra Cowper Brooms Head

Elsmore Matheson Furracabad Stonehenge Newton Boyd Buccarumbi South Grafton Tyndale Sandon

Gilgai Stannifer Maybole Dalmorton Coutts Crossing Pillar Valley Minnie Water

Tingha Ben Lomond Glencoe Warra NP Nymboida Tallawudjah Kungala Wooli

Bundarra Wandsworth Oban Clouds Creek Towallum Glenreagh Corindi Beach Red Rock

Laura Guyra Backwater Wards Mistake Billys Creek Nana Glen Lower Bucca Mullaway Woolgoolga

Baldersleigh Rockvale Tyringham Dundurrabin Coramba Moonee Beach

Yarrowyck Wongwibinda Hernani Deer Vale Ulong Upper Orara Korora Coffs Harbour

ARMIDALE Wollomombi Ebor Majors Pt Dorrigo Bonville Sawtell Big Banana

Uralla Dangarsleigh Hillgrove Jeogla Darkwood Brinerville Thora Raleigh Bellingen

Gostwyck Kentucky Five Day Creek Bostobrick Bowraville Urunga Mylestom

Longford Enmore Georges Junction Comara Warrell Ck Talarm Nambucca Heads Scotts Head

Wollun Bellbrook Taylors Arm Macksville Stuarts Point

Walcha Woolbrook Walcha Road Millbank Eungai Clybucca South West Rocks Arakoon Smoky Cape

Moona Plains Willawarrin Sherwood Gladstone Kinchela Creek Jerseyville Hat Head

Limbri Glen Morrison Tia Trinidad Hill Kookaburra Burnt Bridge KEMPSEY Crescent Head

Aberbaldie Brackendale Yarrowitch Upper Rollans Plains Kundabung OCEAN

Niangala Myrtle Scrub Birdwood Pappinbarra Point Plomer

Carnegie Woolomin Mt Seaview Kindee Pembroke Telegraph Point Limeburners Creek Nature Reserve

Bowling Alley Point Yarras Ellenborough Beechwood Long Flat Port Macquarie

Hanging Rock Byabarra Wauchope Lake Cathie Tacking Point

GREAT DIVIDING RANGE

SOUTH PACIFIC OCEAN

© Hema Maps Pty Ltd

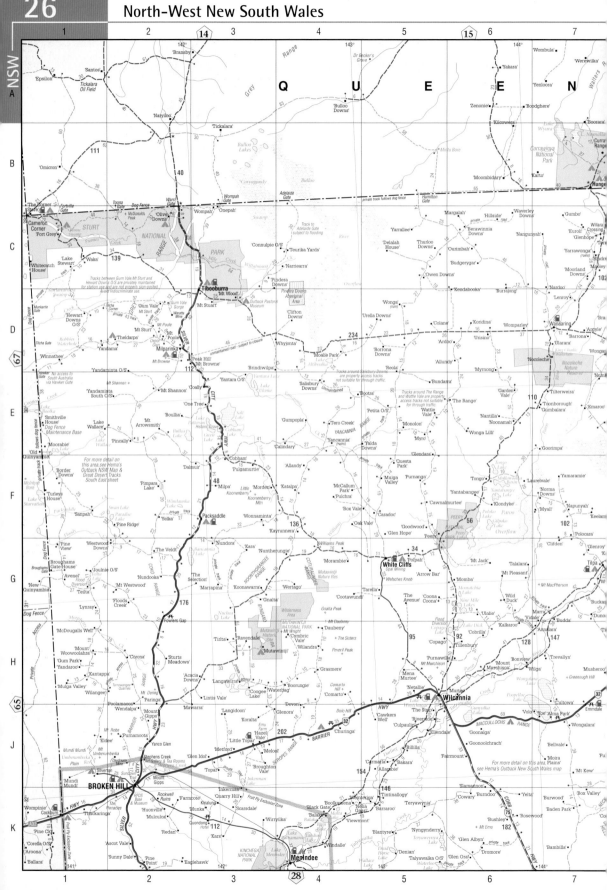

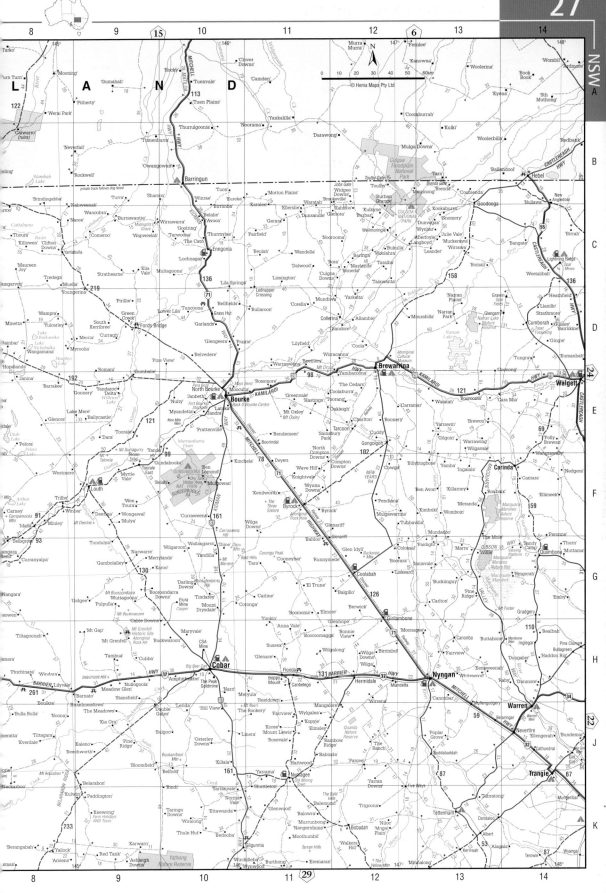

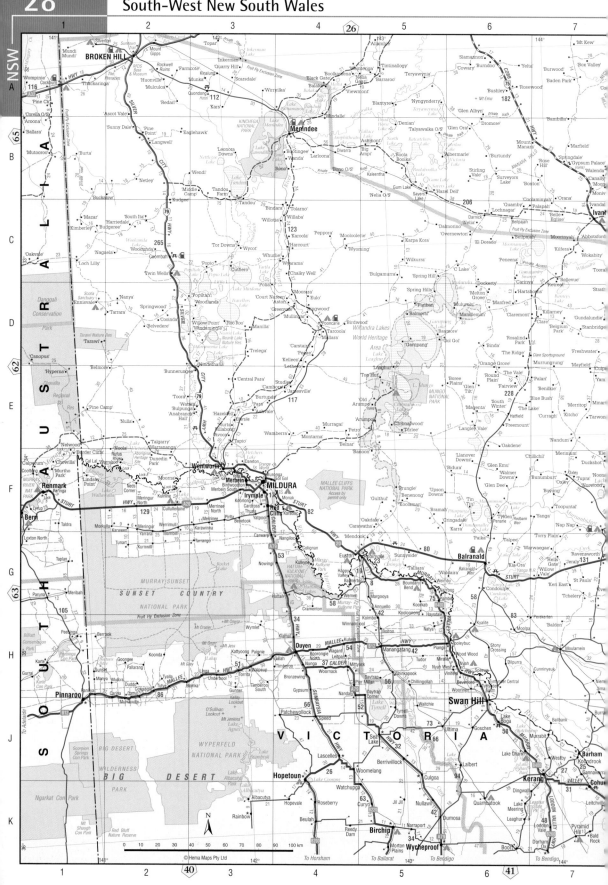

8 9 10 27 11 12 13 14

A — Bloomfield, Belford, Kulwin, Belarabon, Norragee, 'Panjee', 'Yarran Downs', 87, Tabratong, Trangie, Murriberibal, 'Bindi', 'Yarranvale', 'Shuttleton', Old Mining Town, 'Yarra', Balemund, Trigoona, Tottenham, Dandaloo, Albert

B — 'Berangabah', 'Yallock', 'Amiens', Wallangarra, Kajuligah, 'Keewong Farm Holidays 4WD Tours', 'Taringo Downs', 'Wiralong', Gilgunnia, 'Balowra', 'Murrunbong', 'Nangerybone', 'Moothumbi', Bobadah, Niloc, 'Mogal Plain', Walkers Hill, Minnalong, Kerriwah, Alagala, Terowie, Wyanga, 'Warge Rock', Tullamore, Eringon, Numulla, Denmore, 233, 'Moolah', Yathong Nature Reserve, Mt Merrimerriwa, Wagga Tank, 'Coan Downs' Mt Allen, Mt Wilson, Wirchilleba, Burthong, 'Eremaran', 'Tara', 'Marobee', Keriei Hills, Rollings Nature Reserve, Mineral Hill, Burra Burra, Kadungle, Fifield, 86

C — 'Oxford', Conoble, 'Irish Lords', Trida, Wangaroa, Warranary Hill, Roth, Lowlands, 'Gunnigudrie', Nombinnie Nature Res, Round Hill NR, Warkatta Hill, Euabalong West, Euabalong, Murrin Bridge, Caringa, Kiacatoo, Condobolin, Oltha 66, Bogan Gate, Yarrabandai, Gunningbland, Tichborne, Parkes, 42, 94, North Parkes Mine, Trundle, 61, Blow Clear, Goonumbla

D — Wakefield, Killara, 'Mossgiel', 'Borwonnie', Willandra National Park, Merton Q/S, 'Willandra', 99, 'Moolbong', Vieta, Hillston, 92, Merri Merrigal, Lake Cargelligo, Burgooney, Tullibigeal, 'Eurella', 118, 105, Burcher, Wamboyne, Lake Cowal, 68, Garema, 64, Forbes, 100, Wirrinya, Bedgerebong, Daroobalgie, Corridgery, 33, Clearview, Yandembah, 'Mooral', 'Brooklyn', 95, Monia Gap, 70, Hannan, Gubba Nat Res, Gubbata, Kikoira, Thullo, Girral, Weja, Winnunga, Ungarie, Clear Ridge, Marsden, Pullabooka, 24, Caragabal, Piney Range, Widdin Mouna NR, Black Bering NR, Grenfell

E — 'Daisy Plains', 82, 'Natue', Toms Lake', 'Alma', 77, 'Horton Park', Boogul, 'Neobine', 'Gunbar', 'Wongalea', 'Belaly', Goolgowi, 56, Tabbita, Rankins Springs, Erigola, Warran Mnii, Weethalle, 93, West Wyalong, Wyalong, Tallimba, Ruddigore NR, Buddigower, Bellanvi, Alleena, Bland, Barmedman, 68, Quandialla, Bimbi, Brribbaree, 37, Narragal, Thuddungra, Grogan, Milvale, Merungle, 'Wyadra', 'Cowl Cowl', Langtree, Melbergen North', 'Hillview', Naradhan, 60, Woodville, Merriwagga, Allawah, 'Wilkin Grange', Lafydale

F — 'Benara', 'Daracola', 'Embah', 'Nullagong', 24, 113, Warburn, Lake Wyangan, 'Tharbogang', Yoogali, Binya, 85, Barellan, Moombooldool, Kamarah, Beckom, Ariah Park, 14, Pucawan, 72, Combaning, Wallundry, Springdale, Barmedman, 69, Mirrool, Temora, 58, Stockinbingal, BURLEY 29, Griffith, Hanwood, Widgelli, Willbriggie, 38, Murrami, Stoney Point, Gogeldrie, Yanco, 97, Coleambally, Cowabbie West, 64, Methul, Rannock, Murrulbale Hill

G — Hay, Shear Outback, 115, 20, Carrathool, Oxley, Darlington Point, Whitton, Leeton, 57, Narrandera, Big Guttu, Grong Grong, 69, Coolamon, Marrar, Old Junee, 59, Junee Reefs, Frampton, Cootamundra, 55, Dimasere, Bethungra, Illabo, 53, Muttama, 'Sixteen Mile Gums', 'Walgrove', 'Eurolie', Coleambally Irrigation, 'Nyangay', 'Booroorban', 'Wargam'

H — 105, 'Oaklands Park Estate', 119, Moonbara, Steam Plains, 'Moonbah', 'Yanko', Widgiewa, 107, Boree Creek, Greenvale, Yuluma, Brookdale, Gelistoniga, 95, Bullenbong, Millwood, Malebo, Wagga Wagga, Alfred Town, 45, Borambola, Gundagai, 9, Currawarna, Morundah, Lockhart, Milbrulong, French Park, Osborne, Woodend, Uranagong, The Rock, Mangoplah, Yerong Creek, 77, 30, Tumut, Adelong, Gobarralong

J — 'Walgrove', Conargo, Coree, 91, Jerilderie, Mairjimmy, Nyora, Oaklands, Daysdale, Bungowannah, Urana, 45, Lake Cullivel, 107, Bidgeemia, Urangeline, Urangeline East, Pleasant Hills, Ryan, Henty, Cookardinia, Nest Hill, Morven, Culcairn, Holbrook, Westby, Kyeamba, Humula, Carabost, Oberne, Wondalga, Batlow, 74, 105, Deniliquin, Mayrung, Riverina Irrigation, 60, 58, Finley, 36, Berrigan, 58, Blighty, Osborne Well, Tuppal, 'North Tuppal', Morocco, Tocumwal, 37, 92, Savernake, Rennie, Sangar, Coreen, Lowesdale, Burraja, Balldale

K — Echuca, Moama, Wax Museum, Picnic Point, Barmah, Mathoura, Strathmerton, 75, Cobram, Muckatah, Katunga, Nathalia, Numurkah, Katamatite, Yarrawonga, Mulwala, Bundalong, Merton, Corowa, Rutherglen, 44, Esmond, Wahgunyah, Chiltern, Howlong, Jindera, Albury, Table Top, Bungowannah, Wodonga, Bonegilla, Leneva, Tallangatta, Ournie, Corryong, Koetong, 82, Shelley, Cudgewa, Walwa, Jingellic, 65

To Bendigo & Melbourne · To Echuca · To Shepparton · To Benalla · To Wangaratta · Bow-Ironbark Nat Park · To Wangaratta

8 9 10 42 11 12 43 13 14

NSW

South-East New South Wales

Major places: Young, Boorowa, Harden, Cootamundra, Murrumburrah, Gundagai, Tumut, Batlow, Tumbarumba, Khancoban, Thredbo, Jindabyne, Cooma, Berridale, Bombala, Bonang, Delegate

Canberra, Queanbeyan, Australian Capital Territory

Yass, Goulburn, Crookwell, Braidwood, Captains Flat, Bredbo, Nimmitabel, Bega, Eden

Wollongong, Port Kembla, Shellharbour, Kiama, Gerringong, Berry, Nowra, Culburra, Ulladulla, Batemans Bay, Moruya, Narooma, Bermagui, Merimbula, Tathra, Tura Beach, Pambula

Mittagong, Bowral, Moss Vale, Bundanoon, Bomaderry, Milton, Camden, Campbelltown, Picton

KOSCIUSZKO NATIONAL PARK, ALPINE NATIONAL PARK, SNOWY RIVER NATIONAL PARK, MORTON NATIONAL PARK, DEUA NATIONAL PARK, WADBILLIGA NATIONAL PARK, SOUTH EAST FORESTS NATIONAL PARK, BEN BOYD NATIONAL PARK, NAMADGI NATIONAL PARK, BRINDABELLA NATIONAL PARK, BUDAWANG WILDERNESS

VICTORIA

TASMAN SEA

Coral Coast, Shoalhaven Coast, Eurobodalla Coast, Sapphire Coast

Cape Howe

For more details on this area, see Hema's South East New South Wales Map.

N

0 10 20 30 40 50km

© Hema Maps Pty Ltd

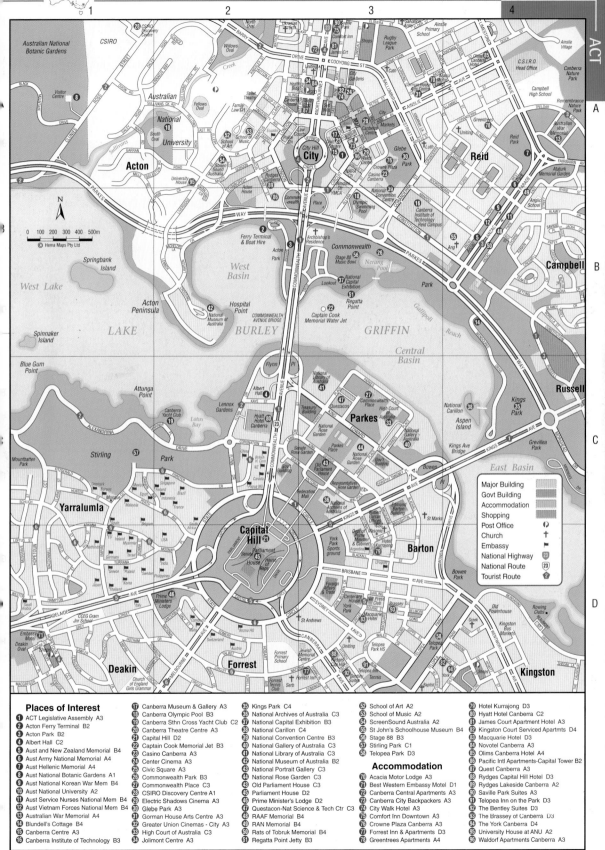

ACT

Places of Interest

1. ACT Legislative Assembly A3
2. Acton Ferry Terminal B2
3. Acton Park B2
4. Albert Hall C2
5. Aust and New Zealand Memorial B4
6. Aust Army National Memorial A4
7. Aust Hellenic Memorial A4
8. Aust National Botanic Gardens A1
9. Aust National Korean War Mem B4
10. Aust National University A2
11. Aust Service Nurses National Mem B4
12. Aust Vietnam Forces National Mem B4
13. Australian War Memorial A4
14. Blundell's Cottage B4
15. Canberra Centre A3
16. Canberra Institute of Technology B3

17. Canberra Museum & Gallery A3
18. Canberra Olympic Pool B3
19. Canberra Sthn Cross Yacht Club C2
20. Canberra Theatre Centre A3
21. Capital Hill D2
22. Captain Cook Memorial Jet B3
23. Casino Canberra A3
24. Center Cinema A3
25. Civic Square A3
26. Commonwealth Park B3
27. Commonwealth Place C3
28. CSIRO Discovery Centre A1
29. Electric Shadows Cinema A3
30. Glebe Park A3
31. Gorman House Arts Centre A3
32. Greater Union Cinemas - City A3
33. High Court of Australia C3
34. Jolimont Centre A3

35. Kings Park C4
36. National Archives of Australia C3
37. National Capital Exhibition B3
38. National Carillon C4
39. National Convention Centre B3
40. National Gallery of Australia C3
41. National Library of Australia C3
42. National Museum of Australia B2
43. National Portrait Gallery C3
44. National Rose Garden C3
45. Old Parliament House C3
46. Parliament House D2
47. Questacon-Nat Science & Tech Ctr C3
48. RAAF Memorial B4
49. RAN Memorial B4
50. Rats of Tobruk Memorial B4
51. Regatta Point Jetty B3

52. School of Art A2
53. School of Music A2
54. ScreenSound Australia A2
55. St John's Schoolhouse Museum B4
56. Stage 88 B3
57. Stirling Park C1
58. Telopea Park D3

Accommodation

70. Acacia Motor Lodge A3
71. Best Western Embassy Motel D1
72. Canberra Central Apartments A3
73. Canberra City Backpackers A3
74. City Walk Hotel A3
75. Comfort Inn Downtown A3
76. Crowne Plaza Canberra A3
77. Forrest Inn & Apartments D3
78. Greentrees Apartments A4

79. Hotel Kurrajong D3
80. Hyatt Hotel Canberra C2
81. James Court Apartment Hotel A3
82. Kingston Court Serviced Apartmts D4
83. Macquarie Hotel D3
84. Novotel Canberra A3
85. Olims Canberra Hotel A4
86. Pacific Intl Apartments-Capital Tower B2
87. Quest Canberra A3
88. Rydges Capital Hill Hotel D3
89. Rydges Lakeside Canberra A2
90. Saville Park Suites A3
91. Telopea Inn on the Park D3
92. The Bentley Suites D3
93. The Brassey of Canberra D3
94. The York Canberra D4
95. University House at ANU A2
96. Waldorf Apartments Canberra A3

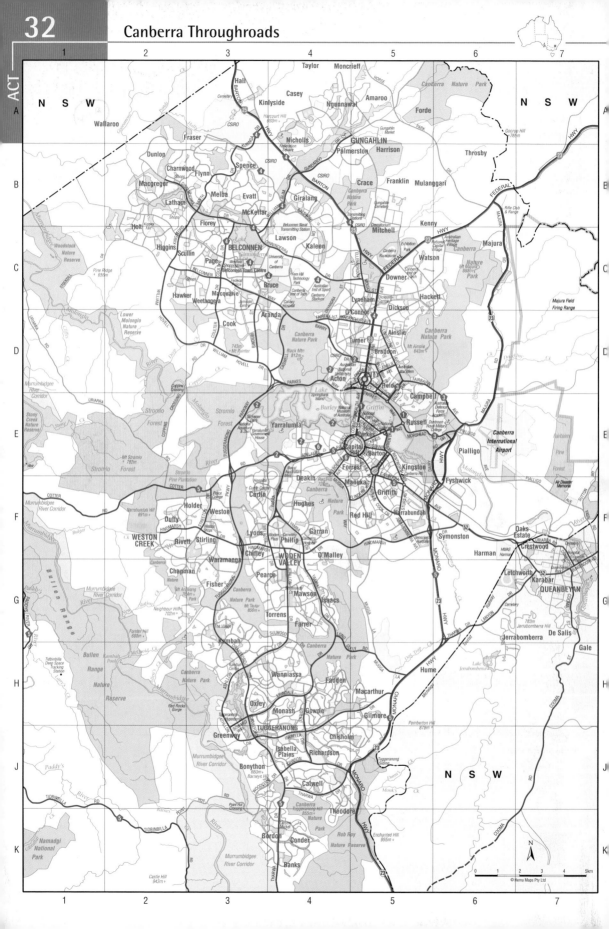

ACT

Victoria

Distances in kilometres

	Ballarat	Bairnsdale	Bendigo	Echuca	Geelong	Hamilton	Melbourne	Mildura	Shepparton	Swan Hill	Traralgon	Wangaratta	Warrnambool
Albury	393	330	282	233	388	555	314	609	178	387	448	72	567
Ballarat		394	121	214	87	174	112	460	241	285	276	319	174
Bairnsdale			430	492	356	568	282	824	404	618	118	308	543
Bendigo				93	177	273	148	404	122	188	312	210	295
Echuca					270	366	210	376	71	154	374	174	388
Geelong						230	74	547	258	365	238	316	187
Hamilton							286	448	395	352	450	483	100
Melbourne								542	184	336	164	242	261
Mildura									447	222	706	550	548
Shepparton										225	348	103	415
Swan Hill											500	328	395
Traralgon												387	425
Wangaratta													493
Warrnambool													

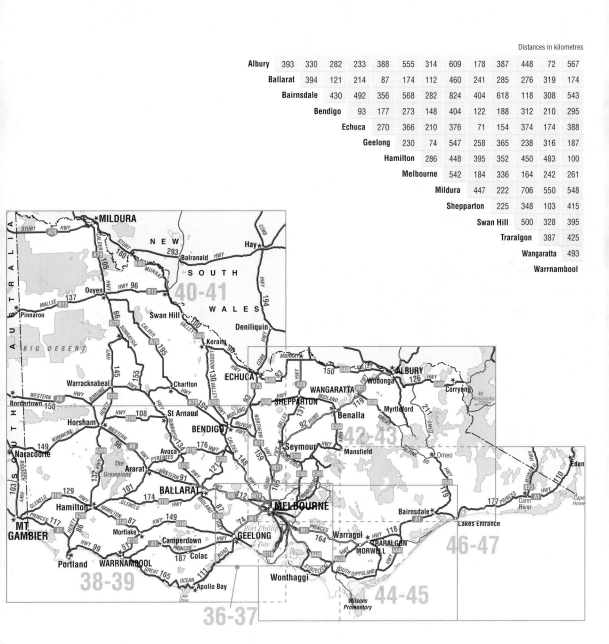

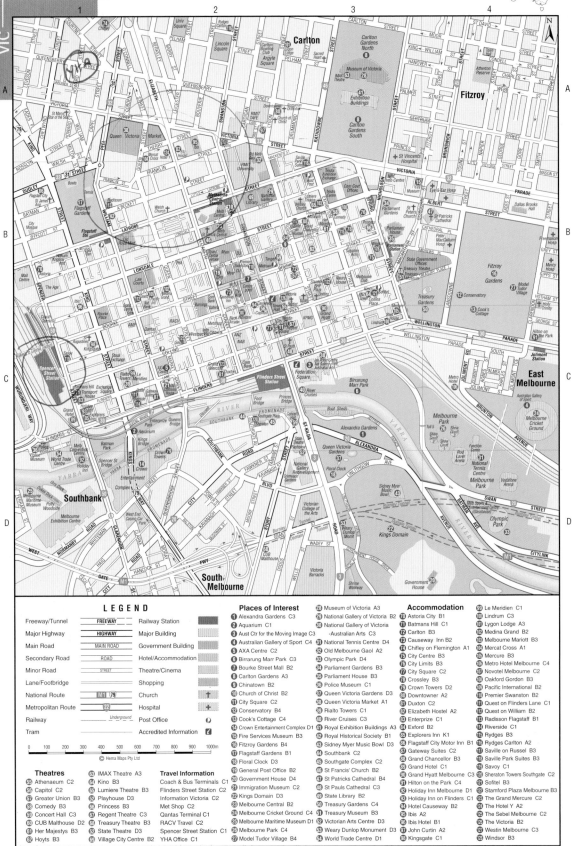

VIC

PORT PHILLIP BAY

CityLink Tollway
For information on CityLink
Tollway day passes and e-TAGs
phone 13 26 29 anytime.

SCALE
0 1 2 3 4 5 6 7 8 9 10km
© Hema Maps Pty Ltd

N

MELBOURNE

AIRPORT

Melbourne Airport Terminal

Tullamarine

ESSENDON AIRPORT

Greenvale, Bulla, Woodlands, Somerton, Coolaroo, Westmeadows, Keilor North, Keilor, Somerton, Campbellfield, Broadmeadows, Thomastown, Epping, Plenty, Mill Park, Plenty, Diamond Creek, Hurstbridge, Kangaroo Ground, Research, Warrandyte State Park, Bundoora, Greensborough, Eltham, Watsonia, Macleod, Fawkner, Kingsbury, Reservoir, Preston, Coburg, Thornbury, Heidelberg, Templestowe, Doncaster, Park Orchards, St Albans, Essendon, Brunswick, Northcote, Braybrook, Sunshine, Carlton, Fitzroy, Collingwood, Kew, Balwyn, Box Hill, Blackburn, Mitcham, Ringwood, Ardeer, Brooklyn, Footscray, Kensington, MELBOURNE, Richmond, Hawthorn, Camberwell, Burwood, Bayswater, Newport, South Melbourne, Port Melbourne, Prahran, Toorak, Armadale, Burwood East, Knox City, Altona, Williamstown, St Kilda, Caulfield, Mt Waverley, Glen Waverley, Scoresby, Altona Meadows, Elwood, Chadstone, Glen Iris, Wheelers Hill, Point Cook, Brighton, McKinnon, Oakleigh, Monash University, Moorabbin, Clayton, Springvale, Noble Park, Dandenong North, Sandringham, Cheltenham, Southland, Dandenong, Doveton, Black Rock, Mentone, Dingley Village, Braeside, Keysborough, Dandenong South, Bangholme, Lyndhurst, Mordialloc, Edithvale, Chelsea, Carrum, Carrum Downs, Seaford, Skye, Cranbourne, Frankston

Hobsons Bay
Altona Bay
Cheetham Wetlands
Point Cook
Beaumaris Bay
Picnic Point
Ricketts Point
Moorabbin Airport
Sandown Racecourse
Springvale Crematorium
Braeside Metropolitan Park

© Hema Maps Pty Ltd

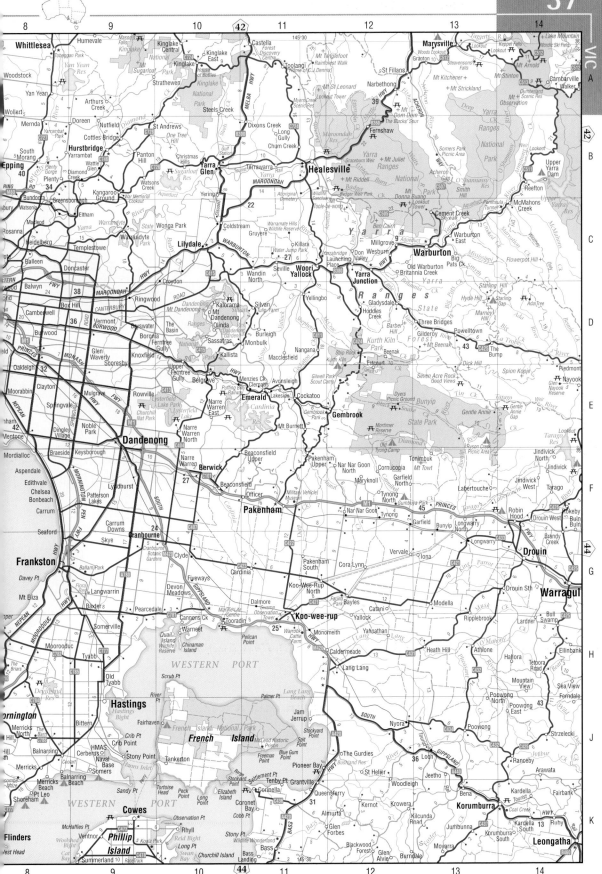

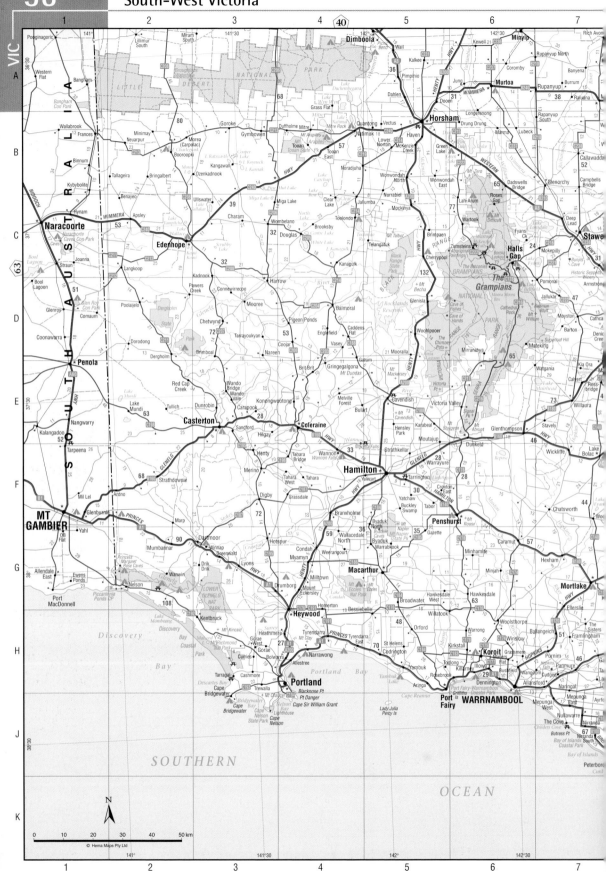

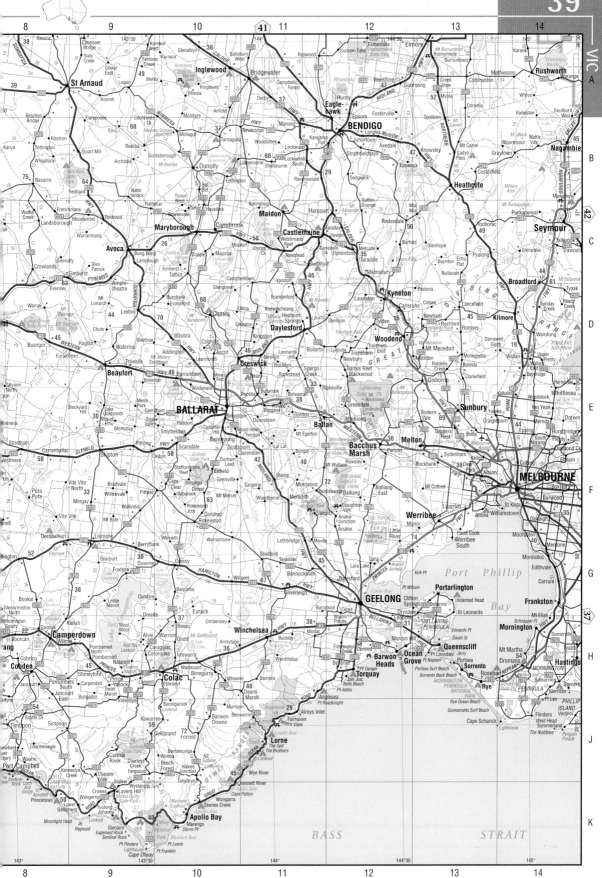

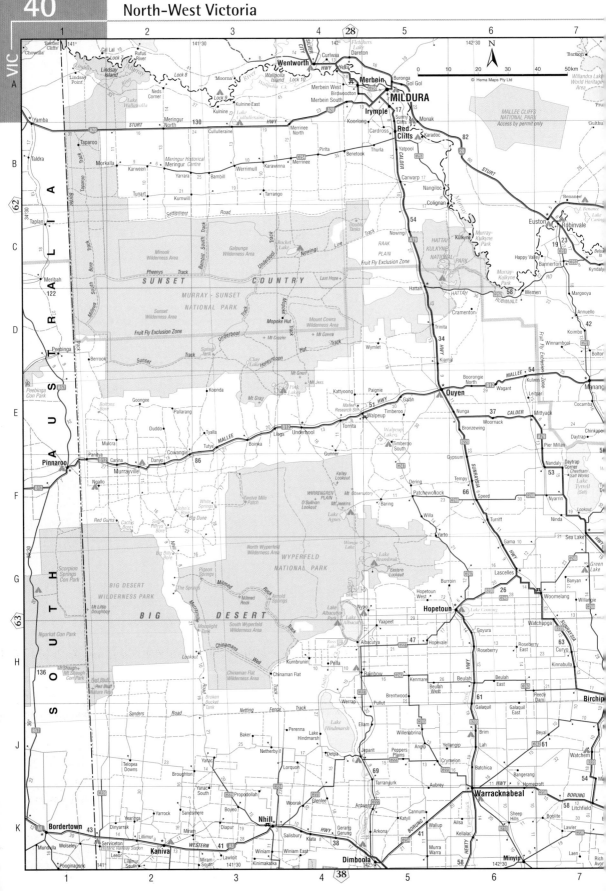

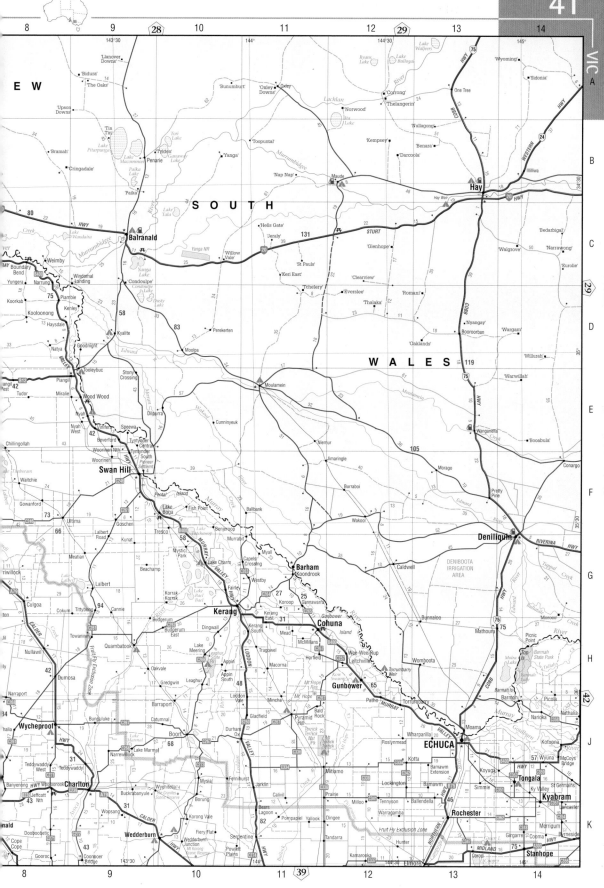

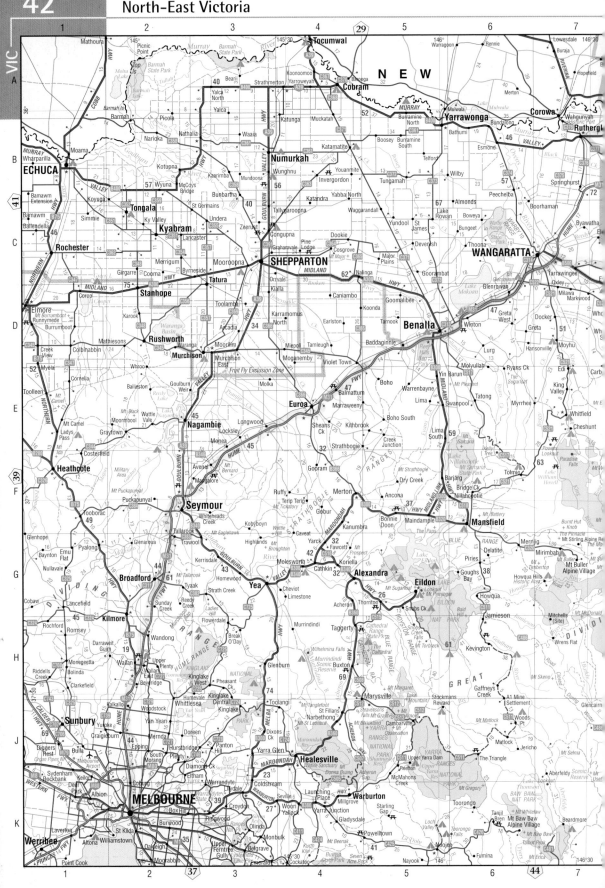

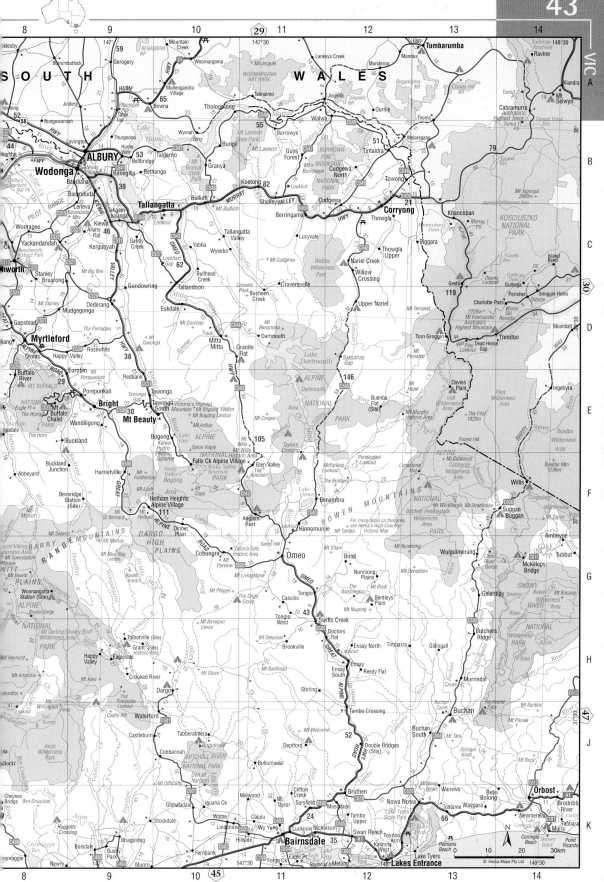

VIC

8 9 10 43 11 12 13 14

A

Mt Tamboritha
Lookout
Glencairn
Mt Wellington
Views
146 30
147
The Pinnacles Lookout
Waterford
Castle Hill
Castleburn
C601
Tabberabbera
Angusvale
147 30
Mt Welcome
Nicholson River
Deptford
Tambo Crossing
52
GREAT ALPINE ROAD OMEO
37 30
Double Bridges (Site)
47

B

C486
Selma
Licola
Cheynes Bridge
Ben Cruachan
54
Avon Wilderness Park
Cobbannah
C601
Den of Nargun
MITCHELL RIVER NATIONAL PARK
Bullumwaal
Melwood
Mt Taylor
Clifton Creek
Sarsfield
24
Mossface
Bruthen
C620
147
'Glenfalloch'
Mt Useful
Scenic Reserve
ardmore

C

n
Walhalla Historic Area
C461
Coopers Creek
Thomson
C486
Glenmaggie Res
Huggetts Crossing
Avon
Freestone Ck
Boisdale
Briagolong
Glenaladale
Stockdale
Iguana Ck
Walpa
Lindenow
C601
C60
Hillside
Calulu
Wy Yung
C603
Lucknow
Nicholson
Bairnsdale
35
Swan Reach
A1
Kalimna West
C605
Tambo Upper
C606
Glenmaggie
Seaton
Newry
Fernbank
C602
Eagle Pt
Paynesville
Metung
Bungo Arm
Lakes Entrance
Maffra
Stratford
Munro
HWY
A1
69
Forge Ck
Raymond Is
Jones Bay
Lake King
38

D

Heyfield
Tinamba
C105
Cowwarr
C105
Bushy Park
C494
C495
Pern
24
C106
Bengworden
Meerlieu
Goon Nure
Wattle Pt
THE LAKES NATIONAL PARK
GIPPSLAND LAKES
Toongabbie
Nambrok
C488
C487
Bundalaguah
C491
C106
Airlie
Clydebank
Holland Landing
Loch Sport
Ninety
Mile
Lake Victoria
Gippsland Lakes Coastal Park
Glengarry
La Trobe
RALGON
PRINCES
A1
49
Rosedale
Kilmany
Wurruk
Sale
Cobains
The Heart
Marley Point
Lake Wellington
Seacombe
Lake Reeve
C105
Longford
C485
Lake Coleman

E

RWELL
hurchill
Loy Yang
C482
Traralgon Sth
C483
Willung
Gormandale
Powers Hill Lookout
HYLAND
Holey Plains State Park
C485
Stradbroke West
C496
Paradise Beach
Golden Beach
The
Ninety

F

Mt Tassie Lookout
Balook
C484
RIDGE
TARRA-BULGA NAT PARK
Carrajung
C453
Won Wron
C482
Darriman
Giffard
72
A440
HWY
Lake Denison
Seaspray
Jack Smith Lake

G

Hiawatha Falls
Jack River
Devon
Greenmount
Yarram
C459
C453
Woodside
Woodside Beach
Reeves Beach
McLaughlins Beach
Binginwarri
Alberton
GIPPSLAND
C452
Tarraville
St Margaret Is
Manns Beach
29
Welshpool
Sunday Is
Port Welshpool
Port Albert
Clonmel Is
Nooramunga Marine & Coastal Park
Snake Is

H

Hunter
Johnny Souey Pt
Wilsons Promontory Marine Park

J

Sealers Cove
Horn Pt
Brown Head
Cape Wellington
Waterloo Bay
Peak House Point

K

STRAIT
N
0 10 20 30km
© Hema Maps Pty Ltd
146 30
147°
147 30
148°
8 9 10 11 12 13 14
39°

VIC

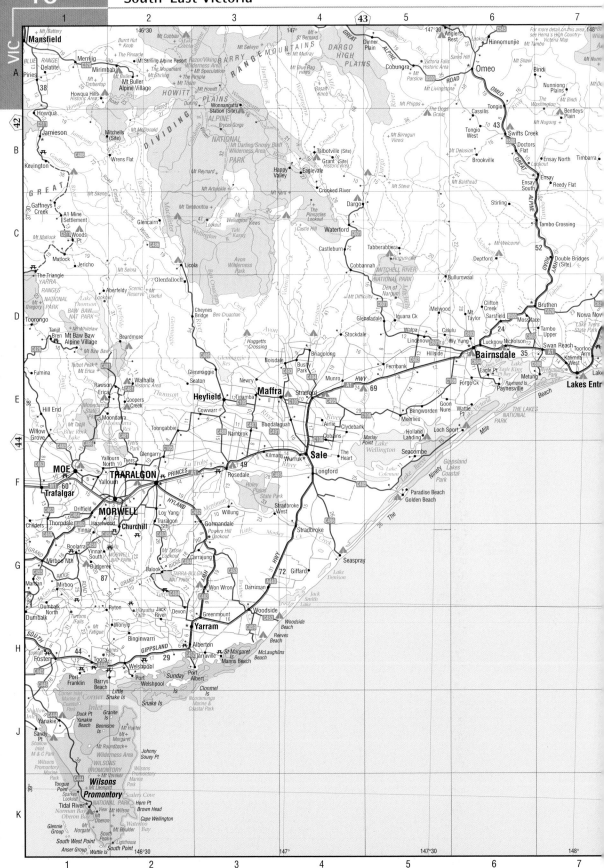

VIC

148°30   Mt Taylor   Mt Tingaringy   148°   149°30   150°
NEW   SOUTH   WALES
Pambula
Lochiel
Pambula Beach
Haycock Point
Egan Peak   Greigs Flat
Maharatta   Burragate   Nethercote
Coolumbooka NR   Mt IMLAY   Towamba
Amboyne   Delegate River   Delegate   73   SOUTH   NAT PK   Boydtown
Tubbut   Dellicknora   Haydens   Craigie   EAST   Eden
McKillops   Bog   Platts   FORESTS   Pericoe   Twofold Bay   Boyds Tower
Bridge   C612   Mt Delegate   Bendoc   NAT PK   Rockton   Mt Imlay   BEN BOYD
Cabanandra   North   Edrom   NATIONAL
Bonang   Lower   Kiah   Saltwater
Bendoc   Narrabarba   Creek
SNOWY   Mt Bendoc   Nungatta   Wonboyn   Reserve
Bowen   Mt Bonang   63   Lake   Bittangabee
Gelantipy   ERRINUNDRA   Lighthouse   Bay
RIVER   Buddah   Genoa   Green Cape
Butchers   NATIONAL   Mt Jersey   Falls   Mt Merragunegin   Nungatta South   Disaster
Ridge   PARK   Goongerah   (COOPRACAMBRA   Ranger   Bay
C603   Errinundra   Chandlers   NATIONAL PARK   Station
River   Creek   Wilderness   Wroxham   NADGEE
96   Mt Ellery   Combienbar   Area)   Wangarabell   NATURE
Murrindal   C612   Noorinbee   Maramingo   Timbillica   Newtons Beach
Raymond   Mt Sardine   North   Hill   RESERVE
Falls   Mt Pinnak   Noorinbee   Genoa   Mallacoota
Buchan   Mt Jack   Tonghi   Genoa   Gipsy   Lookout   Cape Howe
South   Mt Kuark   LIND   Ck   ALFRED   Pt   Fairhaven
Mt Tara   NATIONAL   Rainforest   NATIONAL   Genoa   Cape Howe
Stringer   C616   PARK   Watk   PARK   Peak   Wilderness
Knob   Mt Buck   Club Terrace   Cann   47   A1   Lookout   Area   Cape Howe
Beta   Murrungowar   River   C617   Mallacoota   Lake Barracoota
airewa   C612   Orbost   Bemm River   Mt Bemm   Gabo Island
Bolong   A1   Rainforest   18   Bastion   Lighthouse
Waygara   Bellbird Creek   76   Point
Newmerella   Brodribb   Manorina   Sandpatch   Coast
Tabbara   River   C615   Wilderness   Little Rame
Marlo   Cabbage   23   Lake   Area   Head
Corringle   Tree Creek   Bemm River   Corner   Sandpatch Pt
Beach   Cabbage Tree   Swan   Lake   Tamboon   Lighthouse   Rame
Palms Reserve   Lake   Tamboon   Point Hicks   Petrel   Head
Snowy   Point   Cape Conran   Pearl   Furnell   Inlet   Pt
Inlet   Ricardo   Coastal Park   Point   Sydenham   Wingan
Cape   Inlet   Inlet
Conran   Point Hicks   CROAJINGOLONG   NATIONAL   PARK

W i l d e r n e s s

T A S M A N   S E A

N

0   10   20   30   40   50 km

© Hema Maps Pty Ltd

148°30   149°   149°30   150°

Tasmania

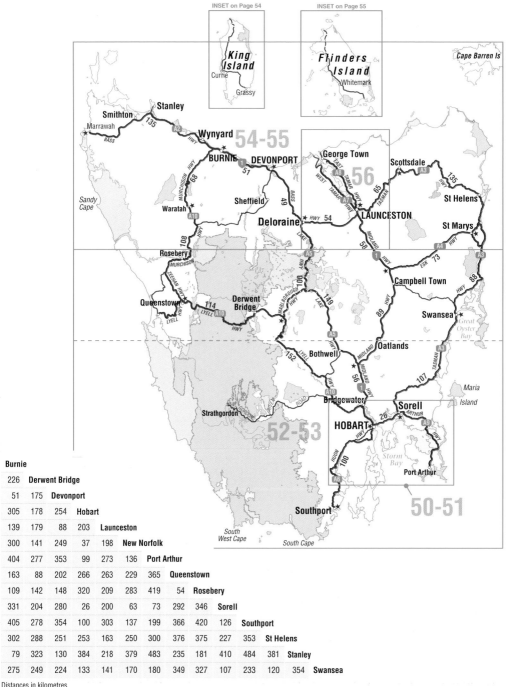

INSET on Page 54

INSET on Page 55

King Island — Currie, Grassy

Flinders Island — Whitemark

Cape Barren Is

54-55

56

52-53

50-51

Stanley, Smithton, Marrawah, Wynyard, BURNIE, DEVONPORT, George Town, Scottsdale, Sheffield, Waratah, Deloraine, LAUNCESTON, St Helens, St Marys, Sandy Cape, Rosebery, Campbell Town, Swansea, Queenstown, Derwent Bridge, Bothwell, Oatlands, Strathgordon, Bridgewater, Sorell, HOBART, Port Arthur, Southport, South West Cape, South Cape, Maria Island

Burnie													
226	**Derwent Bridge**												
51	175	**Devonport**											
305	178	254	**Hobart**										
139	179	88	203	**Launceston**									
300	141	249	37	198	**New Norfolk**								
404	277	353	99	273	136	**Port Arthur**							
163	88	202	266	263	229	365	**Queenstown**						
109	142	148	320	209	283	419	54	**Rosebery**					
331	204	280	26	200	63	73	292	346	**Sorell**				
405	278	354	100	303	137	199	366	420	126	**Southport**			
302	288	251	253	163	250	300	376	375	227	353	**St Helens**		
79	323	130	384	218	379	483	235	181	410	484	381	**Stanley**	
275	249	224	133	141	170	180	349	327	107	233	120	354	**Swansea**

Distances in kilometres

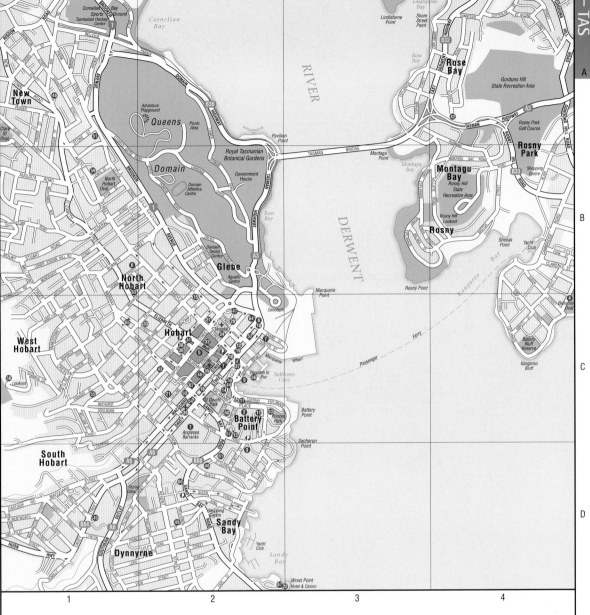

© Hema Maps Pty Ltd

LEGEND

Major Road	**DAVEY STREET**	Shopping Area
Route Number	1 A3	Church
Street	DUKE STREET	Hospital
Lane/Walkway		Park / Reserve
One Way Street	→	Accredited Information
Railway		Post Office

SCALE
0 200m 400m 600m 800m 1km

Places of Interest
1. Anglesea Barracks C2
2. Antarctic Adventure C2
3. Battery Point Area D2
4. Bellerive Oval C4
5. Cat & Fiddle Arcade C2
6. Designer Makers Tasmania B1
7. Franklin Square C2
8. Gas Works Village C2
9. Harbour Cruises C2
10. Hobart Town Hall C2
11. Kelly Steps C2
12. Maritime Museum C3
13. Narryna Heritage Museum C2
14. Parliament House C2
15. Penitentiary Chapel & Courts C2
16. Royal Tennis Centre C2
17. Salamanca Market (Saturday) C2
18. Tasmania Distillery & Museum C2
19. Tasmanian Museum & Art Gallery C2
20. Theatre Royal C2
21. Van Diemens Land Folk Museum C2
22. Wrest Point Casino D2

Services
30. Allport Library & Museum C2
31. Jewish Synagogue C2
32. Police Headquarters C2
33. Post Office C2
34. Qantas C2
35. RACT C2
36. Royal Hobart Hospital C2
37. St Davids Cathedral C2
38. St Helens Hospital C2
39. Tasmanian Visitor Information Centre C2
40. YHA Office C2

Accommodation
40. Blue Hills Motel & Apartments D2
41. Chancellor Inn C2
42. City View Motel A4
43. Corus Hotel Hobart C2
44. Customs House Hotel C2
45. Davey Place Holiday Town Houses D1
46. Doherty's Hotel C2
47. Fountainside Motor Inn C2
48. Graham Court Apartments A1

49. Grosvenor Court Apartments D2
50. Hobart Macquarie Motor Inn C2
51. Hobart Tower Motel A1
52. Hotel Grand Chancellor C2
53. Lenna of Hobart C2
54. Macquarie Manor C2
55. Motel Mayfair C1
56. Oakford on the Pier C2
57. Portsea Terrace C2
58. Quest Waterfront
59. Rydges Hobart B1
60. Salamanca Inn C2
61. St Ives Motel Apartments D2
62. The Astor Private Hotel C2
63. The Lodge on Elizabeth B1
64. The Old Woolstore C2
65. Waratah Motor Hotel C1
66. Woolmers Inn D2
67. Wrest Point Hotel Casino D2

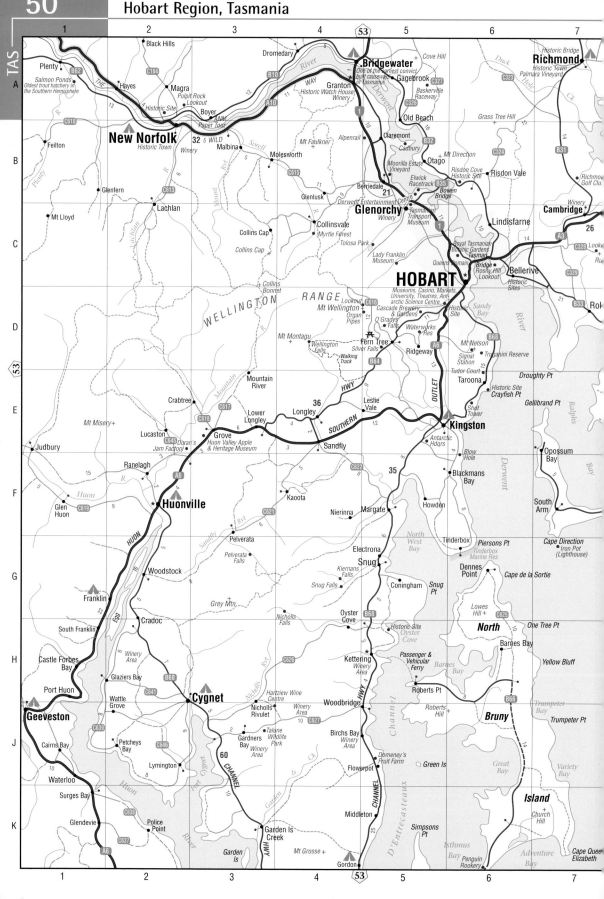

Column and row reference markers (top)
8 9 10 53 11 12 13 14

A B C D E F G H J K

Place names and features

Nugent
Cape Bernier
Point du Ressac
Orielton
Pawleena
Corbetts Lookout
Mt Lord
Penna
Gordon SL
Kellevie
Ragged + Tier
Marion Bay
Wattle Hill
Sorell
Midway Pt
Orani Vineyard
Forcett
Bream Creek
Winery
Copping
Museum
ARTHUR
Convict & Colonial Collection
Cape Paul Lamanon
Tasmania Golf Club
Oyster Farm
Seven Mile Beach Equestrian Centre
Lewisham
Carlton
Blackman Bay
North Bay
Cape Frederick Hendrick
Hobart Airport
Lanherne Golf Club
Sandy Pt
Tiger Head
Dodges Ferry
Seven Mile Beach
Carlton
Roches Beach
Carlton Bluff
Primrose Sands
Tasman Monument
Dunalley
Denison Canal
Lauderdale
Primrose Pt
Fulham Is
Dunalley Bay
Mt Forestier
Frederick Henry
Green Head
Smooth Is
King George Is
Mt Forestier
Forestier
Sandford
Bay
Sloping Is
Whitehouse Pt
Lime Bay Nature Res
73
Wellard Bridge
Cremorne
Mt Augustus
Pipe Clay Lagoon
Mt Stewart
Chronicle Pt
Murdunna
Cape Surville
Tasman National Park
Peninsula
Cape Deslacs
Coal Mines Historic Site
Flinders Bay
Macgregor Peak
Clifton Beach
Mutton Bird Viewing (Summer)
Convict Settlement Ruins
Norfolk Bay
Ck
North West Head
Gwandalan
Garnetts Bridge
Lookout
Tessellated Pavement
Sandford Equestrian Centre
Saltwater River
Deer Pt
Eaglehawk Neck
Officers Quarters & Dogline
Cape Contrariety
Hurdle Bridge
Halfway Bluff
Eaglehawk Bay
Historic Site
Pirates Bay
Betsey Is
Premaydena
Cashs Lookout
Penzance
Tasman Blowhole
Doo Town
Tasman Arch
Devils Kitchen
Mt Communication
Koonya
Taranna
Tasmanian Devil Centre
Waterfall Bay
Outer North Head
Camp Falls
O'Hara Bluff
Auk Pt
Sand Dunes
Tasman National Park
Storm
Nubeena
Tasman
Peninsula
Thumb Pt
Parsons Bridge
Oakwood
Mimosa Falls
Bay
Wedge Bay
White Beach
Bush Mill Railway
Cape Huay
The Lanterns
Wedge Is
Isle of the Dead Historic Site
Fortescue Bay
Highcroft
Port Arthur
Convict Ruins Historic Ghost Tours Ocean Kayaking Tours
Port Arthur
Stormlea
Palmers Lookout
Two Island Bay
Remarkable Cave
Maingon Blowhole
Tasman National Park
Curio Bay
West Arthur Head
Munro Bight
Tasman National Park
Raoul Bay
Black Head
Cape Pillar
Cape Raoul
Maingon Bay
Tasman Is
Chasm Lookout
Lighthouse

Road numbers
A3, 7, 13, C332, C331, 20, 2, 5, C349, A9, 17, C349, 15, C334, A9, HWY, 8, 14, 9, C338, B33, B37, C343, C341, 9, 8, 10, 13, 9, A9, 10, C344, C347, 5, 6

Scale
SCALE
0 5 10 km
© Hema Maps Pty Ltd

N

SOUTHERN

OCEAN

Tullah
Rosebery
MURCHISON
Mt Murchison
Mt Read
Williamsford
Anthony PS
Montezuma Falls
Mt Dundas
Selina
Zeehan
Dundas
Mt Agnew
Museum
Mt Zeehan
Trial Harbour
Granville Harbour
Ahrberg Bay
Lake Pieman
Bastyan PS Dam
Renison Bell
Mt Sedgwick
Henty Glacial Moraine
Mt Beatrice
Lookout
Mt Lyell
Copper Mines
Linda
Chairlift, Museum
Queenstown
Mt Owen
Mt Huxley
Lynchford
Mt Lyell
Crotty Dam
Mt Jukes
Strahan
Wharf Centre
Regatta Pt
Cruise
Ocean Beach
King River Gorge
Darwin Dam
Mt Darwin
Lighthouse
Cape Sorell
Macquarie Hds
Sophia Pt
Liberty Pt
Macquarie
Harbour
Sloop Pt
George Pt
Gould
Sarah Is
Convict Ruins
Kelly Basin
Heritage Landing
Birthday Bay
Varna Bay
Hibbs Bay
Point Hibbs
SOUTHWEST
Mt Lee
Innes Pk
Spero Bay
Endeavour Bay
Christmas Cove
CONSERVATION
High Rocky Pt
Mt Lewis
AREA
Lighthouse
Low Rocky Pt
Elliott Bay
Nye Bay
Elliott Pt
Mulcahy Bay
Brier Holme Head
Mt Hean
Castle Hill
Svenor Pt
Wreck Bay
James Kelly Basin
Payne Bay
North Head
Pt St Vincent
Breaksea Is
Port Davey
Hilliard Head
Stephens Bay
Mutton Bird Is
South West Cape
Telopea Pt
Cox Bluff
Red Pt
De Witt Is
Flat Witch Is
Walker Is
Lighthouse
MAATSUYKER GROUP
Maatsuyker Is

CRADLE MOUNTAIN
LAKE ST CLAIR
NATIONAL PARK
Mt Pelion West
Mt Pelion East
Mt Ossa
Cathedral Mtn
Mt Olympus
Eldon Peak
Eldon Bluff
High Dome
Pyramid Mtn
Mt Hagel
Mt Rufus
Mt Alma
Mt Arrowsmith
Derwent Bridge
Visitor Centre
Victoria Pass
Nelson Valley
LYELL HWY
Franklin River Nature Trail
Mt King William I
King William
Guelph Basin
Mt King William II
Butlers Gorge PS
Mt Hobbhouse
Mt King William III
Frenchmans Cap
FRANKLIN - GORDON
WILD RIVERS
NATIONAL PARK
PART OF WORLD HERITAGE AREA
Goodwins Peak
Mt Hemboldt
Reeds Peak
Clear Hill
Wylds Craig
PRINCE OF WALES RANGE
DENISON RANGE
Gordon Dam
Lake Gordon
Adamsfield
Gate
Old Mine
Pyramid Head
Serpentine Dam
Strathgordon
Teds Beach
Mt Sprent
McPartlan Pass
Frodshams Pass
Creepy Crawly Walk
Mt Wedge
Mt Bowes
Double Peak
Mt Anne
Mt Eliza
Lake Pedder
FRANKLAND RANGE
Lake Judd
Mt Solitary
Lookout
Scotts Peak Dam
Edgar Dam
Mt Hesperus
Mt Orion
West Portal
ARTHUR RANGE
SOUTHWEST NATIONAL PARK
PART OF WORLD HERITAGE AREA
Federation Peak
Ripple Mtn
Mt Narold
Mt Rugby
Bathurst Harbour
Melaleuca Ranger Offe
& Bird Observatory
Mt Counsel
Mt Melaleuca
Mt Karamu
Mt Louisa
Louisa Bay
Havelock Bluff
Ile du Golfe

Bronte Park
Tarraleah

© Hema Maps Pty Ltd

N

0   10   20   30   40 km

HOBART

Campbell Town
Ross
Oatlands
Bothwell
Hamilton
Kempton
New Norfolk
Bridgewater
Richmond
Sorell
Cambridge
Midway Pt
Triabunna
Orford
Swansea
Bicheno
Freycinet Peninsula
Freycinet National Park
Schouten Island
Maria Island
Maria Island National Park
Lauderdale
Kingston
Huonville
Snug
Cygnet
Geeveston
Dover
Southport
Bruny Island
North Bruny
South Bruny
South Bruny National Park
Forestier Peninsula
Tasman Peninsula
Tasman Nat Park
Port Arthur
Nubeena
Eaglehawk Neck
Taranna
Dunalley
Poatina
Conara
Avoca
Bicheno
Douglas-Apsley National Park

Storm Bay
Frederick Henry Bay
Norfolk Bay
Great Oyster Bay
Marion Bay

TASMAN SEA

GREAT WESTERN TIERS CONSERVATION AREA
Buckland Military Training Area

BASS STRAIT

INSET

King Island

Cape Wickham
Victoria Cove
Cape Farewell
Disappointment Bay
Egg Lagoon
New Year Is
Christmas Is
Whistler Pt
Phques
Reekara
Loorana
Yambacoona
Naracoopa
Fraser Bluff
Currie
Pegarah
Grassy
Lymwood
Yarra Creek
Cataraqui Pt
Pearshape
Mt Stanley
Stokes Pt

Cape Keraudren
Cape Rochon
Cape Adamson
Three Hummock Island
S Hummock
Cuvier Bay
Hunter Island
Lighthouse
Steep Is
Bird Is
Stack Is
Walker Island
Trefoil Is
Woolnorth Pt
Hunter Passage
Kangaroo Is
Robbins Island
Guyton Pt
Cape Elie
Cape Grim
Woolnorth
Montagu
Stony Pt
Perkins Island
North Pt
Highfield Historic Site
West Pt
Highfield Pt
Historic Town
Bluff Hill
Montagu
Stanley
The Nut
Circular Head
Smithton
Marrawah
Redpa
Togari
Black River
Port Latta
Crayfish Creek
Rocky Cape
Pebbly Beach
Sisters Beach
Boat Harbour
Wynyard
Seabrook
Somerset
BURNIE
Penguin
Ulverstone
DEVONPORT
Latrobe
Railton
Sheffield
Mole Creek
Waratah
Guildford
Tullah
Rosebery
Zeehan
Queenstown
Strahan
Derwent Bridge
Bronte Park

BASS HWY

MURCHISON HWY

ZEEHAN HWY

LYELL HWY

CRADLE MOUNTAIN
LAKE ST CLAIR
NATIONAL PARK

FRANKLIN - GORDON
WILD RIVERS
NATIONAL PARK

ARTHUR PIEMAN
CONSERVATION AREA

SAVAGE RIVER
NATIONAL PARK

© Hema Maps Pty Ltd

0   10   20   30km

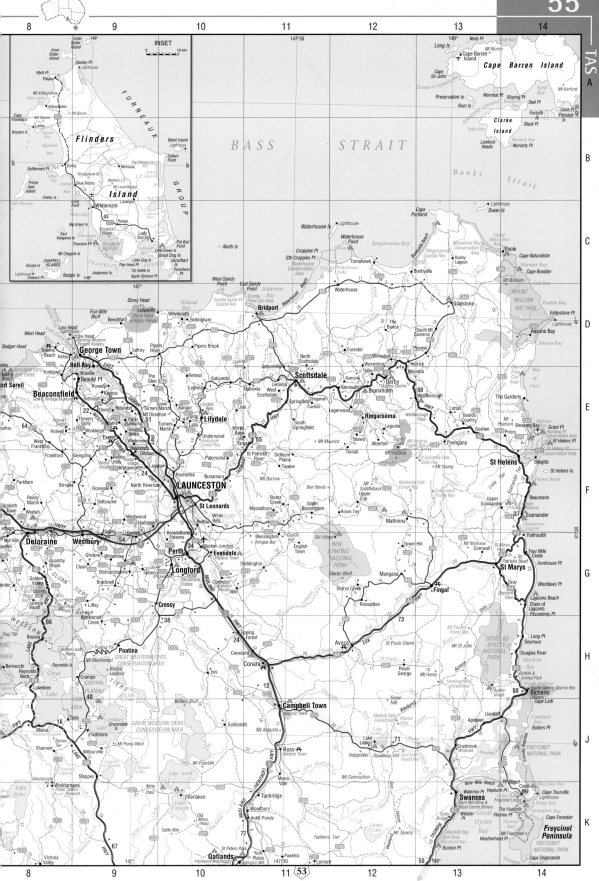

INSET

FURNEAUX

Flinders

Island

GROUP

BASS   STRAIT

Banks   Strait

Cape Barren Island

Clarke
Island

Low Head
George Town
Bell Bay
Beaconsfield

Bridport

Scottsdale

Derby
Branxholm

Ringarooma

The Gardens

St Helens

Lilydale

LAUNCESTON
St Leonards

Deloraine
Westbury
Perth
Evandale
Longford

Cressy

Falmouth

St Marys

Fingal

BEN
LOMOND
NATIONAL
PARK

Avoca

Conara

Bicheno

DOUGLAS
APSLEY
NATIONAL
PARK

Campbell Town

GREAT WESTERN TIERS
CONSERVATION AREA

Ross

Swansea

FREYCINET
NATIONAL
PARK

Freycinet
Peninsula

Oatlands

N

0   5   10km
© Hema Maps Pty Ltd

BASS   STRAIT

West Sandy Point
East Sandy Point
St Albans Bay
Double Sandy Point Coastal Reserve
Granite Pt Con Area

Stony Head
Noland Bay

Lulworth
Weymouth
Bellingham
Bridport

Five Mile Bluff
Beechford
Stony Head Artillery Range
Turquoise Bluff

West Head
Low Head Lighthouse
Devil's (Summer Only)
Port Dalrymple

Greens Beach
Low Head
Maritime Museum
Penguin Rookery

Lefroy
Pipers River
Winery

Pipers Brook Winery

Kelso
Clarence Point
George Town
+Mt George
B82

Lavender Farm

Yorktown
Ilfraville
Bell Bay

Retreat
Golconda
B81
Nabowla

Beauty Point
Winery Area Kayena
Rowella

The Glen
C513
Lebrina
Wineries Tunnel
Wyena

Beaconsfield
Gold & Heritage Museum
A7

Sidmouth
Lower Turners Marsh
Bangor
North Lilydale
Lisle

Batman Bridge
Deviot
Hillwood Winery
Mt Direction

Lilydale
Winery
Lilydale Falls
Mt Arthur

Flowery Gully
Robigana
Paper Beach
Gravelly Beach

Turners Marsh
Karoola
Lalla
Underwood
Myrtle Bank
Targa

Holwell Gorge
Stewarts Hill
Holwell
Winkleigh
Exeter
Winery Area

St Patricks River

West Frankford
Frankford
Glenarry Winery
Notley Hills
Notley Gorge

Brady's Lookout
Waterbird Haven
Grindelwald Swiss Village
Rosevears
Dilston
Patersonia
Nunamara

Birralee
Bridgenorth
Winery Legana
Rocherlea
Mt Edgecombe

Reedy Marsh
Rosevale
North Riverside
Riverside
Mowbray

LAUNCESTON

Selbourne
Lake Trevallyn
Trevallyn State Rec Area
Norwood
St Leonards

Westwood
Hadspen
Entally House
Prospect
Youngtown
White Hills

Deloraine
Exton
BASS HWY
Westbury
Hagley
Carrick
54 HWY
Relbia Winery
Breadalbane
Launceston Airport
Temple Bar

Glenore Winery
Whitemore
Oaks
Pateena
Western Junction
Evandale
Historic Town

Quamby Brook
Cluan
Bishopsbourne
Toilberry
Perth
Longford
Glen Stuart

Golden Valley
Quamby Bluff
Bracknell
Brickendon
Woolmers
Clarendon
Clarendon House
Nile

Jackeys Marsh
Liffey
Liffey Falls
Simmons Plains Car Racing
Cressy

South Australia

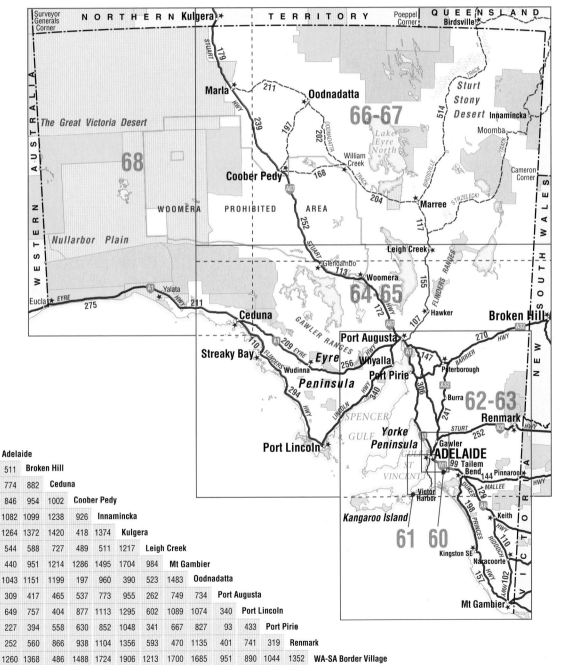

Adelaide												
511	**Broken Hill**											
774	882	**Ceduna**										
846	954	1002	**Coober Pedy**									
1082	1099	1238	926	**Innamincka**								
1264	1372	1420	418	1374	**Kulgera**							
544	588	727	489	511	1217	**Leigh Creek**						
440	951	1214	1286	1495	1704	984	**Mt Gambier**					
1043	1151	1199	197	960	390	523	1483	**Oodnadatta**				
309	417	465	537	773	955	262	749	734	**Port Augusta**			
649	757	404	877	1113	1295	602	1089	1074	340	**Port Lincoln**		
227	394	558	630	852	1048	341	667	827	93	433	**Port Pirie**	
252	560	866	938	1104	1356	593	470	1135	401	741	319	**Renmark**
1260	1368	486	1488	1724	1906	1213	1700	1685	951	890	1044	1352	**WA-SA Border Village**

Distances in kilometres

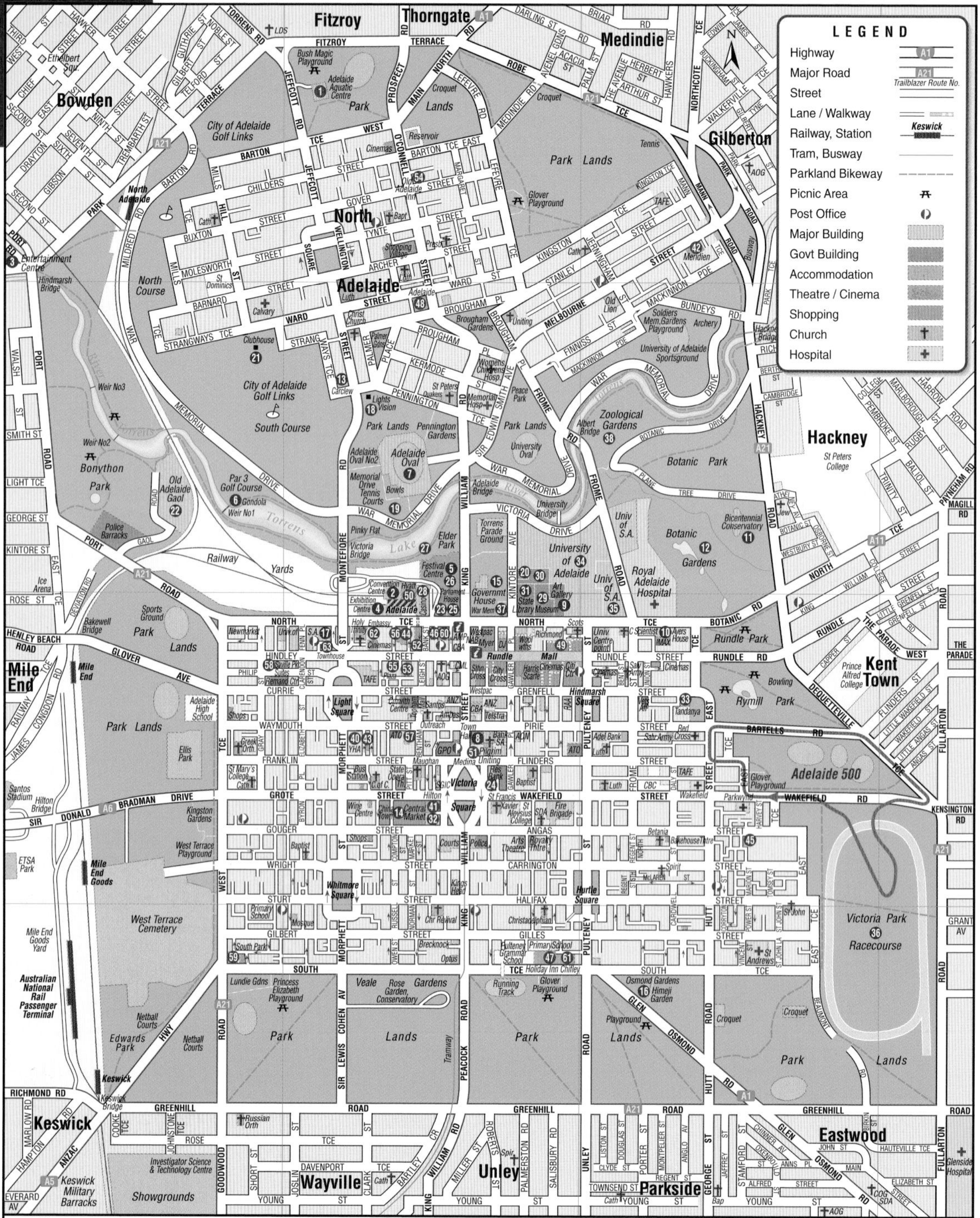
LEGEND
Highway
Major Road
Trailblazer Route No.
Street
Lane / Walkway
Railway, Station
Keswick
Tram, Busway
Parkland Bikeway
Picnic Area
Post Office
Major Building
Govt Building
Accommodation
Theatre / Cinema
Shopping
Church
Hospital
Fitzroy
Thorngate
Medindie
Bowden
Gilberton
North Adelaide
Hackney
Mile End
Kent Town
Keswick
Wayville
Unley
Parkside
Eastwood
Park Lands
Adelaide 500
Victoria Park Racecourse
Botanic Gardens
Rundle Mall
Victoria Square
Light Square
Hindmarsh Square
Hurtle Square
Whitmore Square
Showgrounds
West Terrace Cemetery
0 200 400 600m
© Hema Maps Pty Ltd

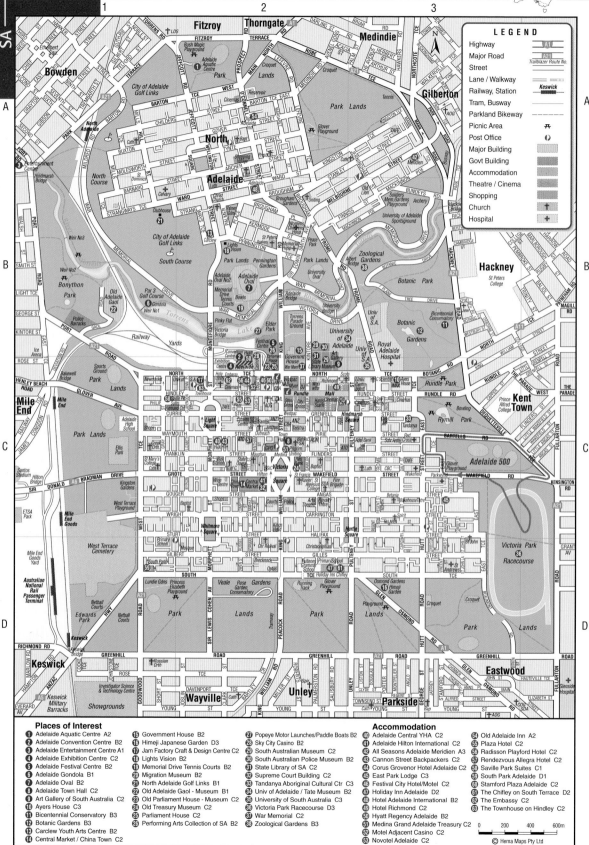

Places of Interest

1. Adelaide Aquatic Centre A2
2. Adelaide Convention Centre B2
3. Adelaide Entertainment Centre A1
4. Adelaide Exhibition Centre C2
5. Adelaide Festival Centre B2
6. Adelaide Gondola B1
7. Adelaide Oval B2
8. Adelaide Town Hall C2
9. Art Gallery of South Australia C2
10. Ayers House C3
11. Bicentennial Conservatory B3
12. Botanic Gardens B3
13. Carclew Youth Arts Centre B2
14. Central Market / China Town C2
15. Government House B2
16. Himeji Japanese Garden D3
17. Jam Factory Craft & Design Centre C2
18. Lights Vision B2
19. Memorial Drive Tennis Courts B2
20. Migration Museum B2
21. North Adelaide Golf Links B1
22. Old Adelaide Gaol - Museum B1
23. Old Parliament House - Museum C2
24. Old Treasury Museum C2
25. Parliament House C2
26. Performing Arts Collection of SA B2
27. Popeye Motor Launches/Paddle Boats B2
28. Sky City Casino B2
29. South Australian Museum C2
30. South Australian Police Museum B2
31. State Library of SA C2
32. Supreme Court Building C2
33. Tandanya Aboriginal Cultural Ctr C3
34. Univ of Adelaide / Tate Museum B2
35. University of South Australia C3
36. Victoria Park Racecourse D3
37. War Memorial C2
38. Zoological Gardens B3

Accommodation

40. Adelaide Central YHA C2
41. Adelaide Hilton International C2
42. All Seasons Adelaide Meridien A3
43. Cannon Street Backpackers C2
44. Corus Grovenor Hotel Adelaide C2
45. East Park Lodge C3
46. Festival City Hotel/Motel C2
47. Holiday Inn Adelaide D2
48. Hotel Adelaide International B2
49. Hotel Richmond C2
50. Hyatt Regency Adelaide B2
51. Medina Grand Adelaide Treasury C2
52. Motel Adjacent Casino C2
53. Novotel Adelaide C2
54. Old Adelaide Inn A2
55. Plaza Hotel C2
56. Radisson Playford Hotel C2
57. Rendezvous Allegra Hotel C2
58. Saville Park Suites C1
59. South Park Adelaide D1
60. Stamford Plaza Adelaide C2
61. The Chifley on South Terrace D2
62. The Embassy C2
63. The Townhouse on Hindley C2

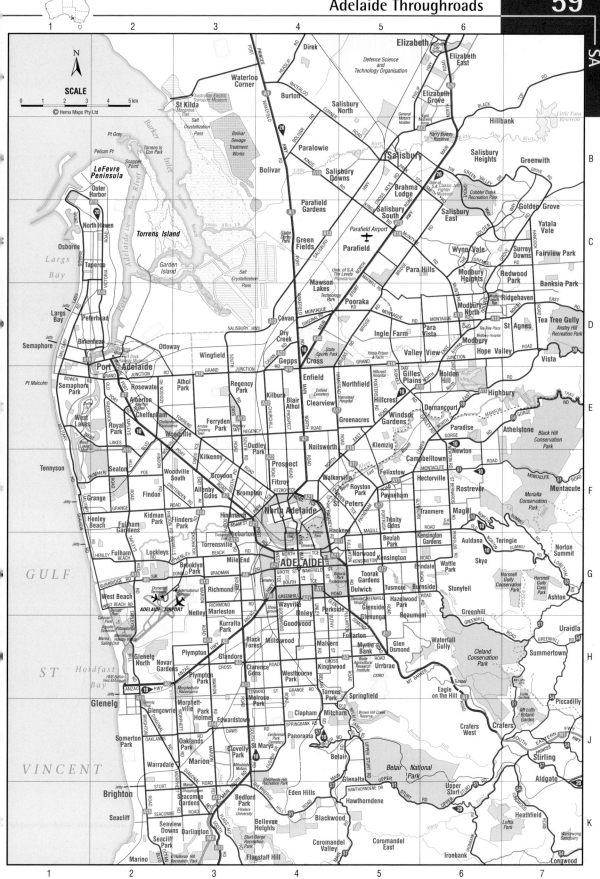

SA

© Hema Maps Pty Ltd

Selected place names and features:

Red Banks, Korunye, Reeves Plains, Wasleys, Templers, Greenock, Daveyston, Nuriootpa, Light Pass, Penrice, Angaston, Maranunga, Seppeltsfield, Wineries, Barossa Valley, Tanunda, Bethany, Menglers Hill, Collingrove Historic Homestead

Lower Light, Two Wells, Lewiston, Buchfelde, Gawler Airfield, Gawler, Sandy Creek, Lyndoch, Rowland Flat, Cranford, Eden Valley, Kaiserstuhl Con Park, Mt Crawford Forest

Port Gawler, Virginia, Penfield, Angle Vale, Munno Para, Uleybury, Yattalunga, Williamstown, Springton, Mt Crawford, Mt Pleasant, Crawford Forest

St Kilda, Bolivar, Burton, Elizabeth, One Tree Hill, Upper Hermitage, Kersbrook, Forreston, Mt Pleasant

Outer Harbor, North Haven, Largs Bay, Port Adelaide, Salisbury, Golden Grove, Para Hills, Modbury, Tea Tree Gully, Lower Hermitage, Inglewood, Chain of Ponds, Gumeracha, Birdwood, Tungkillo

Semaphore, West Lakes, Woodville, Enfield, Ingle Farm, Highbury, Paracombe, Cudlee Creek, Mt Torrens, Lobethal

Tennyson, Grange, Findon, Croydon, Prospect, Walkerville, Campbelltown, Athelstone, Castambul, Montacute, Cherryville, Lenswood, Charleston, Mt Beevor

Henley Beach, Lockleys, Fulham, Thebarton, Norwood, Kensington, Magill, Rostrevor, Norton Summit, Marble Hill, Basket Range, Forest Range, Woodside, Harrogate, Rockleigh

West Beach, ADELAIDE, Burnside, Stonyfell, Ashton, Uraidla, Summertown, Carey Gully, Kenneth Stirling, Army Camp

Adelaide Airport, Unley, Glen Osmond, Cleland Con Park, Piccadilly, Balhannah, Oakbank, Brukunga

Glenelg, Somerton Park, Marion, Mitcham, Brown Hill Creek Rec Park, Crafers, Stirling, Verdun, Ambleside, Hahndorf, Nairne, Dawesley

Brighton, Seacliff, Belair, Blackwood, Bellevue Heights, Coromandel Valley, Aldgate, Bridgewater, Heathfield, Longwood, Ironbank, Mylor, Littlehampton, Mt Barker, Kanmantoo

Marino, Hallett Cove, Flagstaff Hill, Aberfoyle Park, Cherry Gardens, Scott Creek, Bradbury, Biggs Flat, Totness, Disher Hill

Lonsdale, Reynella, Happy Valley, Clarendon, Dorset Vale, Mt Bold Reservoir, Echunga, Wistow, Callington Freeway

O'Sullivan Beach, Christies Beach, Port Noarlunga, Noarlunga Centre, Hackham, Kangarilla, Blewitt Springs, Greenhill, Macclesfield, Hartley, Woodchester

Seaford, Moana, Old Noarlunga, McLaren Flat, Mt Wilson, Paris Creek, Meadows, Rowleys Hill, Kuitpo Forest

McLaren Vale, Wineries

GULF ST VINCENT, Holdfast Bay, Largs Bay, Torrens Island, Gulf St Vincent

Mount Lofty Ranges

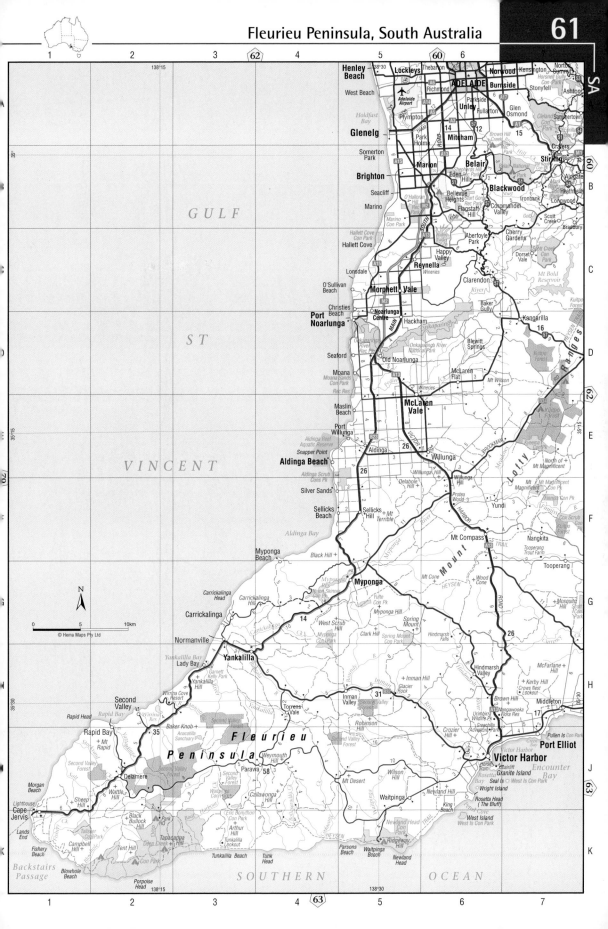

NSW

SA

Adelaide

Renmark · **Berri** · **Loxton** · **Barmera** · **Waikerie** · **Morgan** · **Burra** · **Clare** · **Kapunda** · **Gawler** · **Elizabeth** · **Nuriootpa** · **Angaston** · **Tanunda** · **Murray Bridge** · **Mt Barker** · **Maclaren Vale**

Port Augusta · **Whyalla** · **Port Pirie** · **Port Germein** · **Wilmington** · **Melrose** · **Orroroo** · **Peterborough** · **Jamestown** · **Gladstone** · **Crystal Brook** · **Laura** · **Snowtown** · **Balaklava**

Kadina · **Wallaroo** · **Moonta** · **Maitland** · **Ardrossan** · **Yorke Peninsula** · **Minlaton** · **Yorketown** · **Edinburgh** · **Stansbury** · **Port Vincent** · **Stansbury**

Iron Knob · **Kimba** · **Cleve** · **Cowell** · **Arno Bay** · **Eyre Peninsula** · **Thorn**

GULF ST VINCENT

SPENCER GULF

EYRE HWY · STURT HWY · BARRIER HWY · LINCOLN HWY

Fruit Fly Exclusion Zone

Bookmark Biosphere Reserve · Danggali Conservation Park · Billiatt Con Park · Murray River National Park · Sunset National Park

VICTORIA

Murrayville · Big Desert Wilderness Park · Big Desert · Kaniva · Telopea Downs · Little Desert National Park · Apsley · Edenhope · Langkoop · Casterton · Dartmoor · Glenelg

Scorpion Springs Con Park · Servicetown · Bordertown · Wolseley · Frances · Naracoorte · Lucindale · Penola · Nangwarry · Tarpeena · MT GAMBIER · Port MacDonnell · Cape Northumberland

Keith · Brimbago · Wirrega · Kongal · Willalooka · Lochaber · Kybybolite · Coonawarra · Comaum · Yahl

Tintinara · Coonalpyn · Culburra · Kingston SE · Cape Jaffa · Robe · Beachport · Millicent · Lake Bonney

Meningie · Coorong · Coorong National Park · Younghusband · Magrath Flat · Woods Well · Policemans Point · Salt Creek · Chinamans Well · Tilley Swamp · Mount Benson · Nora Creina · Southend · Carpenter Rocks

Lake Alexandrina · Lake Albert · Milang · Clayton · Narrung · Poltalloch · Goolwa · Middleton · Port Elliot · Victor Harbor · Hindmarsh Is · Encounter Bay · Fleurieu Peninsula · Normanville · Yankalilla · Rapid Bay · Cape Jervis · Cape Delamere

Kingscote · American River · Penneshaw · Kangaroo Island · Flinders Chase National Park · Parndana · Vivonne Bay · Cape Gantheaume Con Park · Remarkable Rocks · Cape du Couedic · Cape Borda · Cape Torrens · Cape Forbin

SOUTHERN OCEAN

Investigator Strait

© Hema Maps Pty Ltd

Scale: 0 10 20 30 40 50 60 70 80km

Yellabinna Regional Reserve

For more detail on this area,
see Hema's Great Desert Tracks
South Central Sheet

Yumbarra Conservation Park

Pureba Conservation Park

Roxby Downs

'Roxby Downs'
Purple Downs

'Mount Vivian'

Woomera

Pimba

Kingoonya
Goodambo
Coondambo
Kultanaby
'Wirraminna'
'Witraminna'
113

TRANS AUSTRALIAN RAILWAY

STUART HWY

Tarcoola
Wilgena
'Malbooma O/S'
Lyons
Malbooma
'Wilgena'
'North Well'
Ferguson

Dog Fence
Mt Finke

Lake Labyrinth
Lake Harris

Lake Gairdner
Lake Gairdner National Park

Lake Everard
'Lake Everard'

'Yerda'

'Kokatha'

'Kondoolka'

Island Lagoon

Lake MacFarlane

Bookabie
Penong
Kowulka
Kevin
Charra
Moule
Koonibba Community
Koonibba
Karawingi Park

Ceduna
Thevenard
Laura Bay
Cape D'Estrees
St Peter Island
Goat Is
Smoky Eye Is
Franklin Is
Denial Bay
Mudamuckla
Nunjikompita
Carawa
Wirrulla
139
Petina
Cungena
Haslam
110

Nuyts Archipelago Con Park
St Francis Is
Point Brown
Streaky Bay

Cape Bauer
Piednippie
Chandada
Poochera
Minnipa
83
Yaninee
Wudinna
Eyre
Peninsula
Kimba
88

Streaky Bay
Point Westall
Calca
Colley
Port Kenny
Mount Damper
Koongawa
Warramboo
Koonibba
Waddikee
125
Venus Bay
Talia
Talia Caves
'Gum Flat'
Kopi
55
Darke Peak
Mangalo
Cleve
115
Cowell

Cape Radstock
Anxious Bay
Walkers Rock
Cape Finniss
Mount Wedge
90
Bramfield
Kappawanta
LOCK
Murdinga
Rudall
Carpa
Port Gibbon

Flinders Island
Ward Is
Colton
Elliston
'Portana'
'Oakdale'
Toolig ie
Verran
Arno Bay
Cape Driver
113

Investigator Group Con Park
Topgallant Isles
Sheringa
Pine Grove
101
81
Hincks Con Park
Warmington
SPENCER

Pearson Isles
Sheringa Beach
Cap Is
Mt Hamilton
Karkoo
Mount Hill
Brooker
Butler Tanks
Port Neill
Cape Hardy

Drummond Point
Mt Drummond
Rocky Island
Kapinnie
Yeelanna
Cockaleechie
Brayfield
Cummins
Lipson
Lipson Cove

Mt Greenly
Coles Point
Point Sir Isaac
Coffin Bay
Reef Point
Coffin Bay National Pk
Point Whidbey
Wangary
Warrow
Coulta
Mt Dutton
Edillilie
White 46
Koppio
65
Yallunda Flat
Tumby Bay
Cape Euler
Winceby Is
Reevesby Is
Sir Joseph Banks Group Con Park
Spilsby Is

Avoid Bay
Point Avoid
Coffin Bay
68
Wanilla
Green Patch
Louth Bay
Poonindie
Louth Is
Boston Point
Boston Island
Boston Bay

Perforated Is
Four Hummocks
Price Is
Whidbey Isles Con Park
Shoal Point
Port Lincoln
Tulka
Lincoln National Park
Macaren Point
Port Donington
Dangerous Reef

Cape Carnot
Liguanea Is
Cape Wiles
Sleaford Bay
Taylor Is
West Point
Williams Is
Thistle Island
Cape Catastrophe
Observatory Point

Waterhouse Point
Wedge Is
South West Rock

Neptune Islands

West Cape
Cape Spencer
Reef Head
Seal Is
Althorpe Islands

Kangaroo Island
Corny Point
Berry Bay
Corny
Daly Head
Formby Bay
Point Margaret
Brown Beach
Royston Head

Marion
Stenhouse
Western River Con Park
Cape Forbin
Cape Torrens
Investigator

SOUTHERN

OCEAN

GULF

N

0   50   100km

© Hema Maps Pty Ltd

SA

NEW SOUTH WALES

VICTORIA

Leigh Creek · Copley · North Mooloolloo · Maynards Well · Balcanoona' · Lake Runbarow · Starvation Lake · Packsaddle

NORTH FLINDERS RANGES

Sliding Rock Mine · 'Warraweena' · Nantawarrina · 'Mulga View' · Lake Elder · Pine View · 'Westwood Downs'

Puttapa · Beltana · Beltana Roadhouse · 'Moorilla' · Patawarta Gorge · 'Narrina' · 'Mooloolloo' + Glass Gorge · Chambers Gorge · Lake Maljanapa · Lake Kuuni · Brougham Gate · 'Quinyambie' · Joulnie O/S · 'Avenel' · 'Telita'

Nilpena · 'Moralana' · Brachina Gorge · St Mary Peak + Mt Caernarvon · 'Willow Springs' · 'Martins Well' · 'Erudina Woolshed' · Lake Namba · Dog Fence · 'Benagarie' · 'Gum Park' · 'Yandaroo' · 'Mulga Valley' · 'Wilangee'

Parachilna · Angorichina Village · 'Aroona' (Ruin) · 'Gum Creek' · Wirrealpa' · 'Frome Downs' · Lake Frome Regional Reserve · LAKE FROME · Lake Karpi · Lake Moko

Motpena · 'Commodore' · Blinman · Flinders Ranges National Park · 'Erudina' · 'Curnamona' · 'Mooleulooloo' · 'Yarramba' · 'Mulyungarie' · 'Eldee' · 'Purnamoota'

Hawker · 'Ravensleigh' Park · Sacred Canyon · 'Arkaba' Wonoka · 'Warcowie' · 'Bibliando' · 'New Baratta' · 'Glenorchy' · 'Strathearn' · Kalkaroo O/S · 'Mundi Mundi' · Fruit Fly Exclusion Zone · Silverton

'Warrakimbo' · 'Partacoona' · Kanyaka Ruins · Cradock · 'Witchitie' · 'Killawarra' · 'Talabity' · BROKEN HILL · The Pinnacles · Silver City HWY

Quorn · Boolcunda · Carrieton · Johnburgh · 'Minburra' · 'Melton' · 'Waukaringa' (Ruins) · 'Weekeroo' · 'Old Boolcoomata' · Wompinie' · Cockburn · 'Cutana' · 'Aroona' · 'Corella O/S' · 'Ascot Vale' · 'Sunny Dale'

Port Augusta · Wilmington · Amyton · Hammond · Eurelia · 'Yalpara' · Meadow Downs' · 'Melton' · 'Winninninnie' · Mannahill · Olary · 'Waiwera' · 'Erunga' · 'Maldorky' · 'Mutooroo' · 'Ballara' · 'Burta'

WHYALLA · Melrose · Booleroo Centre · Orroroo · 'Black Rock' · Dawson · Nackara · 'Parato' · 'Tiverton' · 'Netley Gap' · 'Dlorah Downs' · 'Oulnina' · Benda · 'Wadnaminga' · 'Devonborough Downs' · 'Buckalowie' · 'Mazar' · 'Harriedale' · 'Nagaela' · 'Loch Lilly'

PORT PIRIE · Laura · Jamestown · Peterborough · Yongala · Oodla Wirra · 'Oak Park' · Lilydale' · 'Oakvale'

PORT PIRIE · Crystal Brook · Gladstone · Georgetown · Terowie · 'Loch Winnoch' · 'Faraway Hill' · 'Sturt Vale' · 'Morgan Vale' (ruin) · Danggali Conservation Park · 'Ennisvale' · 'Nanya' · 'Tarrara' · 'Belvedere'

Port Broughton · Redhill · Gulnare · Hallett · 'Collinsville' · 'Kia-Ora' · 'Caroona' · Pine Valley · 'Glenora' · 'Woolgangi' · 'Lords Well' · Bookmark Biosphere Reserve · Tarawi Nature Park · Tarawi

Mundoora · Koolunga · Spalding · 'Booborowie' · Mount Bryan · Mongolata' · 'Old Koomooloo' · 'Canegrass' · 'Hyperna' · Chowilla Regional Reserve · 'Belmore'

Brinkworth · Snowtown · Burra · Redbanks · Chalk Cliffs · 'Koomooloo' · 'Redcliffe' · 'Balah' · Bookmark Biosphere Reserve · 'Pine Camp'

Blyth · Clare · Leighton · Hanson · 'Grassville' · 'Sampsons Well' · 'Bunyung' · 'Nulla'

Wallaroo · Kadina · Bute · Lochiel · Ninnes · Halbury · Mintaro · Black Springs · Florieton · 'Calperum' · Border Cliffs · Lake Victoria · Rufus River

Moonta · Moonta Bay · Port Hughes · Cape Elizabeth · Paskeville · Kulpara · Balaklava · Saddleworth · Marrabel · Morgan · Lock 3 · Lock 2 · Overland Corner · 'Cooltoong' · Renmark · Paringa · Lindsay Point · Cullulleraine

The Gap · Arthurton · Port Wakefield · Bowmans · Owen · Hamley Bridge · Riverton · Hamilton · Sutherlands · Murbko · Cadell · Pooginook Con Park · Waikerie · Moorook · Berri · Loxton · Loxton North · Meringur

Maitland · Ardrossan · Dublin · Lower Light · Kapunda · Nuriootpa · Angaston · Keyneton · Sedan · Blanchetown · Swan Reach · Taplan

Yorke Peninsula · Port Victoria · Minlaton · Port Vincent · Stansbury · Gawler · ELIZABETH · Salisbury · Mt Pleasant · Mannum · Bakara · Mercunda · Galga · Kunlara · 'Wirha' · SUNSET COUNTRY · Murray Sunset National Park

Edithburgh · Yorketown · Stansbury · ADELAIDE · Lobethal · Birdwood · Palmer · Walker Flat · Bowhill · Kalyan · Perponda · Veitch · 'Mantung' · Meribah · Pink Lakes State Park

Brighton · Mt Barker · Hahndorf · Mannum · Sandalwood · Bowaka · Haldon · Karte · Halidon · Fruit Fly Exclusion Zone

McLaren Vale · Strathalbyn · Murray Bridge · Tailem Bend · Karoonda · Kulkami · Mulpata · Pinnaroo · Murrayville · Cowangie

Fleurieu Peninsula · Goolwa · Milang · Lake Alexandrina · Meningie · Coomandook · Ngarkat Con Park · Big Desert Wilderness Park · Wyperfeld National Park

Kingscote · Penneshaw · Victor Harbor · Encounter Bay · Lake Albert · Mt Timothy · Scorpion Springs Con Park · MALLEE HWY

Port Germein · Germein Bay · Yacka · MID NORTH · STURT HWY · BARRIER HWY · SILVER CITY HWY

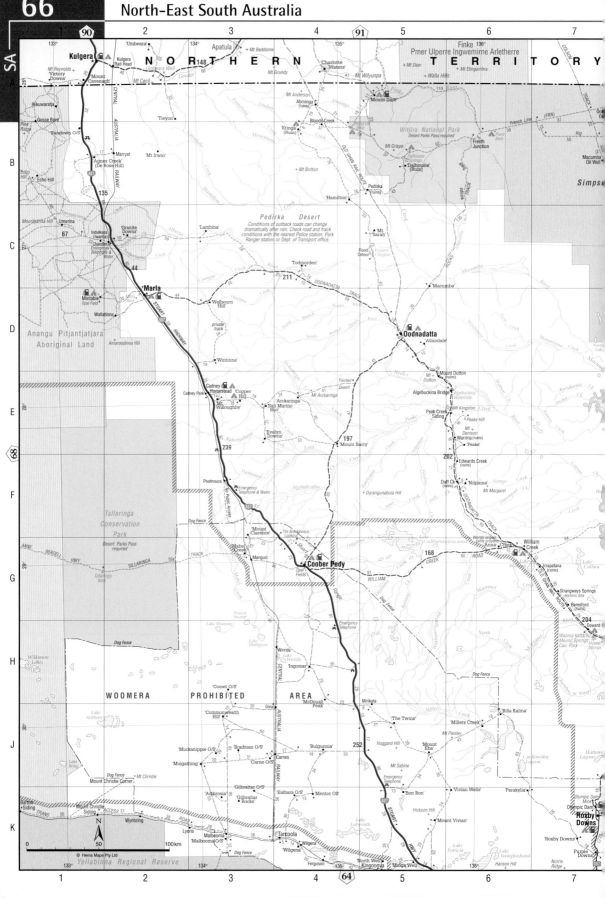

SA

QUEENSLAND

Simpson Desert National Park
Simpson Desert Conservation Park
Desert Parks Pass required
Poeppel Corner
French Line (FRN)
Approdinna Attora Knolls
Rig Road
Rig Road
Poolawanna No.1 Oil Well
Simpson Desert Regional Reserve
Desert Parks Pass required
Lake Gidalda
Lake Poeppel
Lake Tamblyn
QAA Line
Eyre Creek
Nappanerica Big Red Dune
Birdsville
'Roseberth'
'Durrie'
Betoota
BIRDSVILLE DEVELOPMENTAL ROAD
Moona Lake
Shallow Lake
'Planet Downs' Outstation
Haddon Corner
'Pandie Pandie'
Lake Coonimie
'Cadelga' (Ruin)
Lake Short
Lake Etamunbanie
'Nuttall' OS
'Alton Downs'
Andrewilla Waterhole
160
Strzelecki
Desert
'Arrabury'
Lake Uloowaranie
Goyder Lagoon
Inside Track often closed due to flooding
Providence Creek
'Cordillo Downs' Australia's Largest Shearing Shed
Warburton Crossing
Clifton Hills
BIRDSVILLE
308
Lake Marraootanie
Lake Goyder
Lake Toontoowaranie
Yelpawaralinna Track (YLP)
WARBURTON TRACK
(W.B.B.)
Apumurra
Patchawarra Creek
141 DOWNS
Innamincka Regional Reserve
Desert Parks Pass required
Mt Gason Bore
Sturt
Lake Koodianie
Stony
Cooper
Walkers Crossing
Burke & Wills Dig Tree
'Nappa Merrie'
Tirrawarra Oil & Gas Field
Gidgealpa
Innamincka
Cullyamurra Waterhole
'Innamincka'
'Cowarie'
Lake Howitt
Mera Mitta Bore
Desert
Lake Perigundi
Lake Andree
'Kalamurina'
COOPER CREEK TRACK
Koolkootinnie Lake
Kalamurra Lake
'Mulka'
'Mungerannie'
Mungerannie Roadhouse
Lake Kittakittaooloo
Cooper Creek
Lake Warrawakalanna
Moomba Oil & Gas Field
156
Delta Gas Field
Dullingari Oil & Gas Field
'Epsilon'
Lake Eyre National Park
Desert Parks Pass required
Tirari
Lake Ngapakaldi
Lake Ngapakaldi
Desert
Lake Puntawolona
Lake Hope
Big Lake
Lake Moomba
LAKE EYRE NORTH
Ellior Price Con Con
Madigan Gulf
Lake Killalpaninna
Cooper Ck Ferry
Lake Pallamperpunna
'Etadunna'
Lake Koppenoppulana
Cannuwaukaninna Bore
Lake Gregory
Lake Florence
206
Strzelecki
Desert
Lake Mertree
'Merty Merty'
'Omicron'
'Dulkaninna'
BIRDSVILLE TRACK
Strzelecki Regional Reserve
Strzelecki Crossing
'Bollards Lagoon'
Bullards Lagoon
The Corner Store
Cameron Corner
Dog Fence
'Muloorina'
'Clayton'
123
Lake Blanche
'Lindon'
Sturt National Park
Fort Grey
Whitecatch House
'Lake Stewart'
Dog Fence
Lake Harry
Lake Harry (Ruin)
Lake Arthur
Montecollina Bore
'Murnpeowie'
'Blanchewater' (Ruin)
Mount Hopeless
'Old Tilcha' (ruins)
Munkartie Gate
'Hewart Downs'
Tilcha Gate
Lake Callabonna
Finnis Springs
DOONADATTA
Alberrie Creek
Wongianna
Callanna
Marree
'Mundowdna'
Callanna
'Finniss Springs'
OLD GHAN RAIL ROUTE
Mt Distance
Mt Babbage
'Moolawatana'
Fossil Reserve S.A. Museum Entry Permit required
Lake Yanerpi
Lake Cootaburlow
'Winnathee'
Hawkers Gate
No access to South Australia via Hawkers Gate
NSW
194
'Wilpoorinna'
'Farina' (Ruins)
80
Mt Freeling
Mt Fitton
Mt Fitton
Mt Neil
152
'Old Mulga'
Rotten Swamp
'Smithville House'
'Witchelina'
'Mulgaria'
STRZELECKI TRACK
Yudnamutana
Freeling Heights
Mt Painter
'North Mulga'
Paralana Hot Springs
'Moorabie'
Lyndhurst
103
'Avondale'
'Mt Lyndhurst'
Umberatana
Arkaroola
'Wooltana'
'Myrtle Springs'
Leigh Creek Coalfield
Telford
'Depot Springs'
'Owieandana'
Mt Serle
Mt McKinley
Gammon Ranges National Park
Arkaroola
Balcanoona
'Wertaloona'
Lake Frome Regional Reserve
Lake Elder
'Border Downs'
'Turleys House'
Leigh Creek
'North Moolooloo'
Copley
Angepena
'Maynards Well'
Nepabunna
Iga Warta
NORTH FLINDERS RANGES
Nantawarrina
Lake Coontayanta
Starvation Lake
'Pine View'
'Westwood Downs'
Sliding Rock Mine
Warraweena
Nantawarrina
Andamooka
Lake Torrens
Lake Torrens National Park
Beltana
Beltana Roadhouse
Beltana
Puttapa
Lake Frome
Lake Maljanapa

QUEENSLAND

NSW

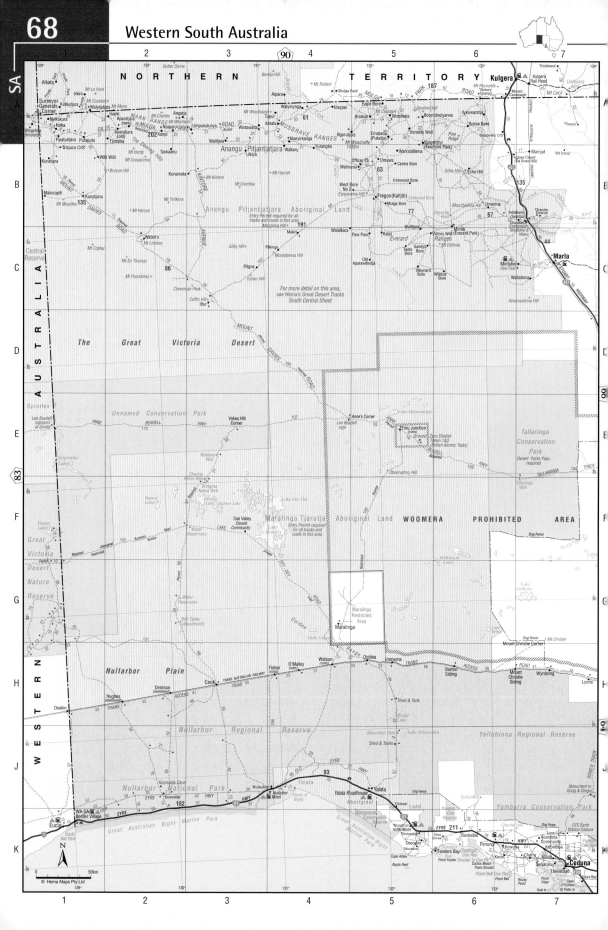

Western Australia

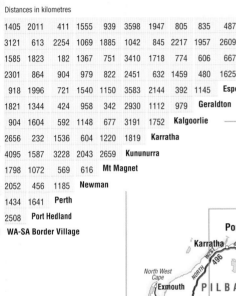

Distances in kilometres

1405	2011	411	1555	939	3598	1947	805	835	487	1315	342	2624	Albany
3121	613	2254	1069	1885	1042	845	2217	1957	2609	1477	2436	Broome
1585	1823	182	1367	751	3410	1718	774	606	667	1086	Bunbury
2301	864	904	979	822	2451	632	1459	480	1625	Carnarvon
918	1996	721	1540	1150	3583	2144	392	1145	Esperance
1821	1344	424	958	342	2930	1112	979	Geraldton
904	1604	592	1148	677	3191	1752	Kalgoorlie
2656	232	1536	604	1220	1819	Karratha
4095	1587	3228	2043	2659	Kununurra
1798	1072	569	616	Mt Magnet
2052	456	1185	Newman
1434	1641	Perth
2508	Port Hedland
WA-SA Border Village

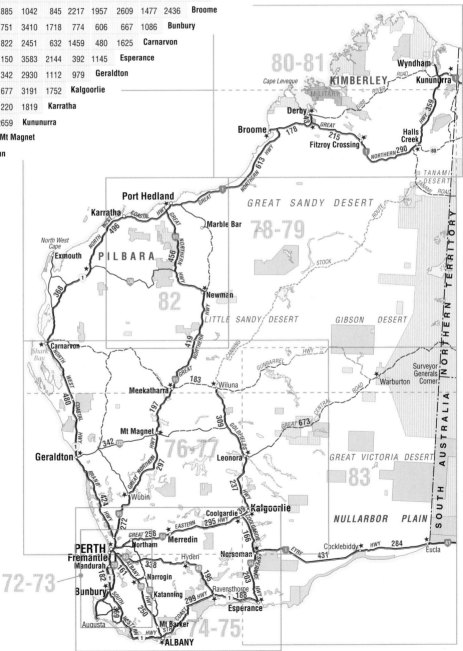

Northbridge

West Perth

Perth Oval

East Perth

Wellington Square

Queens Gardens

Kings Park

The Narrows

Mill Point

Point Belches

Point Lewis

Milyu

Nature

Heirisson Island

SWAN

Perth   Water

RIVER

Windsor Park

Res

Sir South Perth

James

Mitchell

Park

Zoological Gardens

Langley Park

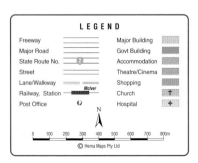

LEGEND

Freeway	Major Building
Major Road	Govt Building
State Route No.	Accommodation
Street	Theatre/Cinema
Lane/Walkway	Shopping
Railway, Station	Church
Post Office	Hospital

N

0 100 200 300 400 500 600 700 800m

© Hema Maps Pty Ltd

Places of Interest

1 Allan Green Plant Conservatory B2
2 Art Gallery of WA A3
3 Barracks Archway B1
4 Forrest Chase B3
5 Government House B3
6 Hay Street Mall B2
7 Horseshoe Bridge A2
8 Kings Park B1
9 Kings Park Lookout C1
10 Murray Street Mall B2
11 Old Council House B3
12 Old Court House B3
13 Old Mill C1
14 Old Observatory B1
15 Old Perth Boys School B2
16 Parliament House B1
17 Perth Concert Hall B3
18 Perth Entertainment Centre A2
19 Perth Inst. of Contemporary Art A3

20 Perth Mint B4
21 Perth Town Hall B3
22 Scitech Discovery Centre A1
23 St Georges Cathedral B3
24 St Marys RC Cathedral B3
25 State Library of Western Australia A3
26 Swan Bells B2
27 The Cloisters B2
28 The Deanery B3
29 WA Museum A3
30 War Memorial C1

Accommodation

35 Carlton Hotel B4
36 Chateau Commodore Hotel B3
37 Criterion Hotel B3
38 Crowne Plaza Perth C4
39 Duxton Hotel B3
40 Emerald Hotel B1
41 Globe Hotel B2

42 Goodearth Hotel C4
43 Grand Central Backpackers B3
44 Holiday Inn City Centre B2
45 Hotel Grand Chancellor A2
46 Hotel Milligan A2
47 Hyatt Regency Perth C4
48 Ibis Hotel B2
49 Kings Perth Hotel B3
50 Melbourne Hotel B2
51 Mercure Hotel B3
52 Novotel Langley Hotel B3
53 Old Brisbane Hotel A3
54 Park Inn International B3
55 Parmelia Hilton Int. Hotel B2
56 Perth Ambassador Hotel B4
57 Perth City Hotel B4
58 Royal Hotel B2
59 Rydges Perth Hotel B2
60 Sheraton Perth Hotel B3
61 The Sebel of Perth B3
62 Wentworth Plaza Hotel B2

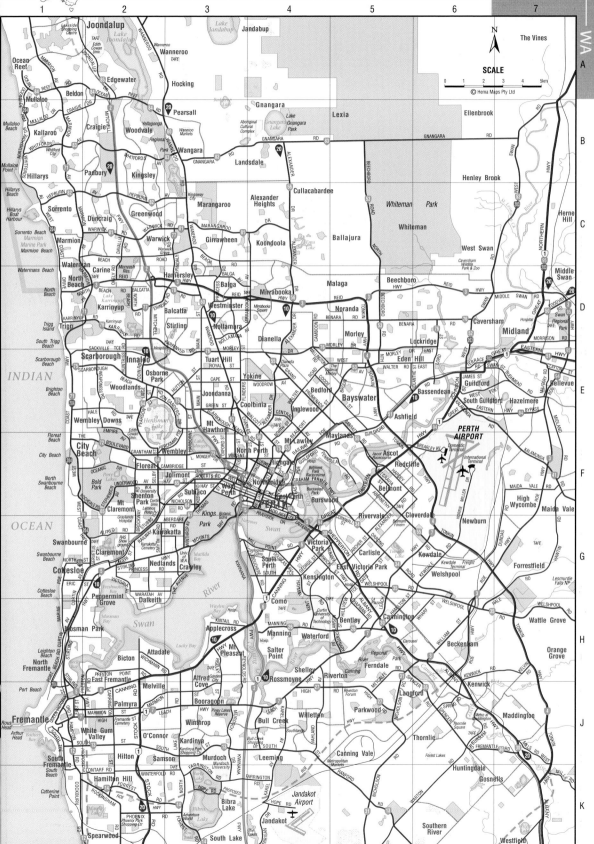

WA

WA

Grid columns: 8 9 10 11 12 13 14
Grid rows: A B C D E F G H J K

Major towns and places:

Wagin, Williams, Highbury, Plesseville, Quindanning, Quindanning, Collie, Darkan, Duranillin, Bokal, Boscabel, Kojonup, Frankland, Rocky Gully, Carrolup, Carnecabup, Harvey, Wokalup, Benger, Brunswick Junction, Australind, Bunbury, Picton, Capel, Donnybrook, Boyup Brook, Mayanup, Bridgetown, Manjimup, Pemberton, Quinninup, Dinninup, Hester, Greenbushes, Balingup, Mullalyup, Kirup, Grimwade, Lowden, Mumballup, Shotts, Collie Cardiff, McAlinden, Noggerup, Brookhampton, Argyle, Gwindinup, Dardanup, Boyanup, Elgin, Ludlow, Wonnerup, Busselton, Dunsborough, Yallingup, Margaret River, Witchcliffe, Karridale, Augusta, Nannup, Jarrahwood, Carlotta, Pemberton, Deanmill, Jardee, Palgarup, Quinninup

Cape Naturaliste, Cape Leeuwin, Flinders Bay, Hamelin Bay, Cape Freycinet, Cape Hamelin, Cowaramup, Gracetown, North Point, Prevelly

Geographe Bay

Highways: SOUTH WESTERN HWY, BUSSELL HWY, COALFIELDS HWY, BROCKMAN HWY, VASSE HWY, MUIRS HWY, STEWART ROAD, WHICHER ROAD

Scale: 50 km

© Hema Maps Pty Ltd

N (compass)

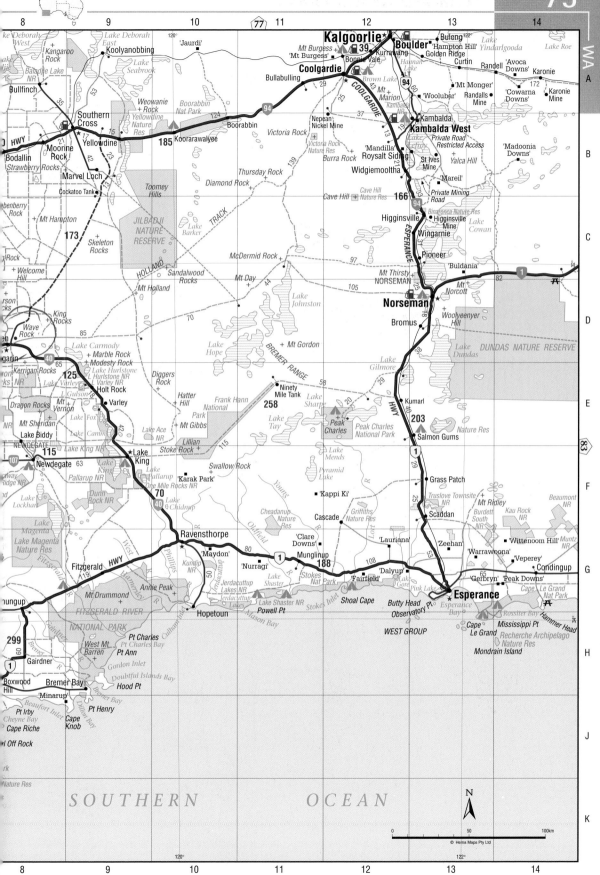

WA

SOUTHERN OCEAN

N

0   50   100km

© Hema Maps Pty Ltd

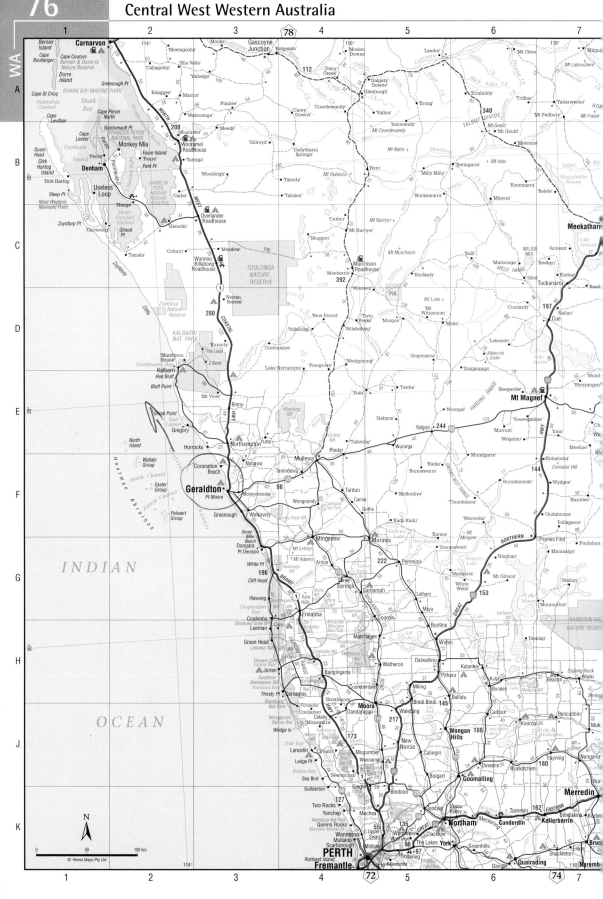

WA

INDIAN

OCEAN

0   50   100 km

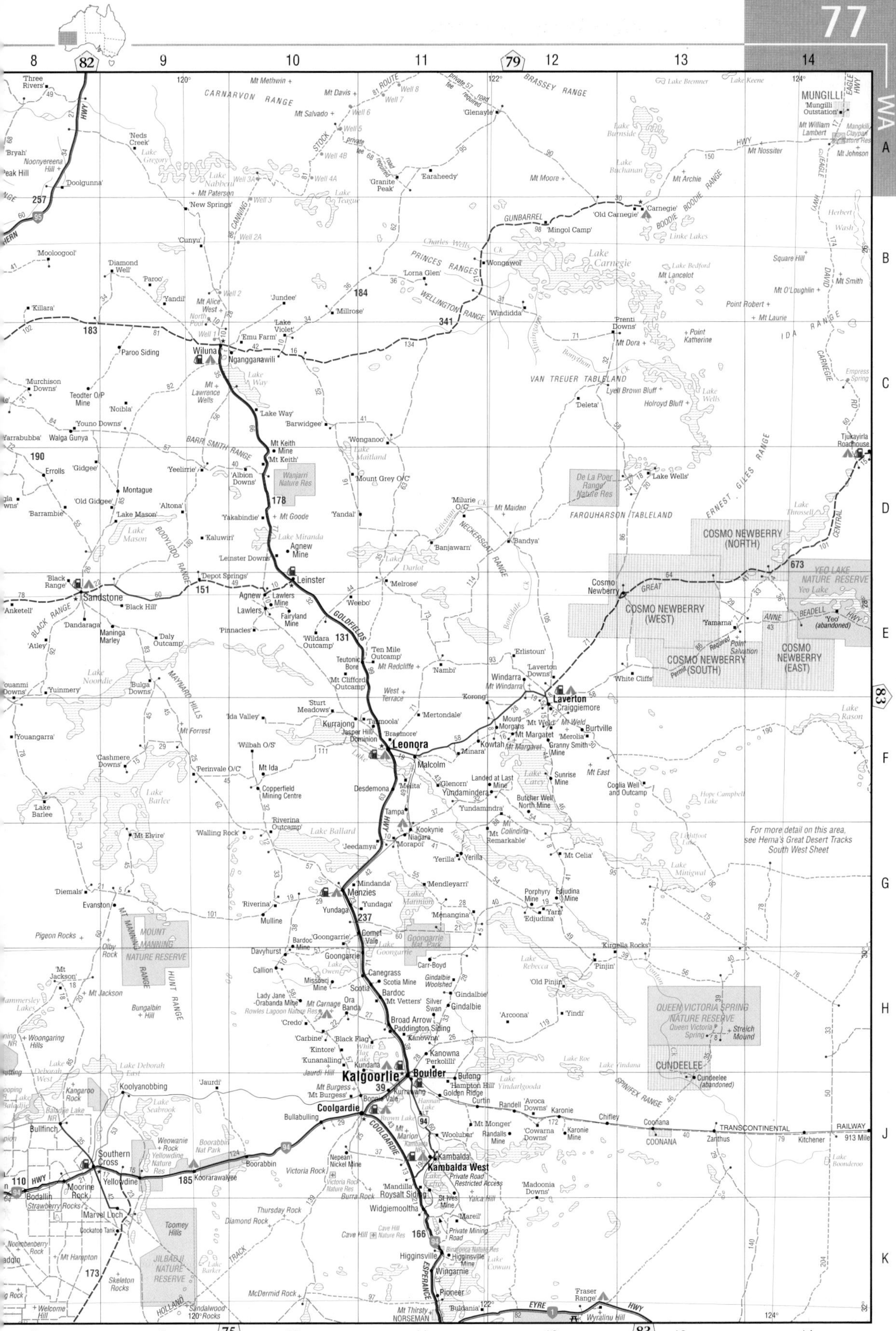
8
9
10
11
12
13
14
A
B
C
D
E
F
G
H
J
K
82
79
83
75
CARNARVON RANGE
BRASSEY RANGE
Mt Methwin
Mt Davis
Mt Salvado
'Glenayle'
'Three Rivers'
'Neds Creek'
Lake Gregory
'Bryah'
Noonyereena Hill
Peak Hill
'Doolgunna'
Lake Nabberu
Mt Paterson
'New Springs'
'Granite Peak'
'Earaheedy'
Lake Teague
Mt Moore
Lake Burnside
Lake Buchanan
Mt Archie
MUNGILLI
'Mungilli Outstation'
Mt William Lambert
Mt Nossiter
Mt Johnson
'Carnegie'
'Old Carnegie'
GUNBARREL
'Mingol Camp'
BOODIE BOODIE RANGE
Linke Lakes
Lake Carnegie
'Wongawol'
PRINCES RANGES
'Lorna Glen'
WELLINGTON RANGE
'Windidda'
'Cunyu'
'Mooloogool'
'Diamond Well'
'Paroo'
'Yandil'
Mt Alice West
North Pool
'Jundee'
'Millrose'
'Killara'
'Emu Farm'
'Lake Violet'
Wiluna
Nganganawili
Paroo Siding
Lake Bedford
Mt Lancelot
Square Hill
Mt O'Loughlin
Mt Smith
Point Robert
Mt Laurie
IDA RANGE
'Prenti Downs'
Mt Dora
Point Katherine
VAN TREUER TABLELAND
Lyell Brown Bluff
Holroyd Bluff
Lake Wells
'Deleta'
Empress Spring
'Murchison Downs'
Teodter O/P Mine
'Noibla'
Mt Lawrence Wells
Lake Way
'Lake Way'
'Barwidgee'
'Youno Downs'
'Yarrabubba'
Walga Gunya
BARR SMITH RANGE
Mt Keith Mine
'Mt Keith'
'Wonganoo'
Lake Maitland
Tjukayirla Roadhouse
Errolls
'Gidgee'
'Yeelirrie'
'Albion Downs'
Wanjarri Nature Res
'Mount Grey O/C'
De La Poer Range Nature Res
'Lake Wells'
ERNEST GILES RANGE
Montague
'Old Gidgee'
'Altona'
'Barrambie'
'Lake Mason'
'Yakabindie'
Mt Goode
'Yandal'
'Milurie O/C'
Mt Maiden
FARQUHARSON TABLELAND
Lake Throssell
Lake Mason
BOOYLGOO RANGE
'Kaluwiri'
Lake Miranda
Agnew Mine
'Leinster Downs'
'Banjawarn'
NECKERSCALL RANGE
'Bandya'
COSMO NEWBERRY (NORTH)
CENTRAL
'Black Range'
Sandstone
'Depot Springs'
Leinster
Agnew
Lawlers Mine
Lawlers
Fairyland Mine
'Melrose'
'Weebo'
Lake Darlot
Cosmo Newberry
GREAT
COSMO NEWBERRY (WEST)
YEO LAKE NATURE RESERVE
Yeo Lake
'Yeo' (abandoned)
ANNE
BEADELL
HWY
'Anketell'
'Black Hill'
BLACK RANGE
'Dandaraga'
Maninga Marley
'Daly Outcamp'
'Pinnacles'
'Wildara Outcamp'
GOLDFIELDS
'Ten Mile Outcamp'
Mt Redcliffe
'Erlistoun'
'Yamarna'
Point Salvation
COSMO NEWBERRY (SOUTH)
COSMO NEWBERRY (EAST)
'Atley'
Lake Noondie
'Bulga Downs'
MAYNARD HILLS
Teutonic Bore
'Nambi'
'Laverton Downs'
Windarra
Mt Windarra
'White Cliffs'
'Mt Clifford Outcamp'
West Terrace
'Korong'
Laverton
Craiggiemore
'Yuinmery'
'Youanmi Downs'
'Ida Valley'
'Sturt Meadows'
'Mertondale'
Mount Morgans
'Mt Weld'
Mt Weld
Burtville
Lake Rason
'Youangarra'
Mt Forrest
Kurrajong
'Tarmoola'
Jasper Hill Dominion
'Braemore'
Leonora
Mt Margaret
'Minara'
Kowtah
'Merolia'
Granny Smith Mine
'Wilbah O/S'
'Cashmere Downs'
'Perinvale O/C'
Mt Ida
Malcolm
Mt East
Sunrise Mine
Lake Carey
Landed at Last Mine
'Glenorn'
Yundamindera
Coglia Well and Outcamp
Copperfield Mining Centre
Desdemona
'Melita'
Butcher Well North Mine
'Yundamindra'
Hope Campbell Lake
Lake Barlee
'Lake Barlee'
'Riverina Outcamp'
Lake Ballard
Tampa
Kookynie
Niagara
'Morapoi'
'Jeedamya'
'Mt Remarkable'
Mt Colindina
'Walling Rock'
'Mt Elvire'
'Yerilla'
Yerilla
'Mt Celia'
Lightfoot Lake
For more detail on this area, see Hema's Great Desert Tracks South West Sheet
Lake Minigwal
'Mindanda'
'Mendleyarri'
'Diemals'
Evanston
'Riverina'
Menzies
Yundaga
'Yundaga'
Lake Mariinon
'Menangina'
Porphyry Mine
Edjudina Mine
'Yarri'
'Edjudina'
Mulline
Pigeon Rocks
MOUNT MANNING NATURE RESERVE
Olby Rock
'Goongarrie'
Comet Vale
Lake Goongarrie
Goongarrie Nat Park
Bardoc Mine
Davyhurst
Goongarrie
Carr-Boyd
'Kirgella Rocks'
'Pinjin'
Lake Rebecca
'Mt Jackson'
Mt Jackson
Callion
Canegrass
Scotia Mine
Missouri Mine
Scotia
Lake Owen
Gindalbie Woolshed
'Old Pinjin'
HUNT RANGE
Lady Jane
Orabanda Mine
Bardoc
'Mt Vetters'
'Gindalbie'
Gindalbie
Silver Swan
QUEEN VICTORIA SPRING NATURE RESERVE
Queen Victoria Spring
Streich Mound
Bungalbin Hill
Rowles Lagoon Nature Res
Mt Carnage
Ora Banda
'Credo'
'Arcoona'
'Yindi'
Hammersley Lakes
Woongaring Hills
Broad Arrow
Paddington Siding
'Carbine'
'Black Flag'
White Flag Lake
'Kanowna'
'Kintore'
'Kunanalling'
Kundana
Kanowna
'Perkolilli'
Lake Roe
Lake Yindana
Lake Deborah East
Lake Deborah West
Jaurdi Hill
'Jaurdi'
Kalgoorlie
Boulder
Bulong
Lake Yindarlgooda
CUNDEELEE
Cundeelee (abandoned)
Koolyanobbing
Kangaroo Rock
'Hampton Hill'
Golden Ridge
SPINIFEX RANGE
Lake Seabrook
Mt Burgess
'Mt Burgess'
Boorara Vale
Kurrawang
Hannan Lake
Baladjie Lake
Coolgardie
Brown Lake
Curtin
Randell
'Avoca Downs'
Karonie
Chifley
Coonana
COONANA
TRANSCONTINENTAL RAILWAY
Zanthus
Kitchener
913 Mile
Bullfinch
Bullabulling
Mt Marion
'Mt Monger'
Randalls Mine
'Wooluba'
'Cowarna Downs'
Karonie Mine
Weowanie Rock
Yellowdine Nature Res
Boorabbin Nat Park
Boorabbin
Victoria Rock
Nepean Nickel Mine
Kambalda
Kambalda West
Lake Boonderoo
Southern Cross
Yellowdine
Koorarawalyee
Victoria Rock Nature Res
Private Road Restricted Access
Moorine Rock
Bodallin
Strawberry Rocks
Burra Rock
'Mandilla'
Roysalt Siding
Yaica Hill
'Madoonia Downs'
Lake Lefroy
St Ives Mine
Widgiemooltha
Thursday Rock
Marvel Loch
Toomey Hills
Diamond Rock
'Mareil'
Cockatoo Tank
Cave Hill
Cave Hill Nature Res
Private Mining Road
Noombenberry Rock
Mt Hampton
JILBADJI NATURE RESERVE
Lake Barker
Higginsville
'Higginsville'
Binaronca Nature Res
Lake Cowan
Wingarnie
Skeleton Rocks
McDermid Rock
Pioneer
'Fraser Range'
Welcome Hill
HOLLAND TRACK
Sandalwood Rocks
'Buldania'
Mt Thirsty
NORSEMAN
EYRE HWY
Wyralinu Hill
COOLGARDIE
ESPERANCE
120°
122°
124°
30°
32°

WA

© Hema Maps Pty Ltd

0 50 100 150km

INDIAN

OCEAN

For more detail on this area,
see Hema's map of The Pilbara

Port Hedland

DAMPIER ARCHIPELAGO

Montebello Islands

Dampier Wickham
Karratha Roebourne

Barrow Island

GREAT SANDY ISLAND NATURE RESERVE

Whim Creek

Marble Bar

Onslow

YANDEYARRA

Pannawonica

North West Cape

Exmouth

Learmonth

PILBARA

Fortescue River Roadhouse

Nullagine

Wittenoom

Tom Price

Paraburdoo

Newman

JIGALONG

CAPE RANGE NAT PARK
NINGALOO MARINE PARK

Coral Bay

TROPIC OF CAPRICORN

For more detail on this area,
see Hema's map of The Pilbara

Cape Cuvier

Quobba

Carnarvon

Gascoyne Junction

MOUNT JAMES

SHARK BAY MARINE PARK

Monkey Mia

Denham

Useless Loop

Meekatharra

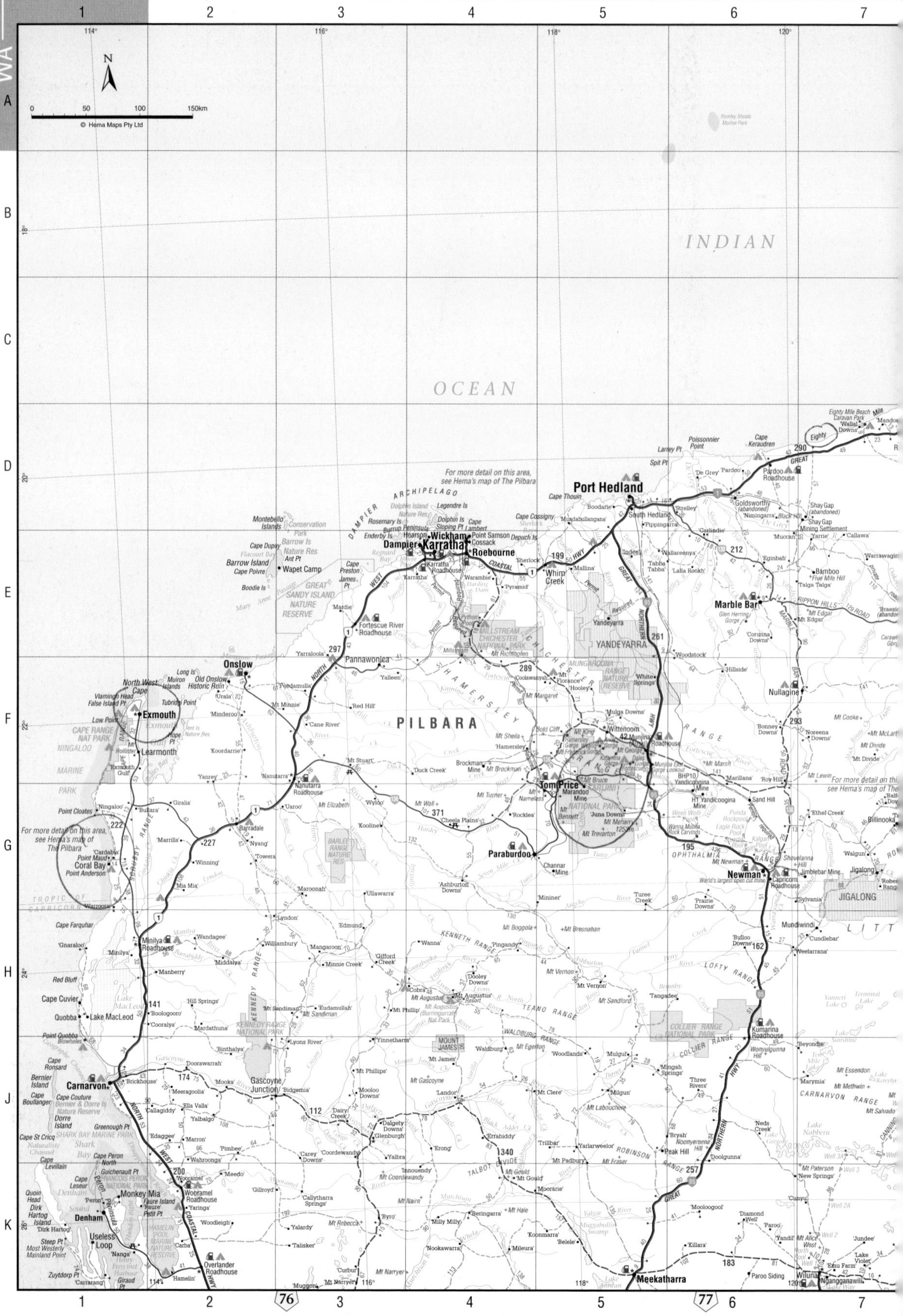

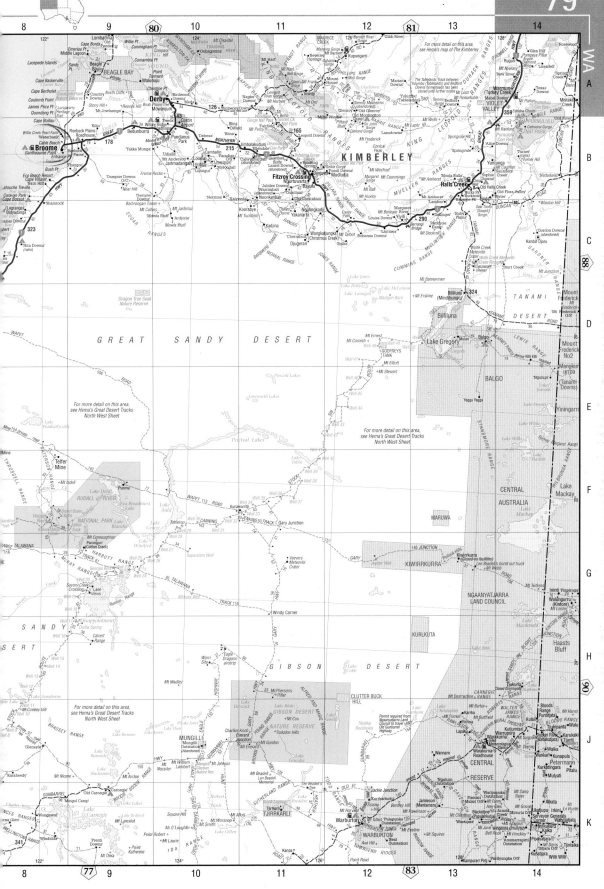

WA

N

0   50km
© Hema Maps Pty Ltd

INDIAN

OCEAN

For more detail on this area,
see Hema's map of The Kimberley

BONA...

Coronatio
Island

Br
Brunswick

HEYWOOD
ISLANDS

Champagny Is

Augustus Is
Camden Sound
Wilson Point   Kun
Kuri Bay   M
Deception Bay   Kuri Bay
Hall Point   KUNML

Wedge Hill

Mt Fr

Montgomery
Islands

BUCCANEER ARCHIPELAGO

Cockatoo
Is   Kingfisher
Koolan Is   Is   Collier
Koolan   Bay

Doubtful Bay

Hidden Is

WOTJALUM

Horizontal
Waterfall

Walcott Inlet

Strickland Bay

Yule
Entrance

Goose Channel

Sunday Strait

Old Yampi Sound

Cone Bay

Talbot Bay

McLARTY RANGE

ONE ARM
POINT   Sunday
Is
Cape Leveque   SUNDAY IS
Koolaman Tourist
Complex
One Arm   Mt Disaster
LOMBADINA   Point   MILITARY
Lombadina   TRAINING
Lombadina Pt   'Oobagooma   AREA
Thomas Bay
Willie Pt
Cape Borda   Old
Pender   Cunningham Pt
Middle Lagoon   Compass Hill
Emeriau Pt Pender
Bay   Comambie Pt
Lacepede Islands   KING
Sandy   Disaster
Pt   Beagle   Point
Bay   BEAGLE BAY   SOUND
Cape Baskerville   Point
Carnot Bay   private   Torment
Walunuju
Cape Bertholet
North Cliffs
Coulomb Point   'Country Downs'
Coulomb Point Nature Reserve   Christine Pt
James Price Pt   Derby 'Birdwood
Quondong Pt   Downs' 'Meda'
Cape Boiliau   'Mt Jowlaenga'   Boab Prison Tree
Mowanjum

'Kilto'   178 Bedunburra
Willie Creek Pearl Farm
'Waterbank' Roebuck Plains
Roadhouse
Broome   'Yeeda'   Curtin
Cable Beach   Willare Bridge Airport
Gantheaume Point   Roadhouse
Entrance Pt   'Roebuck   Minnie Bridge   Pandanus Park
Plains'   Willare Bridge
Roebuck Bay
Thangoo   'Yakka Munga'
Bush Pt
'Udialla'
Eco Beach Resort
Cape Villaret   'Dampier Downs   'Mt Anderson' Loom
'Barn Hill'   O/C'   Jarlmadangah LOOMA
Cape Latouche Treville   Near Hill   'Liveringa'
Port Smith Caravan Park
False Cape Bossut   'Dampier
Cape Bossut (Lagrange)   Downs'
Bidyadanga   Barbrongan Tower +
Admiral Bay 'Shamrock'   Mt Collins
'Frazier Downs'   Mowla Bluff
Cape Jaubert 323   Mowla Bluff
Desault Bay
Cape Missiessy

Koolan

43

126

Blina
Oilfield
'Blina'

'Debesa'

NORTHERN Jimbalak
215   Elle

Camballin
22
'Paradise O/S'
LOOMA 'Calwyny
'Myroodah' (abandon
'Luluigui'
Frome Rocks +

Noonk
'Nerrima' 110 Kalyeeda
Koorabye

Mt Jarlemai
'Ardjorie' Mt Tuckfie

Ka

EDGAR

RANGES

'Nita Downs'
(ruins)

'Anna
Plains'

16

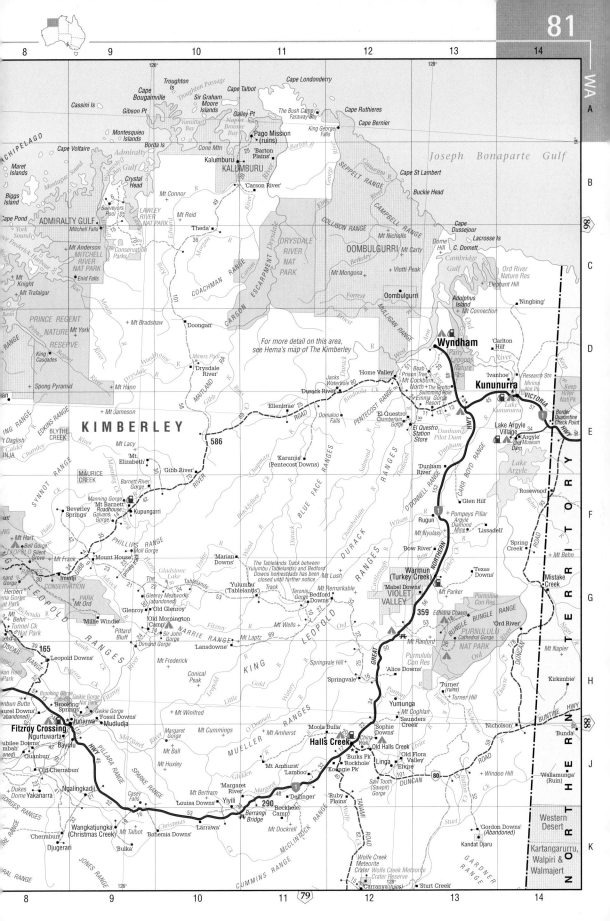

8   9   10   11   12   13   14

A

B

98

C

D

E

TERRITORY

F

G

H

J

88

K

NORTHERN

KIMBERLEY

Joseph Bonaparte Gulf

Cape Londonderry
Cape Talbot
Cape Bougainville
Sir Graham Moore Islands
Cape Ruthieres
Cape Bernier
Galley Pt
The Bush Camp Faraway Bay
King George Falls
Cassini Is
Gibson Pt
Montesquieu Islands
Cape Voltaire
Borda Is
Cone Mtn
Pago Mission (ruins)
Cape St Lambert
Buckie Head
Cape Dussejour
Lacrosse Is
Maret Islands
Crystal Head
Kalumburu
'Barton Plains'
Cape Domett
Dome Hill
Biggs Island
KALUMBURU
'Carson River'
Cape Pond
ADMIRALTY GULF
Mt Connor
Mt Reid
Theda'
Mt Nicholls
Mt Carty
Cambridge Gulf
Ord River Nature Res
Elephant Hill
Mt Anderson
Mitchell Falls
Enid Falls
OOMBULGURRI
Adolphus Island
Mt Connection
'Ningbing'
Mt Knight
Mt Trafalgar
Mt Mongona
Viotti Peak
King Cascades
Spong Pyramid
Mt Bradshaw
Mt York
'Doongan'
WYNDHAM
'Carlton Hill'
'Ivanhoe'
Research Stn
Mitchell River Nat Park
Mt Hann
Miners Pool
'Drysdale River'
'Home Valley'
Boab Prison Tree
Mt Cockburn North
The Grotto
Mt Jameson
Jacks Waterhole
Durack River
Emma Gorge Resort
KUNUNURRA
Lake Kununurra
VICTORIA
Border Quarantine Check Point
586
'Mt Elizabeth'
'Gibb River'
Ellenbrae
Oomaloo Falls
El Questro
Chamberlain Gorge
El Questro Station Store
Dunham Pilot Dam
Lake Argyle Village
Argyle'
Ord Museum Dam
Manning Gorge
'Mt Barnett Roadhouse'
Galvans Gorge
Kupungarri
'Karunjie' (Pentecost Downs)
'Dunham River'
'Glen Hill'
Rosewood'
'Beverley Springs'
Mt Lacy
'Lissadell'
MAURICE CREEK
Barnett River Gorge
Rugun
Pompeys Pillar
Argyle Diamond Mine
'Spring Creek'
Mt Behn
Moll Gorge
'Marian Downs'
Mt Nyulasy
'Bow River'
Mount House'
The Tablelands Track between Yulumbu (Tablelands) and Bedford Downs homesteads has been closed until further notice.
WARMUN (Turkey Creek)
'Texas Downs'
Mistake Creek
Gladstone Lake
Tablelands
'Yulumbu' (Tablelands)
Teronis Gorge
Mt Lush
Mt Remarkable
'Mabel Downs'
VIOLET VALLEY
Mt Parker
'Ord River'
Millie Windie'
Glenroy Meatworks (abandoned)
'Glenroy'
'Old Glenroy'
Bedford Downs'
Echidna Chasm
PURNULULU Con Res
359
Cathedral Gorge
'Old Mornington Camp'
Mt Wells
Mt Radford
PURNULULU NAT PARK
Mt Napier
Pittard Bluff
Sir John Gorge
Dimond Gorge
'Lansdowne'
Mt Laptz
Springvale Hill
'Alice Downs'
'Kirkimbie'
165
Leopold Downs'
Conical Peak
'Springvale'
'Turner' (ruins)
Turner Hill
Brooking Gorge
'Fossil Downs'
Geikie Gorge
Yumunga
'Nicholson'
FITZROY CROSSING
Brooking Springs
Junjuwa
Mudludja
Mt Coghlan
'Saunders Creek'
'Bunda'
Ngurtuwarta
Bayulu
Margaret Gorge
Mt Cummings
Mt Amherst
'Moola Bulla'
'Sophie Downs'
HALLS CREEK
Old Halls Creek
'Old Flora Valley'
'Wallamunga' (Ruin)
Ngalingkadji
Mt Ball
Mt Huxley
Linga
'Elvire'
Yakanarra
'Old Cherrabun'
Mt Bertram
Mt Amhurst
'Lamboo'
'Burks Pk' 'Rockhole'
Koangie Pk
80
Windoo Hill
Dukes Dome
'Margaret River'
Yiyili
Dellinger
'Ruby Plains'
Saw Tooth (Sawpit) Gorge
Wangkatjungka (Christmas Creek)
Rockhole Camp
'Bohemia Downs'
'Larrawa'
Berrangi Bridge
Mt Dockrell
Western Desert
'Cherrabun'
Djugerari
'Bulka'
Wolfe Creek Meteorite Crater
Wolfe Creek Meteorite Crater Reserve
'Gordon Downs' (Abandoned)
Kandat Djaru
Kartangarurru, Walpiri & Walmajert
'Sturt Creek'
'Carranya' (ruins)

For more detail on this area, see Hema's map of The Kimberley

290
79

WA

1 2 3 4 5 6 7

N

0 50km
© Hema Maps Pty Ltd

For more detail on this area,
see Hema's map of The Pilbara

Port Hedland

Wickham
Karratha
Dampier
Roebourne

DAMPIER ARCHIPELAGO
Dolphin Island Nature Res
Legendre Is
Rosemary Is
Dolphin Is
Sloping Pt
Cape Lambert
Point Samson
Cossack
Burrup Peninsula
Hearson
Enderby Is
Depuch Is
Regnard Bay
Cape Preston
Maree Pool
Karratha Roadhouse
'Karratha'
'Warambie'
'Pyramid'

Cape Thouin
'Boodarie'
South Hedland
'Mundabullangana'
Cape Cossigny
Sherlock Bay
Cape Keraudren
Eighty Mile Beach
GREAT
Poissonnier Point
Larrey Pt
Spit Pt
'De Grey'
'Pardoo'
Pardoo Roadhouse
Goldsworthy (abandoned)
'Nimingarra'
Shay Gap (abandoned)
Shay Gap Mining Settlement
'Muccan'
'Callawa'
'Yarrie'
'Carlindie'
'Eginbah'
Bamboo
Five Mile Hill
'Talga Talga'

'Strelley'
'Pippingarra'
'Indee'
'Wallareenya'
Tabba Tabba
'Lalla Rookh'

RIPPON HILLS RD
Mt Edgar
'Mt Edgar'

Marble Bar

MARBLE BAR ROAD

Glen Herring Gorge
'Corunna Downs'
'Hillside'

Nullagine

Fortescue River Roadhouse

Pannawonica
'Yalleen'

Python Pool
MILLSTREAM CHICHESTER NATIONAL PARK
Millstream
Mt Richthofen
'Coolawanyah'
Mt Florance
'Hooley'
Mt Margaret

CHICHESTER RANGE
MUNGAROONA RANGE NATURE RESERVE
Yandeyarra
YANDEYARRA
'Woodstock'
'White Springs'

PILBARA

HAMERSLEY RANGE
'Karratha'
'Duck Creek'
Brockman Mine
Mt Brockman
Mt Sheila
'Hamersley'
Bold Cliff
Hamersley Gorge
Mt Frederick
Mt King
Weano Gorge
Knox Gorge
Kalamina Gorge
Mt George
Fortescue Falls
'Mulga Downs'
Wittenoom
Munjina (Auski) Roadhouse
Munjina East
Gorge Lookout
'Marillana'
'Roy Hill'
Mt Marsh
Mt Lewin

For more detail on this area,
see Hema's map of The Pilbara

Tom Price
Mt Nameless
Mt Turner
Marandoo Mine
KARIJINI NATIONAL PARK
Mt Bruce
'Juna Downs'
Mt Bennett
Mt Meharry 1253m
Mt Trevarton
'Rocklea'

BHP10 Yandicoogina Mine
H1 Yandicoogina Mine
Sand Hill
Weeli Wolli Pool
Wanna Munna Rock Carvings
Punda Rockpool
Eagle Rock Pool
Kalgan Pool
Shovelanna Hill
Jimblebar Mine

'Wyloo'
Mt Wall
'Cheela Plains'
'Kooline'

Paraburdoo
Channar Mine

BARLEE RANGE NATURE RES
'Ullawarra'

OPHTHALMIA RANGE
Mt Newman
Newman
World's largest open cut mine
Capricorn Roadhouse

TROPIC OF CAPRICORN
'Ashburton Downs'
'Mininer'
'Mt Boggola'
Mt Bresnahan
'Prairie Downs'
Turee Creek
'Sylvania'

JIGALONG
Mundiwindi
'Cundlebar'

'Edmund'
'Wanna'
'Gifford Creek'
KENNETH RANGE
'Pingandy'
Mt Vernon
'Mt Vernon'
Mt Sandford
'Tangadee'
'Bulloo Downs'
'Weelarrana'

'Yinnetharra'
Cobra
Dooley Downs
Mt Augustus Resort
Mt Augustus (Burringurrah) Nat Park
'Mt Phillip'
TEANO RANGE
'Mt James'
MOUNT JAMES
'Waldburg'
WALDBURG RANGE
Mt Egerton
'Woodlands'
'Mulgul'
COLLIER RANGE NATIONAL PARK
LOFTY RANGE
Kumarina Roadhouse
'Beyondie'
Yanneri Lake
Wonyulgunna Hill
Ten Mile Lake
Mt Essendon
'Marymia'
'Mingah Springs'
Mt Gascoyne

COLLIER RANGE
NORTHERN HWY
GREAT

76   77

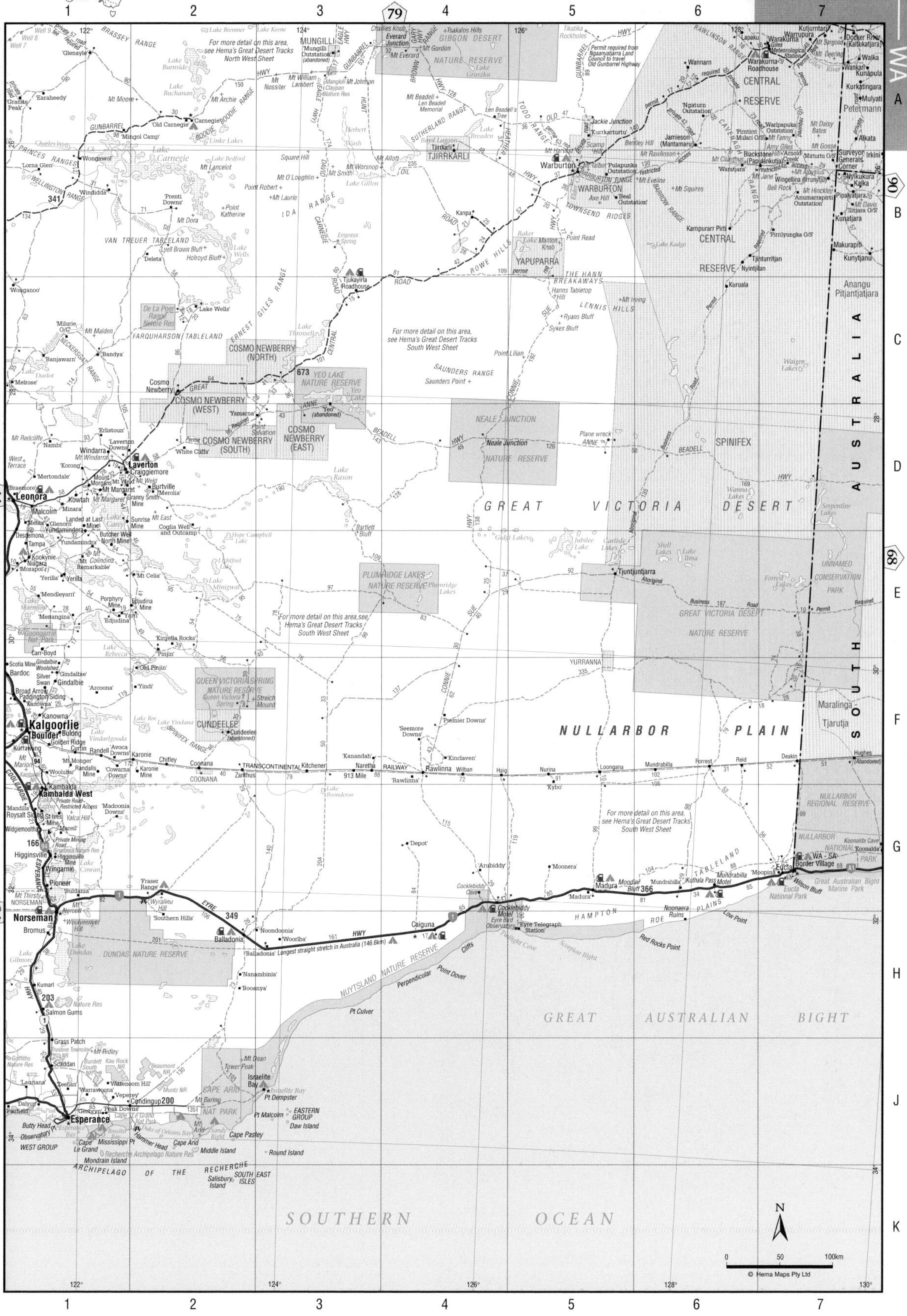

WA

WESTERN AUSTRALIA

SOUTH AUSTRALIA

GIBSON DESERT

GIBSON DESERT NATURE RESERVE

CENTRAL RESERVE

CENTRAL RESERVE

WARBURTON

TJIRRKARLI

YAPUPARRA

Anangu Pitjantjatjara

COSMO NEWBERRY (NORTH)

COSMO NEWBERRY (WEST)

COSMO NEWBERRY (SOUTH)

COSMO NEWBERRY (EAST)

YEO LAKE NATURE RESERVE

673

NEALE JUNCTION NATURE RESERVE

SPINIFEX

GREAT VICTORIA DESERT

GREAT VICTORIA DESERT NATURE RESERVE

PLUMRIDGE LAKES NATURE RESERVE

Tjuntjuntjarra

UNNAMED CONSERVATION PARK

Maralinga

Tjarutja

QUEEN VICTORIA SPRING NATURE RESERVE

CUNDEELEE

Leonora

Malcolm

Laverton

Kalgoorlie
Boulder

Kambalda West

NULLARBOR PLAIN

NULLARBOR REGIONAL RESERVE

NULLARBOR NATIONAL PARK

TRANSCONTINENTAL RAILWAY

Rawlinna   Wiban   Haig   Nurina   Loongana   Forrest   Reid   Deakin   Hughes

Border Village

WA - SA

Norseman

DUNDAS NATURE RESERVE

Balladonia

Caiguna

Cocklebiddy

Madura

Mundrabilla

Eucla

HAMPTON TABLELAND

ROE PLAINS

Fraser Range

Esperance

NUYTSLAND NATURE RESERVE

CAPE ARID NAT PARK

Israelite Bay

Cape Arid

Cape Le Grand

GREAT   AUSTRALIAN   BIGHT

ARCHIPELAGO OF THE RECHERCHE

SOUTH EAST ISLES

SOUTHERN   OCEAN

N

0   50   100km

© Hema Maps Pty Ltd

Northern Territory

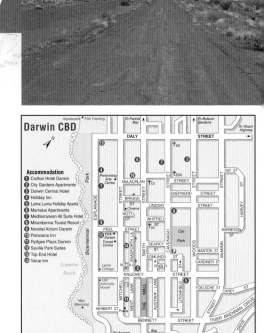

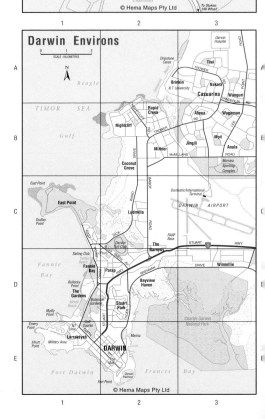

	Alice Springs									
Ayers Rock	448									
Barrow Creek	730	282								
Borroloola	922	1652	1204							
Camooweal	753	699	1429	981						
Darwin	1439	986	1234	1964	1516					
Jabiru	254	1415	962	1210	1940	1492				
Katherine	300	324	1115	662	910	1640	1192			
Kulgera	1466	1766	1790	1255	1478	556	322	274		
Mataranka	1361	105	405	429	1010	557	805	1535	1087	
Nhulunbuy	708	2069	705	1005	1029	1718	1265	1513	2243	1795
Tennant Creek	1290	582	779	687	987	1011	476	699	223	953	505

Distances in kilometres

Darwin CBD

Accommodation
1. Carlton Hotel Darwin
2. City Gardens Apartments
3. Darwin Central Hotel
4. Holiday Inn
5. Luma Luma Holiday Aparts
6. Marrakai Apartments
7. Mediterranean All Suite Hotel
8. Mirambeena Tourist Resort
9. Novotel Atrium Darwin
10. Poinciana Inn
11. Rydges Plaza Darwin
12. Saville Park Suites
13. Top End Hotel
14. Value Inn

© Hema Maps Pty Ltd

Darwin Environs

© Hema Maps Pty Ltd

DARWIN

MELVILLE ISLAND

Tiwi

Paru
Ngulu
Pickertaramoor
Conder Pt
Cobham Bay
Cape Keith
Napier Bay
Cape Gambier

COBOURG MARINE PARK
Greenhill Is
Morse Is
Endyalgout Is
Murgenella

Van Diemen Gulf

WELLINGTON RANGE

Mt Permain +
Tor Rock +
Cooper

Clarence Strait

NW Vernon Is
East Vernon Is
SW Vernon Is
Gunn Pt
Cape Hotham

Cape Hotham Forestry Res
Djukbinj Nat Park
Cape Hotham Sector
Chambers Bay
Pt Stuart Coastal Res
Pt Stuart
Finke Bay
West Alligator Head
Barron Is
Field Is
Pt Farewell
Mt Borradaile +

Kakadu

Beagle Gulf
Shoal Bay
Lee Pt
Hope Inlet
Koolpinyah
Woolner
Lake Finnis
'Lake Finnis'
'Swim Ck'
Shady Camp
Swim Ck Con Res
'Carmor Plain'
Pt Stuart Wilderness Lodge

KAKADU
MAGELA PLAIN
Gunbalanya (Oenpelli)
Ubirr
Cannon Hill
Jabiluka
Border Store
Boat Cruise

DARWIN
Radio Transmitting Stn
Mandorah
COX PENINSULA
Belyuen
Port Darwin
Palmerston
Howard Springs
Black Jungle Con Res
Djukbinj Nat Park
Marrakai Sector
Melaleuca
Alecs Hole
'Munmarlary'
'Mudginberri'
Jabiluka Mineral Lease
Ranger Mineral Lease
Gagudju Crocodile Hotel

Channel Is
Ida Bay
Belyuen
Burge Pt
Bynoe
Harbour
Berry Springs
Wildlife Park
Noonamah
Humpty Doo
Middle Point
Bird Sanc
Beatrice Hill
Helens Ck
Opium Ck
St Stuart Wilderness Lodge
Four Mile Hole
Two Mile Hole
Bowali Visitor Centre
Kakadu Holiday Village
Jabiru
Mt Brockman
Koongarra Mineral Lease

'Finniss River'
Tumbling Waters
Darwin River Dam
Manton Dam Pk
Acacia Store
Corroboree Park Inn
ARNHEM
Wildman River Wilderness Lodge
Corroboree Billabong
Rockhole
Delta Sector
Mary River
Wildman Sector
219
36
HWY
KAKADU NATIONAL PARK
Gagudju Cooinda Lodge
Yellow Water
Nourlangie Rock
Mt Cahill

'Woolaning'
'Wangi'
Wangi Falls
Florence Falls
Batchelor
Banyan
'Sargents'
'Stapleton'
Rum Jungle
War Cemetery
Adelaide River
'Annaburroo'
Bark Hut Inn
McKinlay Sector
JIM
JIM
ROAD
Mundogie Hill
Spring Peak
Mt Partridge
Maguk Gorge
Table Top
Mt Gilruth +
Deaf Adder

LITCHFIELD NAT PARK
Mt Finniss
'Mt Ringwood'
Mt Bundey
Mt Ringwood
Mt Douglas
Mt Masson
Goodparla
209
21
Kakadu
Jim Jim Falls
Twin Falls
Koolpin Gorge

Reynolds
Tolmer Falls
Robin Falls
Mt Tymn
Mt Paqualin
Ban Ban Springs
Mt Ellison
Mt George
'Mary River'
Mary River Roadhouse
Tent Hill
Gunlom (UDP) Falls
'El Sherana'
'Gimbat'
Mt Evelyn

Mt Raymond
23
STUART
Brooks Creek
Grove Hill
Hayes Creek
120
Mt Smith
'Douglas'
Tjuwaliyn
Douglas Hot Springs Nature Pk
Emerald Springs
'Esmerelda'
Mt Porter
Mt Gardiner
Mt Davis
Coronet Hill
Coronation Hill
KAKADU
Gunlom
PARK

'Woolianna'
Mt Thomas
'Perry's'
'Mango Farm'
Nauiyu
Banyan Farm'
Daly River
Mt Haywood
Mt Nancar
'Tipperary'
Douglas Daly Exp Stn
Butterfly Gorge Nature Park
Douglas Daly Park
1
Pine Creek
'Bonrook'
McCarthy Hill
Ranford Hill
Two Sisters
Mt Stow +
Mt Ebsworth +
Mt Lambell +

Mt Boulder
ROCK CANDY RANGE
Mt Muriel
'Ooloo'
Mt Briggs
Ooloo Crossing
'Jindare'
'Lewin Springs'
Cullen
Barnjarn
Mt Todd
NITMILUK NATIONAL PARK
Mt Harvey +
Mt David +
Manyallaluk
Mt Felix +
Manyallaluk (Eva Valley)

Daly
Fish
Umbrawarra Gorge
Mt Giles
91
Edith Falls
Mt Lambell +
Jawoyn
Katherine Gorge
'Fish River'
WINGATE MOUNTAINS
Wagiman
'Claravale'
Hornet Hill
Katherine
Jawoyn
Maranboy Police Stn
Barunga
Beswick

Upper Daly
'Florina'
Katherine
Historic Springvale Homestead
'Manbulloo'
Mt Shepherd
STUART
Gas

'Dorisvale'
Mullens Ridge
Tindal
RAAF Base
Cutta Cutta Caves
105
Fish River Reserve
Mt Pearce +
Yubulyawun
Flora River Nature Park
Croker Hill
'Scott Creek'
Butchers Hill +
126
Mt Armstrong
Mt Freda
VICTORIA
HWY
1
Proposed Railway
Pipeline
Gas
'Mataranka'
Mataranka
Mt Barwolla
'Wombungi'
'Lakefield'
Fitzmaurice

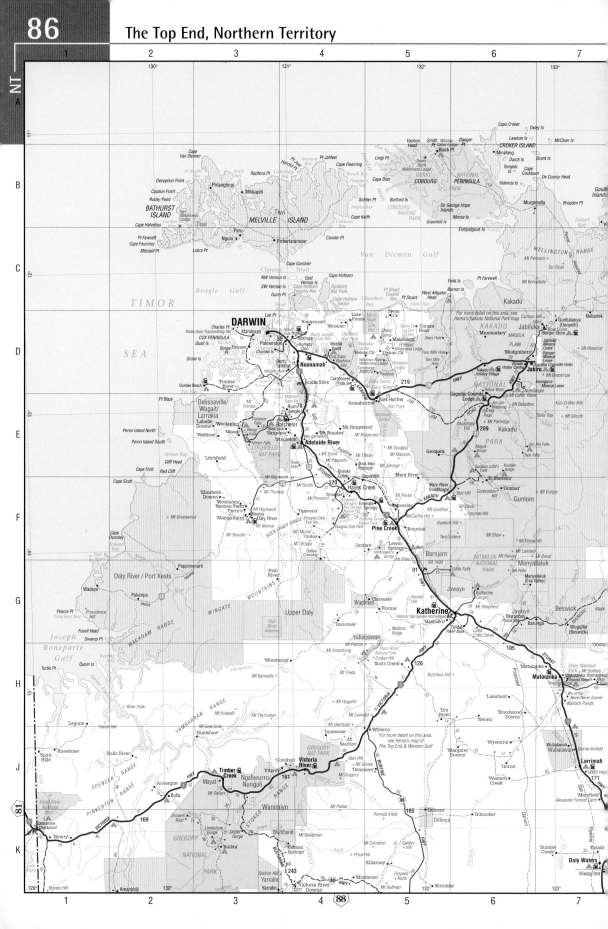

8 9 10 11 12 13 14

134° 135° 136° 137°

A

Rimbija Is
Cape Wessel

11°

B

ARAFURA SEA

Wessel Islands
Marchinbar Is

Cumberland Strait

Stevens Is
Guluwuru Is

Drysdale Is
North West Crocodile Is
Raragala Is
Truant Is
Wigram Is

C

Cuthbert Pt
Braithwaite Pt
Hawkesbury Pt
Nth East Pt
Skirmish Pt
False Pt
Cape Stewart
Mooroongga Is
Elcho Is
Alger Is
Pt Napier
Cunningham Islands
The English Company's Islands
Cape Wilberforce
Bromby Islands

Junction Bay
Rolling Bay
Boucaut Bay
Ji-Marda
Rabuma Is
Howard Is
Galiwinku
Inglis Is
Flinders Pt
Probable Is
Bremer Is

12°

Goomadeer
165
Maningrida
Gochin Jiny Jirra
Yathalamarra
Milingimbi
Castlereagh Bay
Banyan Is
Mapurru
Buckingham Bay
Mallison Is
Everett Is
Rorruwuy
Nhulunbuy
Yirrkala

D

Nangalala
Ramingining
'Old Arafura' (ruins)
Lake Evella
Gapuwiyak
Arnhem Bay
Dhalinybuy
GOVE PENINSULA
Cape Arnhem
Port Bradshaw

Manmoyi
Mirrnatja
Gurrumuru
FREDERICK HILLS
'Mt Alexander' (ruins)
Garrthalala
Birany Birany
Pt Alexander

13°

E

ARNHEM LAND
Arnhem Land
Emu Springs
Mt Fleeming
Mt Caledon
Cape Grey
Bald Bay
Bald Pt

GULF

Baniyala
Round Hill Is
Cape Shield
Isle Woodah
Nicol Is
Pt Arrowsmith

14°

705
Weemol
Bulman
Mt Catt
Mt Catt
Black Mountain
Mt Murumba
Mt Stretton
Mt Rankin
Morgan Is
Jalma Bay
Blue Mud Bay
Burney Is
Hawknest Is
Chasm Is
North Point Is
North East Isles

F

Mountain Valley
Mt Bridges
Mt Bray
Mt Leane
Cape Barrow
Bennet Bay
Bustard Is
Bickerton Is
Winchelsea Is
Milyakburra
North East Isles

OF

Alyangula
Umbakumba

GROOTE EYLANDT
Angurugu
Ilyungmadja Pt

Mainoru
Wharnell Bluff
Mt Throsby
Mt Furrer
Mt Bagster
Mt Phillip
Mt Favenc
Mt Chapman
Three Graces

G

Mt Karmain
DOWNERS RANGE
COLLERA MTNS
PARSONS RANGE
Tasman Pt
South Pt
Cape Beatrice

Numbulwar
Sandy Is
Edward Is

CARPENTARIA

BLACK RANGE
Buddawarka
Urapunga
Ngukurr
Roper Bar
Mt Eclipse
Mt Boxall
Port Roper
Limmen Bight
Maria Is

H

'Moroak'
Mt Eleanor
Mt Price
Bringund
Yutpundji-Djindiwirritj
'Roper Valley'
Mt St Vidgeon
'St Vidgeon' (ruins)
Marra
Beatrice Is

15°

ROPER
176
Mt Forrest
Mt Hughes
Mt Davidson
Mt Kelly
Hodgson Downs
Miniyeri
'Hodgson Downs'
'Mason Bluff'
Limmen Bight Fishing Camp
Maria Lagoon

For more detail on this area, see
Hema's Top End & Western Gulf map

N

0 50 100km
© Hema Maps Pty Ltd

'Hodgson River'
'Nutwood Downs'
'Minamia' (Cox River)
Alawa
372
'Nathan River'
The Four Archers
Rosie
Wurralibi
Sir Edward Pellew Group
Barranyi National Park
North Is
Cape Vanderlin

J

'Lorella Springs'
Port for McArthur River Mine
Bing Bong
Bing Bong Loading Facility
West Island
Watson Is
Centre Is
South West Is
Vanderlin Is
Wurralibi
Port McArthur

HODGSON RIVER
Mt Joe
King Ash Bay
'Manangoora'

TAWALLAH RANGE
Jandanku
'Bauhinia Downs'
Borroloola
Narwinbi
Warby
'Greenbank'

K

16°

CARPENTARIA
HWY
1
'Broadmere'
'Tanumbirini'
'Tawallah'
'Billengarrah'
117
Carabirini Con Res
Bukalara Rock
McArthur River Mine (HYC)
McArthur River
Mt Featherton
'Seven Emu'

8 9 10 11 12 13 14
134° 135° 136° 137° 138°

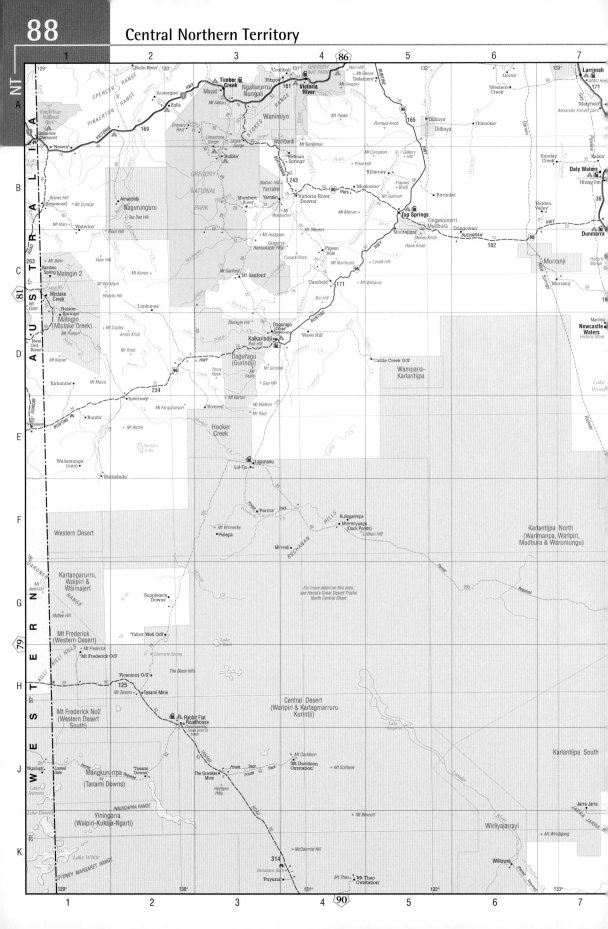

8 9 10 87 11 12 13 14

GULF OF CARPENTARIA

NT

134° 135° 136° 137° 138°

A

'Hodgson River'
'Nutwood Downs'
Alawa
'Minamia' ('Cox River')
Nathan River'
372
'Lorella Springs'
Wurralibi
Sir Edward Pellew Group
Barranyi National Park
North is   Cape Vanderlin
Vanderlin is
Wurralibi
Port for McArthur River Mine
Bing Bong
Bing Bong Loading Facility
West Island
Watson Is
South West Is
Port McArthur
Centre
'Manangoora'

RIVER ROAD
HODGSON
CARPENTARIA HWY 82
'Amungee Mungee'
'Beetaloo'
Tanumbirini
HWY 1 269
'O.T. Downs'
Jandanku
'Bauhinia Downs'
'Billengarrah'
Broadmere'
Tawallah'
Borroloola
Narwinbi
Mt Feathertop
King Ash Bay
Warby
'Greenbank'
'Seven Emu'

B

57

CARPENTARIA
FAVENC RANGE
Cape Crawford
McArthur River'
117
Carahbri Con Res
Bukalara Rock
McArthur River Mine (HYC)
'Spring Creek'
Garawa
254
'Pungalina'

Cape Crawford
'Balbirini'
The Lost City
ABNER RANGE
'Mallapunyah'
Robinson River
'Calvert Hills'
Redbank Mine
'Wollogorang'

C

'Kiana'

For more detail on this area, see Hema's Top End & Western Gulf map

Wampaya
Lia
Shandon Downs (Ruins)
'Wallhallow'
11
CHINA WALL
'Benmara'
Permit

D

'Ucharonidge'
'Mungabroom'
'Cresswell Downs'
CALVERT ROAD 16
Waanyi / Garawa

E
'Powell Creek (Jangirulu)'
Renner Springs
'Helen Springs'
STOCK ROUTE BARKLY 16
'Eva Downs'
Anthony Lagoon
373
Corella Creek
Murun Murula
Mussellbrook
Mussellbrook Mine Camp
CARRARA RANGE
'Highland Plains'

F
Muckaty 242
'Banka Banka'
'Brunchilly'
'Brunette Downs'
Rockhampton Downs'
Connells Lagoon Conservation Reserve
'Connell Lagoon'
Mittiebah
'Mittiebah'
'Alexandria'
'Old Herbert Vale'

G
Warumungu
Likkaparta
John Flynn Memorial
Roadhouse
Three Ways
The Pebbles
187
BARKLY
Warumungu
Prentice Lake
Lone Star Hill
'Alroy Downs'
Burdugu
'Gallipoli'
'Herbert Vale'

H
Tennant Creek
'Peko Mine'
Gold Mine Tours, Gold Stamp Battery, Museum, Overland Telegraph Station
Copper & Gold Mines
Barkly Homestead
BARKLY HWY
Wakaya
Wunara
'Soudan'
'Avon Downs'
265
Camooweal
Camooweal Caves Nat Park
Police Stn
Rockland
Nowranie

Arruwurra
'Burramurra'
'Old Wooroona'
164
Wooroona
Austral Downs'

J
McLaren Creek
Mungkarta
Devils Marbles
Devils Marbles Con Reserve
Wauchope
Singleton'
Whistle Duck Creek
'Epenarra' Wutunugurra
'Kurundi'
Mt Cairns
Canteen Creek (Orwaitilla)
DAVENPORT RANGE NAT PARK
Anurrete
'Annitowa'
Mt Michael
'Arcadia'

K
Wycliffe Well
Ali-Curung
Warrabri
'Murray Downs'
Elkedra
'Hatches Creek' (Ruins)
Alpurrurulam
Lake Nash
'Georgina'
109
STUART HWY
Scarr Hill

0 50km
© Hema Maps Pty Ltd

NT

1 2 3 4 (88) 5 6 7

A

'Ngulupi' • 129° Locked Gate • Lake Jeavons
Mangkururrpa (Tanami Downs) • 'Tanami Downs' • 130° • The Granites Mine • Private Track • 131° • 'Mt Davidson Outstation' • + Mt Solitaire • 132° • 133° • + Jarra Jarra
INNINGARRA RANGE • Hordern Hills • TANAMI • Lander River • JARRA JARRA
Yiningarra (Walpiri-Kukaja-Ngarti) • + Mt Bennett • Wirliyajarrayi • + Mt Windiajong • Connel
Lake White • SYDNEY MARGARET RANGE • Lake Denni

B
314 • + McDiarmid Hill • + Mt Theo • 'Mt Theo Outstation' • Willowra • + Mt Rennie • + Mt Peake
Lake Mackay • Renahans Bore • 'Puyurra' • Chilla Well (Abandoned) • Sowden Hill • 'Chilla Well' • + Mt Patricia • Mount Barkly (Pawu) (Private Road)
Mala (Tjilla-Warlpiri) • Pawu

C
Lake Mackay • + Mt Singleton • + Mt Doreen (Ruins) • + Mt Hardy • 'Mt Denison' • 'Coniston' • + Mt Treachery • + Mt Stafford • + Nancy Hill • Ti-Tree (Nturiya) • Ti-Tree
Yuendumu • Quartz Hill • + Mt Gaidner • Pmar Jutun
'Vaughan Springs' • TREUER RANGE • + Mt Davenport • Yuendumu • Yalpirakinu (Mount Allen) • Uldira Hill • + Mt Firmiss • Pine Hill
GILES RANGE • + Mt Leichhardt • REYNOLDS RANGE

D
Mt Nicker + • Nirrippi • + Mt Carey • Waite Creek Settlement • + Mt Gurner • Yunkanjini • + Wayililinypa O/S • Yarripilangu O/S • 152 • Laramba • Napperby • + Mt Freeling • + Mt Boothby
Lake Mackay • + Mt Cockburn • Newhaven • Central Mount Wedge • + West Bluff • + Hammond • Tilmouth Roadhouse
Ngalurrtja • + Central Mt Wedge • + Mt Harris

E
Ininti • Pinpirnga • Len Beadell marker • Sandy Blight Junction • 'Tjukil' • Illili • Papunya (Fuel) • 'Derwent' • 110 • Narwietooma • Rubunja
ROAD • Walungurra (Kintore) • Tietkens Tree • Willie Rockhole • 'Warren Creek Bore' • 'New Bore' • Inyalinga • 'Blackwater' • 'Utanbaura' • Bunghara Mt Zeil 1531m • 'Glen Helen' • + Mt Chapple • 'Milton Park' • 'Anbula'
Mt Leisler • 255 • Required • Mount + Mt Liebig • 'Mt Larrie' • MACDONNELL • + Mt Hay • 'Hamilton Downs'
Mt Strickland • Liebig • + Mt Edward • Kunparrka (Haasts Bluff) • WEST MACDONNELL NATIONAL PARK

F
331 • 'Ualki' • Neunman • Haasts Bluff • + Mt Udor • 'Kunkayunti' • Yatemans Bore Gas • Merenie Bluff • Kulpitarra • Redbank Gorge Mt Sonder • 71 • Ormiston Gorge • Serpentine Gorge • Ellery Ck Big Hole • DRIVE
Lake Macdonald • Mt Main • BONYTHON RANGE • + Mt Forbes • Mt Solitary + • Camels Hump • Pipeline • Glen Helen Resort • Roulpmaulpma • Ellery Creek • Ellery Creek Nature Park • LARAPINTA • WATERHOUSE
Lake Hopkins • Sandy Blight Required • + Wonnan Rocks • 155 Required ROAD • Talalultuma • Rodna • 43 • Hermannsburg • Injarrtnama • Wallace Rockhole
For more detail on this area, see Hema's Great Desert Tracks North Central Sheet • + Mt Winter • + Laycocks Hill • GARDINER RANGE • Merenie Oil & Gas Field • Ipolera • Areyonga (Permit Only) • Pitlantara Bluff • Finke Gorge • + Mt Keartland

G
Tjukurla (Closed Community) • + Mt Harris + • + Mt Carruthers • Lake Neale • + Mt Oilient • + Mt Cowie • + Mt Tucker • WATARRKA NATIONAL PARK • Carmichael Crag • Kings Canyon • Kings Canyon Resort • Kings Creek • 103 • Urrampinyu Ilijitjara • + Mt Lewis • Tempe Downs • Boggy Hole • Stuarts
Lake Amadeus • + Mt Levi • GEORGE GILL RANGE • Finke River • + Mt Levi • Ambalindum • FINKE GORGE NATIONAL PARK • JAMES RANGE • Henbury Meteorite Con Res 14.5 Ha • Henbu

H
Bloods Range (Puntitjata) • + Mt Harris + • Tjuninanta • Karukaki • + Mt Currie • Katiti • Yowa Bluff • Henbury • Palmer Valley • The Twins
Kutjurntari • Kulail • RANGE • Petermann • Kings Canyon • GILES • 99 •
'Mt Taylor' • BLOODS RANGE • Walu • Lake Amadeus • LURITJA HWY • 64 • GILES • 36
Kaltukatjara (Docker River) • Lasseter's Cave • PETERMANN RANGES • 259 TJUKARURU • Required • ROAD • LASSETER • HWY • BASEDOW RANGE • KERNOT

I
Wirnpura • Tjunti • Puta Puta • Mt Phillips • Ngamgur • Connellan Airport • 138 • Angas Downs • Mt Ebenezer • Imanpa • Mount Ebenezer • 110 • Eridunda Desert Oaks Motel & Roa
Mt Deering O/S • Walka • Wankari • Kunapula • Urilpila • Yulara Resort • Kata Tjuta • Curtin Springs • Mount Ebenezer • Eridunda
Pitalu • + Mt McCulloch • Kata Tjuta (The Olgas) • Uluru • Kata Tjuta • LASSETER HWY • STUART HWY • Karinga

J
Pilakatal • + Katamala Cone • Pirnulpakalarinitja • Uluru (Ayers Rock) • ULURU - KATA TJUTA NATIONAL PARK • + Mt Conner • 'Eridunda O/S (Lyndavale)' • 74
Stevenson Peak • + Butler Dome

K
Mt Daisy Bates • Alkata • + Mt Le Hunt • Benda Hill • + Mt Robert • 'Mulga Park' • 188 • + Mt Reynolds • Victory Downs • Mount Cavenagh
'Mirturtu O/S' • Mt Gosse • Surveyor Generals Corner • Ukatjupa • + Mt Cockburn • Alpara • MULGA PARK ROAD • Walyinynga • Ulaypai • Eagle Bore • Womikata • Boorndoolynga • Ilykuwaratjala • Gosse Bore • Kulgera
Irkini • Kurkutjara • + Mt Mann • Angatja • Umpukulunya • Amata • 61 • Araleun • STUART HWY • Sandown O/S
Irrunytju (Wingellina) • Nyilikura • Aparatjara (new) • Mt Charles • Mt Whinham • Wintawatu • MUSGRAVE RANGES • Ngarutjara • Donalds Well
Mt Hinckley • Kalka • Pipalyatjatja • Putaputa • Aparatjara (old) • 202 Kanpi • Umpukulunya • + Mt Woodroffe • Pine Ridge • Yunyarinyi (Kenmore Park) • Agnes Cr
'Anumarapitji O/S' • Tjitjatara O/S • Tjintalka • Mt Hardy • Walitjara • Manyirkanga • Yurangka • Pukatja (Ernabella) • (De Ro
TOMKINSON RANGE • 129° • Kenatjara • Willi Willi • Tankaanu • Ulkiya • 131° • Anangu Pitjantjatjara • Wallany • Warrabilinna • 132° • 133°

SOUTH • AUSTRALIA • WESTERN • (79)

8 9 89 11 12 13 14

NT

Kurundi 'Burramurra' 'Wooroma'
Devils Marbles Con Reserve 'Austral Downs' Buckley R
Mt Cairns Canteen Creek (Orwaitilla) **Arruwurra** Mt Michael
Wauchope Singleton Whistle Duck Creek 'Arcadia'
DAVENPORT RANGE NAT PARK Old Police Stn Waterhole Mine Ruins **Anurrete** 'Lake Nash'
Wycliffe Well 'Hatches Creek' (Ruins) Alpurrurulam (Fuel)
Ali-Curung 'Murray Downs' 'Annitowa' 'Georgina'
Warrabri 'Elkedra' SANDOVER HWY + Scarr Hill
109 'Irrmarne Irrmarne' 'Argadargada'
arrow Creek 307 Mt Hogarth For more detail on this area, see Hema's Great Desert Tracks North East Sheet
Tara Neutral Junction **Ampilatwatja** 'Ammaroo'
'Stirling' **Alyawarra & Katitja** private road 'Ooratippra'
Wilora Mt Tops HWY
90 **Angarapa** Arlparra Store 'Derry Downs' 'Manners Creek'
Atnelyey Mt Stott 'Arapunya' Tobermorey
(Ti-Tree) Urapuntja (Utopia) 'MacDonald Downs' HWY 32
'Woolla Downs' (ruins) Lirdan Peak 'MacDonald Downs Outstation' 'Lucy Creek' **Anatye** 219 Urlampe
'Chianina' 243 Mt Michael DULCIE RANGES NAT PARK + Mt Pozieres
'Woodgreen' 'Delmore Downs' Box Hole/Meteorite Crater PLENTY Tarlton Downs 'Marqua'
Arno Peak 'Waite River' 'Mount Swan' 'Dneiper' JERVOIS RANGE + Mt Reinecke
69 Red Cliff 'Delney' Irrirlree 'Huckitta' 'Jinka' 'Jervois' + Mt Tietkens Mt Woods TOKO RANGE
Mendip Hill Mt Swan 203 HWY + Mt Smith Mt Wooldridge Twin Hills
Engawala 'Bushy Park' Harts Range Police Stn + Mt Eaglebeak Mt Winnecke Cravens Peak
'Alcoota' 'Mount Riddoch' HARTS RANGE 'Atula' Mt Barrington
The Garden Atnheve Mt Pfitzner Mt Mary **Atnetye** Mt Knuckey
Mt Laughlen Mt Ridgoch Mt Campbell 'Quartz Hill' (ruins) Mt Gardner
'Ambalindum' Claraville + Mt Lionel Lake Caroline
68 **Alice Springs** Arltunga Arltunga Resort 'Indiana'
106 Ross River Resort Ruby Gap Nature Pk Two Hills
MACDONNELL RANGES 12
Emily Gap Corroboree Rock Cons Res N'dhala Gorge Nat Pk 'Atnarpa'
Pine Gap Jessie FERGUSON RANGE 'Ringwood' Limbla'
81 Ltyentye Apurte (Santa Teresa) 'Todd River' 'Numery'
Santa Teresa Mt Oorramina **Pmere Nyente**
106 'Deep Well' Todd River Downs' Oneill Point
Mowelanne Oak Valley 'Allambi'
Hugh River Rodinga (ruin) OLD ANDADO TRACK *Simpson*
Maryvale Titjikala Mt Frank 238 SIMPSON DESERT NATIONAL PARK
Mt Charlotte For more detail on this area, see Hema's map of the Red Centre, and Great Desert Tracks North East sheet *Desert* For more detail on this area, see Hema's Central Australia map, and Great Desert Tracks North East sheet
137 'Idracowra' Bundooma (ruin) MAC CLARK (ACACIA PEUCE) CONSERVATION RESERVE
'Horseshoe Bend' + Colson Pinnacle
Rumbalara (ruin) Permit Required from QNPWS LINE
122 'Andado' 'Old Andado'
'Lilla Creek' Lambert's Centre of Australia Mt Peebles N 50 100km
148 **Finke** (Aputula) 'New Crown' © Hema Maps Pty Ltd
Apatula Mt Gordon Mt Beddome **Finke** Pmer Ulperre Ingwemirne Arletherre Poeppel Corner
'Eringa' (abandoned) Charlotte Waters' 'Mt Dare' Mt Etiegumbra Walls Hills
'Mt Irwin' **AUSTRALIA** SIMPSON DESERT REGIONAL RESERVE SIMPSON DESERT CONSERVATION PARK
Ibunpa (ruin) Freeth Junction FRENCH LINE WAA LINE

8 9 66 10 11 12 67 13 14

92 913 Mile – Beaconsfield

A

913 Mile WA 77 J14 83 F3
A1 Mine Settlement VIC 42 H6 44 A7 46 C1
Abbeyard VIC 43 F8
Abbotsbury NSW 21 E9
Abbotsford NSW 19 E4
Abbotsham TAS 54 E6
Abercorn QLD 7 A9
Abercrombie NSW 22 H5
Abercrombie River Nat Park NSW 22 J6 30 A5
Aberdeen NSW 23 C8
Aberfeldy VIC 42 J7 44 B7 46 D1
Aberfoyle Park SA 60 J2 61 C6
Abergowrie QLD 11 F13
Abminga SA 66 A4 91 K9
Acacia Ridge QLD 3 H4 5 E9
Acacia Store NT 85 D2 86 D4
Acheron VIC 42 G4
Acland QLD 7 F10
Acraman Creek Con Park SA 64 D3
Actaeon Island TAS 53 K9
Acton ACT 31 A1 32 D4
Adaminaby NSW 30 F2
Adamsfield TAS 52 F7
Adavale QLD 13 K11 15 C11
Addington VIC 39 D10
Adelaide SA 59 G4 60 G2 61 A6 62 F7 65 J10
Adelaide CBD SA 58
Adelaide River NT 85 E2 86 E4
Adelong NSW 29 H14 30 D1
Adjungbilly NSW 30 D1
Admiral Bay WA 79 C8 80 J2
Adolphus Island WA 81 C13
Advancetown QLD 5 C13
Adventure Bay TAS 53 J10
Afterlee NSW 25 B12
Agery SA 62 H5 65 G9
Agnes Banks NSW 20 G7
Agnes Banks Nature Res NSW 20 G7
Agnes Water QLD 9 J12
Agnew WA 77 E10
Agnew Mine WA 77 D10
Ahrberg Bay TAS 54 H2
Aileron NT 90 D7
Ailsa VIC 40 K6
Ainslie ACT 32 D5
Aireys Inlet VIC 36 K1 39 J11
Airlie VIC 45 D11 46 E4
Airlie Beach QLD 9 B8
Akuna Bay NSW 19 A6
Alawa NT 84 B3
Alawoona SA 62 B6 65 J13
Albacutya VIC 28 K3 40 H4
Albany WA 74 K6
Albany Creek QLD 3 B2 4 F7
Albany Island QLD 16 B2
Albatross Bay QLD 16 F1
Alberrie Creek SA 67 H8
Albert NSW 22 C1 27 K13 29 A13
Albert Park VIC 36 D7
Alberton QLD 5 C10
Alberton SA 59 E2 60 F1
Alberton TAS 55 E12
Alberton VIC 45 G9 46 H2
Albion QLD 3 D4
Albion VIC 36 C6 39 F13 42 K1 44 B1
Albury NSW 29 K12 43 B9
Alcomie TAS 54 C3
Alderley QLD 3 D3
Aldersyde WA 72 A5
Aldgate SA 59 J7 60 H4 61 B7
Aldinga SA 61 E5 62 F7 65 K10
Aldinga Beach SA 61 E4 62 F7 65 K9
Aldinga Scrub Con Park SA 61 E4
Alectown NSW 22 E2
Alexander Heights WA 71 C4
Alexander Morrison Nat Park WA 76 H4
Alexandra VIC 42 G4
Alexandra Bridge WA 73 J13
Alexandra Headland QLD 4 D1 7 E13
Alexandra Hills QLD 5 D8
Alford SA 62 G4 65 G9
Alfords Point NSW 19 H3
Alfred Cove WA 71 H3
Alfred Nat Park VIC 47 C12
Alfred Town NSW 29 H13
Algebuckina Bridge SA 66 E5
Alger Island NT 87 C11
Algester QLD 3 J4
Alice NSW 7 K12 25 C12
Alice QLD 8 H3 13 F13
Alice Springs NT 91 F8
Ali-Curung NT 89 K9 91 A9
Alkata NT 68 A1 79 K14 83 A7 90 J1
Allambie NSW 19 D6
Allans Flat VIC 43 C9
Allansford VIC 38 H7
Allanson WA 73 F9
Alleena NSW 29 E13
Allen Island QLD 10 D3
Allenby Gardens SA 59 F3
Allendale East SA 38 G1 63 B14
Allestree VIC 38 H4
Allies Creek QLD 7 D9
Allora QLD 7 H11
Allworth NSW 23 D11
Alma SA 62 F5 65 H10
Almaden QLD 11 E11
Almonds VIC 42 C6
Almoola QLD 8 C6
Almurta VIC 37 K12 44 F4
Alonnah TAS 53 J10
Aloomba QLD 11 D13
Alpara NT 68 A4 90 K4
Alpha QLD 8 H4 13 F14
Alpine Nat Park VIC 30 J1 43 F10 46 B3
Alpurrurulam NT 12 A1 89 K14 91 A14
Alstonville NSW 7 K13 25 C14
Althorpe Islands SA 63 J8 64 K7
Alton QLD 6 H6
Alton Nat Park QLD 6 H6
Altona VIC 35 E1 36 D6 39 F13 42 K1 44 C1
Altona Meadows VIC 35 E1
Alum Cliffs State Res TAS 54 F7
Alva Beach QLD 8 A6
Alvie VIC 39 H9
Alyangula NT 87 F12
Amamoor QLD 7 D12
Amanbidji NT 86 K2 88 B2
Amaroo ACT 32 A5
Amata SA 68 A4 90 K4
Ambarvale NSW 21 E11
Amberley QLD 5 H9
Ambleside SA 60 H4
Amboola QLD 6 D3
Amboyne VIC 43 G14 47 A9
Ambrose QLD 9 H11
Amby QLD 6 E4
Amelup WA 74 H7
Amen Corner SA 63 J8 65 K8
American River SA 63 H9
Amherst VIC 39 C10
Amity QLD 4 B7 7 G13
Amoonguna NT 91 F8
Amosfield NSW 25 B10
Amphitheatre VIC 39 C9
Ampilatwatja NT 91 C10
Amyton SA 62 F1 65 A9
Anakie QLD 8 H6
Anakie VIC 36 E2 39 F12
Anakie East VIC 36 E2
Anakie Junction VIC 36 D2 39 F12
Ancona VIC 42 F5
Andamooka SA 67 K8
Anderson VIC 44 G3
Anderson Island TAS 55 C9
Ando NSW 30 H3
Andover TAS 53 D11
Andrews QLD 5 B14
Andrews SA 62 F4 65 F10
Anembo NSW 30 F4
Angahook Lorne State Park VIC 39 J11
Angaston SA 60 A7 62 E6 65 H10
Angatja SA 68 A2 90 K3
Angellala QLD 6 D1 13 K14
Angip VIC 40 J5
Angle Vale SA 60 C3
Anglers Rest VIC 43 F11 46 A5
Anglesea VIC 36 K2 39 H11
Angorichina Village SA 65 B10
Angourie NSW 25 E13
Angurugu NT 87 F12
Anna Bay NSW 23 E11
Anne's Corner SA 68 E5
Annerley QLD 3 F4 5 E8
Annuello VIC 28 G5 40 D7
Anser Group VIC 44 K7 46 K1
Anson Bay NT 86 E2
Ansons Bay TAS 55 D14
Antarrengenge NT 91 C9
Antill Plains QLD 8 A5 11 H14
Antill Ponds TAS 53 C11 55 K11
Antwerp VIC 40 K5
Anula NT 84 B3
Anxious Bay SA 64 F4
Aparatjara (new) SA 68 A2 90 K2
Aparatjara (old) SA 68 A2 90 K2
Apollo Bay VIC 39 K10
Appila SA 62 F2 65 E10
Appin NSW 21 E12 23 J8 30 A7
Appin VIC 41 H10
Appin South VIC 41 H10
Apple Tree Flat NSW 22 D6
Applecross WA 71 H3
Apslawn TAS 53 B13 55 J13
Apsley TAS 53 D10
Apsley VIC 38 C2
Aquila Island QLD 9 E9
Arabella QLD 13 K14 15 D14
Arakoola Nature Res NSW 24 D7
Arakoon NSW 25 J12
Araleun SA 68 A5 90 K5
Araluen NSW 30 E5
Aramac QLD 8 G2 13 E12
Aramara QLD 7 C11
Arana Hills QLD 3 C2
Aranda ACT 32 D4
Ararat VIC 39 D8
Aratula QLD 5 J12 7 H12
Arawata VIC 37 J14
Arcadia NSW 19 A3 20 D6
Arcadia VIC 42 D3
Archdale VIC 39 B9
Archer River Roadhouse QLD 16 G3
Archerfield QLD 3 G3 5 E9
Archies Creek VIC 44 G4
Ardeer VIC 35 D1
Ardglen NSW 23 B8
Ardlethan NSW 29 F12
Ardno VIC 38 F2
Ardrossan SA 62 G5 65 H9
Areyonga NT 90 G6
Argents Hill NSW 25 H12
Argyle WA 73 G10 74 G3
Ariah Park NSW 29 F13
Aringa VIC 38 H5
Arkaroola SA 67 J11
Arkona VIC 40 K5
Arlparra NT 91 C9
Arltunga NT 91 F9
Arltunga Historic Res NT 91 F9
Armadale VIC 35 E4
Armadale WA 72 F4 74 D3
Armatree NSW 22 A3 24 K1
Armidale NSW 25 G9
Armstrong VIC 38 D7
Armuna QLD 8 B6
Armytage VIC 39 H10
Arncliffe NSW 19 G4
Arno Bay SA 62 K4 64 G7
Arnold VIC 39 A10
Arrino WA 76 G4
Artarmon NSW 21 C8
Arthur East WA 73 B10
Arthur Pieman Con Area TAS 54 F2
Arthur Point QLD 9 F9
Arthur River TAS 54 D1
Arthur River WA 73 B9 74 F5
Arthurs Creek VIC 37 A9
Arthurs Lake TAS 53 B9 55 J9
Arthurs Seat State Park VIC 36 J7 39 H14 44 F1
Arthurton SA 62 H5 65 H8
Arthurville NSW 22 D3
Arundel QLD 5 B12
Ascot QLD 3 D4 4 E7
Ascot VIC 39 D10
Ascot WA 71 F5
Ashbourne SA 63 F8 65 K10
Ashbury NSW 21 C9
Ashfield NSW 21 C9
Ashfield WA 71 E5
Ashford NSW 25 D8
Ashgrove QLD 3 D3
Ashley NSW 24 D5
Ashmore QLD 5 B12
Ashton SA 59 G7 60 G4 61 A7
Ashville SA 63 D8 65 K11
Aspen Island ACT 31 C4
Aspendale VIC 37 F8
Aspley QLD 3 B4 4 E7
Aspley VIC 63 A12
Asquith NSW 20 D7
Astrebla Downs Nat Park QLD 12 G5
Athelstone SA 59 E7 60 F3
Atherton QLD 11 D12
Athlone VIC 37 H13 44 E5
Athol Park SA 59 E3
Atitjere NT 91 E10
Atnelyey NT 91 C9
Attadale WA 71 H2
Attunga NSW 24 H7
Aubigny QLD 7 G10
Aubrey VIC 40 K5
Auburn NSW 19 F3 21 D9
Auburn SA 62 F5 65 G10
Auburn River Nat Park QLD 7 C9
Audley NSW 19 K3 21 C10
Augathella QLD 6 C1 13 J14 15 C14
Augusta WA 73 J14 74 J2
Augustus Island WA 80 D7
Auldana SA 59 G6
Aurukun Community QLD 16 G1
Austinmer NSW 21 C13
Austinville QLD 5 C14
Austral NSW 21 F10
Australia Plains SA 62 E5 65 G11
Australind WA 73 G9
Avalon NSW 20 B6
Avalon Beach VIC 36 F3
Avenel VIC 42 F3
Avenue SA 63 C12
Avisford Nature Res NSW 22 D5
Avoca TAS 53 A12 55 H12
Avoca VIC 39 C9
Avoca Beach NSW 20 B4
Avoid Bay SA 64 H5
Avon SA 62 F5 65 H9
Avon Plains VIC 38 A7
Avon Valley Nat Park WA 72 E2 74 C3 76 K5
Avondale QLD 7 A11 9 K12
Avonsleigh VIC 37 E11
Axedale VIC 39 B12
Ayr QLD 8 A6
Ayrford VIC 38 J7
Ayton QLD 11 B12

B

Baalijin Nature Res NSW 25 G11
Baan Baa NSW 24 G5
Babel Island TAS 55 B10
Babinda QLD 11 E13
Bacchus Marsh VIC 36 B3 39 E12
Back River Nature Res NSW 23 A9 25 K8
Backstairs Passage SA 61 K1 63 G8
Backwater NSW 25 F10
Baddaginnie VIC 42 D5
Baden TAS 53 D11
Badgebup WA 74 G6
Badger Island TAS 55 C8
Badgerys Creek NSW 21 F9
Badgingarra WA 76 H4
Badgingarra Nat Park WA 76 H4
Badja NSW 30 F4
Badu Island QLD 16 A1
Baerami NSW 23 D8
Baerami Creek NSW 22 D7
Bagdad TAS 53 E10
Bago Bluff Nat Park NSW 23 A13 25 K11
Bagot Well SA 62 E5 65 H10
Bailieston VIC 39 A14 42 E2
Bailup WA 72 E2
Baird Bay SA 64 E3
Bairnsdale VIC 43 K11 45 C13 46 D6
Bajool QLD 9 H10
Bakara SA 62 C6 65 J12
Baker VIC 40 J3
Baker Gully SA 60 J2 61 C6
Baker Lake WA 83 B5
Bakers Creek QLD 9 D8
Bakers Hill WA 72 D2
Bakers Swamp NSW 22 E4
Baking Board QLD 7 E8
Baladjie Lake Nature Res WA 75 A8 77 J8
Balaklava SA 62 F5 65 G9
Balbarrup WA 73 E13
Balcatta WA 71 D3 72 G3
Bald Hills QLD 3 A3
Bald Island WA 74 K7
Bald Knob NSW 25 E10
Bald Knob QLD 4 F2
Bald Rock VIC 28 K7 41 J11
Bald Rock Nat Park NSW 7 K11 25 C10
Baldry NSW 22 E3
Balfe's Creek QLD 8 B3 11 J13
Balfour TAS 54 E2
Balga WA 71 D3
Balgo WA 79 D13
Balgowan SA 62 H5 65 H8
Balgowlah NSW 19 D6 21 B8
Balgownie NSW 21 D14
Balhannah SA 60 G5 62 E7 65 J10
Balingup WA 73 F11 74 G3
Balkuling WA 72 B3
Balladonia WA 83 H2
Balladoran NSW 22 B3
Ballajura WA 71 C5
Ballalaba NSW 30 E4
Ballan VIC 36 B2 39 E11
Ballan North VIC 36 A2
Ballandean QLD 25 B10
Ballangeich VIC 38 H7
Ballarat VIC 39 E10
Ballark VIC 36 C1
Ballbank NSW 28 J7 41 F11
Balldale NSW 29 K11 42 A7
Ballendella VIC 41 K13 42 C1
Balliang VIC 36 D3 39 F12
Balliang East VIC 36 D3 39 F12
Ballidu WA 76 H6
Ballimore NSW 22 C4
Ballina NSW 7 K14 25 C14
Bally Bally WA 72 B4
Balmain NSW 19 F5 21 C8
Balmattum VIC 42 E4
Balmoral NSW 19 E6 21 B8 21 G14
Balmoral QLD 3 E5
Balmoral VIC 38 D4
Balnarring VIC 37 J8 39 H14 44 F2
Balnarring Beach VIC 37 J8
Balook VIC 45 F8 46 G2
Balranald NSW 28 G6 41 C9
Balwyn VIC 35 D5 37 D8
Bamaga QLD 16 B2
Bamawm VIC 41 K13 42 C1
Bamawm Extension VIC 41 J13 42 B1
Bambaroo QLD 11 G13
Bambill VIC 28 G2 40 B3
Bamboo WA 78 E7 82 C7
Bamboo Spring NT 88 C1
Bamborough Island QLD 9 E10
Bambra VIC 39 H11
Ban Ban Springs QLD 7 C10
Banana QLD 9 K10
Bancroft QLD 7 A9 9 K11
Bandiana VIC 43 B9
Bandon NSW 22 G2
Bandon Grove NSW 23 C10
Banealla SA 63 B9
Bangadilly Nat Park NSW 22 K7 30 B6
Bangalow NSW 7 K13 25 B14
Bangerang VIC 40 J6
Bangham SA 38 A1
Bangham Con Park SA 38 A1 63 A11
Bangholme VIC 35 H6
Bangor NSW 21 C10
Bangor TAS 55 E10 56 D5
Baniyala NT 87 E12
Banks ACT 32 K4
Banks Strait TAS 55 B13
Banksia Beach QLD 4 D4
Banksia Park SA 59 D7
Banksmeadow NSW 19 H6
Bankstown NSW 19 G2 21 D9
Bannaby NSW 22 K6 30 B5
Bannerton VIC 28 G5 40 C7
Bannister NSW 22 K5 30 B4
Bannister WA 72 D6 74 E4
Bannockburn VIC 36 F1 39 G11
Banora Point NSW 5 A14
Banyabba Nature Res NSW 25 D12
Banyan VIC 40 G7
Banyan Island NT 87 C10
Banyena VIC 38 A7
Banyenong VIC 41 K8
Banyo QLD 3 C5
Barabon QLD 11 K9 13 A9
Baradine NSW 24 H3
Barakee Nat Park NSW 23 A11 25 K9
Barakula QLD 7 D8
Baralaba QLD 9 J9
Baranduda VIC 43 B9
Barcaldine QLD 8 H2 13 F12
Bardoc WA 77 H11 83 F1
Bardoc Mine WA 77 G10
Bardon QLD 3 E3
Barduthulla QLD 13 K14 15 C14
Barellan NSW 29 F12
Barfold VIC 39 C12
Bargara QLD 7 A12 9 K13
Bargo NSW 21 F13 22 J7 30 A7
Bargo State Rec Park NSW 21 G14
Barham NSW 28 J7 41 G11
Baring VIC 40 F5
Baringhup VIC 39 C11
Barjarg VIC 42 F5
Bark Hut Inn NT 85 D4 86 E5
Barkly Homestead NT 89 H11
Barkstead VIC 39 E11
Barlee WA 73 G13
Barlee Range Nature Res WA 78 G3 82 G1
Barmah VIC 29 K9 41 H14 42 A2
Barmah Island VIC 41 H14 42 A2
Barmah State Park VIC 41 H14 42 A2
Barmedman NSW 29 F13
Barmera SA 62 B5 65 H13
Barmundu QLD 9 J11
Barnawartha VIC 43 B8
Barnes Bay TAS 50 H6 53 H10
Barneys Lake NSW 28 D7
Barongarook VIC 39 J10
Barooga NSW 29 K10 42 A4
Barool Nat Park NSW 25 E11
Baroota SA 62 G2 65 E9
Barpinba VIC 39 G10
Barraba NSW 24 G7
Barrabool VIC 36 G2 39 G11
Barradale WA 78 G2
Barramunga VIC 39 J10
Barranyi Nat Park NT 87 J13 89 A13
Barraport VIC 41 J10
Barratta QLD 8 A5
Barren Grounds Nature Res NSW 23 K8 30 C7
Barrington NSW 23 B11
Barrington TAS 54 F7
Barrington Tops Nat Park NSW 23 C10
Barringun NSW 15 K13 27 B10
Barrogan NSW 22 F3
Barron Gorge Nat Park QLD 11 D12
Barron Island NT 85 B5 86 C6
Barrow Creek NT 91 B8
Barrow Island WA 78 E2
Barrow Island Nature Res WA 78 E3
Barry NSW 22 G5
Barry NSW 23 A10 25 K8
Barrys Beach VIC 44 H7 46 H1
Barrys Reef VIC 39 E12
Barton ACT 31 D3 32 E5
Barton SA 68 H6
Barton VIC 38 D7
Barton Nature Res NSW 22 F4
Barton Siding SA 66 K1
Barunga NT 85 J7 86 G7
Barunga Gap SA 62 G4 65 G9
Barwell Con Park SA 64 F5
Barwell Con Res SA 64 F5
Barwon Downs VIC 39 J10
Barwon Heads VIC 36 H4 39 H12
Baryulgil NSW 25 D12
Bascombe Well Con Park SA 64 F5
Basket Range SA 60 G4
Basket Swamp Nat Park NSW 7 K11 25 C11
Bass VIC 37 K11 44 F3
Bass Hill NSW 21 D9
Bass Landing VIC 37 K11
Bass Strait TAS VIC 39 K12 44 K5 54 B3 56 A3
Bassendean WA 71 E6
Batchelor NT 85 E2 86 E4
Batchica VIC 40 J6
Bateau Bay NSW 20 B3
Batehaven NSW 30 F6
Batemans Bay NSW 30 F5
Batesford VIC 39 G12
Bathumi VIC 42 B6
Bathurst NSW 22 F5
Bathurst Bay QLD 16 H5
Bathurst Island NT 86 B2
Batlow NSW 29 J14 30 E1
Battery Point TAS 49 C2
Bauhinia QLD 9 K8
Baulkham Hills NSW 19 D2 21 E8
Bauple QLD 7 C12
Baw Baw Nat Park VIC 42 K6 44 B7 46 D1
Bawley Point NSW 30 E6
Baxter VIC 37 G9
Bay of Fires Con Res TAS 55 E14
Bay of Islands Coastal Park VIC 38 J7
Bayles VIC 37 G12 44 E4
Bayley Island QLD 10 D3
Baynton VIC 39 C13 42 G1
Bayswater VIC 35 E7 37 D9
Bayswater WA 71 E5
Bayulu WA 79 B11 81 J9
Bayview NSW 19 B7 20 B6
Bayview Haven NT 84 D2
Beachamp VIC 41 G9
Beachmere QLD 4 E5
Beachport SA 63 C13
Beachport Con Park SA 63 C13
Beacon WA 76 H7
Beaconsfield NSW 19 G5
Beaconsfield TAS 55 E8 56 D2

Beaconsfield – Bramston Beach 93

Beaconsfield VIC 37 F10 44 D3
Beaconsfield Upper VIC 37 F11
Beagle Bay WA 79 A9 80 F4
Beagle Gulf NT 85 B1 86 C3
Bealiba VIC 39 B9
Bearbung NSW 22 A4 24 K2
Beardmore VIC 42 K7 45 C8 46 D2
Beargamil NSW 22 E2
Bearii VIC 42 A3
Bears Lagoon VIC 41 K11
Beatrice Island NT 87 H11
Beaudesert QLD 5 E12 7 H13
Beaufort VIC 39 E9
Beaufort WA 73 B10
Beaumaris TAS 55 F14
Beaumont SA 59 H5
Beaumont Nature Res WA 75 F14 83 J2
Beauty Point TAS 55 E9 56 D2
Beazleys Bridge VIC 39 A8
Bebeah NSW 20 D1
Beckenham WA 71 H6
Beckom NSW 29 F12
Bedarra Island QLD 11 F13
Bedford WA 71 E4
Bedford Park SA 59 K3
Bedgerebong NSW 29 D14 22 F1
Bedourie QLD 12 G4
Bedunburra WA 79 B9 80 H5
Beeac VIC 39 H10
Beech Forest VIC 39 J10
Beechboro WA 71 D5
Beechford TAS 55 D9 56 B3
Beechmont QLD 5 D14
Beechwood NSW 23 A13 25 K11
Beechworth VIC 43 C8
Beechworth Historic Park VIC 43 C8
Beecroft NSW 20 D7
Beedelup Nat Park WA 73 F14 74 J3
Beekeepers Nature Res WA 76 G3
Beela WA 73 F9
Beenak VIC 37 D12
Beenleigh QLD 5 D10 7 G13
Beerburrum QLD 4 F3 7 F13
Beerwah QLD 4 F2 7 E12
Bega NSW 30 H5
Beggan Beggan NSW 22 K2 30 B1
Beilpajah NSW 28 C6
Bejoording WA 72 D1
Belair SA 59 J4 60 H2 61 B6
Belair Nat Park SA 59 J5 60 H3 61 B7
Belalie North SA 62 E2 65 E10
Belaringar NSW 22 B1 27 J13
Belbora NSW 23 C12
Belconnen ACT 32 C3 30 D3
Belconnen Town Centre ACT 32 C3
Beldon WA 71 A1
Belgrave VIC 37 E10 42 K3 44 C3
Bell NSW 22 G7
Bell QLD 7 E10
Bell Bay TAS 55 D9 56 C2
Bellambi NSW 21 C13
Bellara QLD 4 D4
Bellarine VIC 36 G5 39 G13
Bellarwi NSW 29 F13
Bellata NSW 24 E5
Bellbird NSW 23 E9
Bellbird Creek VIC 47 D10
Bellbird Park QLD 5 F9
Bellbrae VIC 36 J2 39 H12
Bellbridge VIC 43 B9
Bellbrook NSW 25 H11
Bellenden Ker QLD 11 D13
Bellerive TAS 50 C6 53 F11
Bellevue WA 71 E7
Bellevue Heights SA 59 K4 60 H2 61 B6
Bellingen NSW 25 G12
Bellinger River Nat Park NSW 25 G12
Bellingham TAS 55 D10 56 B5
Bellmere QLD 4 F4
Bellmount Forest NSW 30 C3
Belltrees NSW 23 B9
Belmont NSW 23 F10
Belmont QLD 3 F6
Belmont VIC 36 G2
Belmont WA 71 F5
Belmore NSW 19 G4 21 C9
Belmunging WA 72 B3
Beloka NSW 30 H2
Belowra NSW 30 G4
Belrose NSW 20 B7
Belsar Island VIC 40 C7
Beltana SA 65 A10 67 K10
Beltana Roadhouse SA 65 A10 67 K10
Belton SA 65 D10
Belyando Crossing QLD 8 E5 13 B14
Belyuen NT 85 C1 86 D3
Bemboka NSW 30 H4
Bemm River VIC 47 D10
Ben Boyd Nat Park NSW 30 J5 47 A14
Ben Bullen NSW 22 F6
Ben Halls Gap Nat Park NSW 23 A9 25 K8
Ben Lomond NSW 25 F9
Ben Lomond Nat Park TAS 55 G12
Bena NSW 29 D13
Bena VIC 37 K13 44 F5
Benalla VIC 42 D5
Benambra VIC 43 F11
Benambra Nat Park NSW 29 K13 43 A9
Benandarah NSW 30 E6
Benaraby QLD 9 J11
Benayeo VIC 38 C2
Bencubbin WA 74 A6 76 J7
Bendalong NSW 30 D6
Bendemeer NSW 25 H8
Bendick Murrell NSW 22 J3 30 A2
Bendidee Nat Park QLD 7 H8 24 A7
Bendigo VIC 39 B12
Bendoc VIC 30 K3 47 A10
Bendoc North VIC 47 A11
Bendoc Upper VIC 30 K3
Bendolba NSW 23 D10
Beneree NSW 22 G4
Benetook VIC 28 F3 40 B4
Benger WA 73 G9
Bengerang NSW 6 K6 24 C4
Bengworden VIC 45 C12 46 E5
Beni NSW 22 C4
Benjeroop VIC 41 F10
Benjinup WA 73 E11
Benlidi QLD 8 K2 13 G11
Bennison Island VIC 44 H7 46 J1
Benowa QLD 5 B13
Bensville NSW 20 B4
Bentinck Island QLD 10 D3
Bentley NSW 25 B13
Bentley WA 71 H5
Bentleys Plain VIC 43 G12 46 B7
Benwerrin VIC 39 J11
Berajondo QLD 9 K12
Berala NSW 21 D9
Berambing NSW 20 J7 22 G7
Beremboke VIC 36 C2
Beresfield NSW 23 E10
Beresford SA 66 G7
Bergalia NSW 30 F5
Berkeley Vale NSW 20 B3
Berkshire Park NSW 20 F7
Bermagui NSW 30 H5
Bermagui South NSW 30 H5
Bernacchi TAS 53 A8 55 H8
Bernier and Dorre Island Nature Res WA 76 A1 78 J1
Bernier Island WA 76 A1 78 J1
Berowra NSW 19 A4 20 C6
Berowra Heights NSW 19 A5
Berowra Valley Regional Park NSW 19 A4 20 D7
Berowra Waters NSW 20 D6
Berri SA 28 F1 62 B5 65 H13
Berridale NSW 30 G2
Berriedale TAS 50 B5
Berrigan NSW 29 J10
Berrilee NSW 20 D6
Berrima NSW 22 K7 30 B6
Berringa VIC 39 F10
Berringama VIC 43 C11
Berriwillock VIC 28 J5 41 G8
Berrook VIC 28 H1 40 D1 62 A7 65 J13
Berry NSW 30 C7
Berry Springs NT 85 D2 86 D4
Berrybank VIC 39 G9
Berwick VIC 37 F10 44 D3
Bessiebelle VIC 38 H5
Bet Bet VIC 39 B10
Beta QLD 8 H4 13 F13
Bete Bolong VIC 43 K14 47 D8
Bethanga VIC 43 B9
Bethania QLD 3 K6
Bethany SA 60 B6
Bethungra NSW 22 K1 29 G14
Betoota QLD 12 J5 14 C3 67 A14
Betsey Island TAS 51 G8 53 G11
Beulah TAS 54 F7
Beulah VIC 28 K4 40 H6
Beulah East VIC 40 H6
Beulah Park SA 59 G5
Beulah West VIC 40 H5
Bevendale NSW 22 K4 30 B3
Beverford VIC 28 H6 41 E9
Beveridge VIC 39 E14 42 H2
Beveridge Station (site) VIC 43 F9
Beverley WA 72 C4 74 D4
Beverly Hills NSW 19 G4 21 C9
Bewong NSW 30 D6
Bews SA 63 B8 65 K12
Bexhill NSW 25 B13
Bexley NSW 21 C9
Beyal VIC 40 J7
BHP10 Yandicoogina Mine WA 78 F6 82 F5
Biala NSW 22 K4 30 B3
Biamanga Nat Park NSW 30 H5
Bibbenluke NSW 30 J3
Biboohra QLD 11 D12
Bibra Lake WA 71 K3
Bicheno TAS 53 A14 55 H14
Bickerton Island NT 87 F12
Bicton WA 71 H2
Biddaddaba QLD 5 D12
Biddon NSW 22 A4 24 K2
Bidgeemia NSW 29 J11
Bidyadanga (Lagrange) WA 79 C8 80 J2
Big Bush Nature Res NSW 29 F13
Big Desert Wilderness Park VIC 28 J2 40 G2 63 A9 65 K14
Big Green Island TAS 55 C9
Big Heath Con Park SA 63 B12
Big Pats Creek VIC 37 C13
Bigga NSW 22 H4 30 A3
Biggara VIC 43 C13
Biggenden QLD 7 B11
Biggs Flat SA 60 H4
Biggs Island WA 81 B8
Bilambil NSW 5 B14 25 A14
Bilbaringa SA 60 C4
Bilgola NSW 20 DC
Billiatt Con Park SA 28 H1 62 B7 65 J13
Billiluna (Mindibungu) WA 79 D13
Billimari NSW 22 G3
Billinga QLD 5 A14
Billinooka WA 78 G7
Billinudgell NSW 25 B14
Billys Creek NSW 25 F11
Biloela QLD 9 J10
Bilpin NSW 20 J6 23 G8
Bilyana QLD 11 F13
Bimberamala Nat Park NSW 30 E6
Bimbi NSW 22 H2 29 E14
Binalong NSW 22 K3 30 B2
Binalong Bay TAS 55 E14
Binaronca Nature Res WA 75 C13 77 K11 83 G1
Binbee QLD 8 B6
Binda NSW 22 J5 30 A4
Bindango QLD 6 E4
Bindarri Nat Park NSW 25 G12
Bindi VIC 43 G12 46 A7
Bindi Bindi WA 76 H5
Bindoon WA 72 F1 74 B3 76 K5
Bingara NSW 24 E7
Bingil Bay QLD 11 E13
Binginwarri VIC 45 G8 46 H2
Biniguy NSW 24 D6
Binjour QLD 7 B10
Binjura Nature Res NSW 30 G3
Binna Burra QLD 5 D14 7 H13 25 A13
Binnaway NSW 22 A5 24 K4
Binnaway Nature Res NSW 22 A5 24 K4
Binningup WA 73 G9 74 F2
Binnu WA 76 E3
Binnum SA 38 B1 63 A11
Binya NSW 29 F11
Birany Birany NT 87 D12
Birchip VIC 28 K5 40 H7
Birchs Bay TAS 50 J4 53 H10
Bird Island TAS 54 B1
Birdsville QLD 12 K3 14 C1 67 A11
Birdwood NSW 23 A12 25 K11
Birdwood SA 60 E6 62 E6 65 J10
Birdwoodton VIC 28 F3 40 A4
Biriwal Bulga Nat Park NSW 23 A12 25 K10
Birkdale QLD 3 F7 5 D8
Birkenhead SA 59 D1
Birnam Range QLD 5 E12
Birralee QLD 8 C6
Birralee TAS 55 F8 56 G2
Birrego NSW 29 H12
Birregurra VIC 39 H10
Birri Lodge QLD 10 C3
Birriwa NSW 22 C5
Birrong NSW 19 F2
Birru QLD 5 J9
Bishopsbourne TAS 55 G9 56 J3
Bittern VIC 37 J9
Black Andrew Nature Res NSW 30 C2
Black Forest SA 59 H3
Black Hill SA 62 D6 65 J11
Black Hill Con Park SA 59 E7 60 F3
Black Hills TAS 50 A2 53 F9
Black Jungle Con Res NT 85 C2 86 D4
Black Mountain NSW 25 G9
Black Mountain Nat Park QLD 11 B12 16 K6
Black Point NT 86 B5
Black Range State Park VIC 38 C5
Black River TAS 54 C3
Black Rock SA 62 E2 65 E10
Black Rock VIC 35 G4 36 E7
Black Springs NSW 22 H6
Black Springs SA 62 E4 65 G10
Black Swamp NSW 25 C11
Blackall QLD 8 J3 13 G12
Blackbraes Nat Park QLD 8 A1 11 H10
Blackbull QLD 10 F7
Blackburn VIC 35 D6
Blackbutt QLD 7 E11
Blackdown Tableland Nat Park QLD 9 H8
Blackfellows Caves SA 63 B14
Blackheath NSW 21 K8 22 G7
Blackmans Bay TAS 50 F6 53 G10
Blacksmith Island QLD 9 C8
Blackstone (Papulankutja) WA 79 K13 83 B7
Blacktown NSW 19 D1 21 E8
Blackville NSW 22 A7
Blackwater QLD 9 H8
Blackwater Mine QLD 8 H7
Blackwood SA 59 K4 60 H3 61 B6 62 F7 65 J10
Blackwood VIC 39 E12
Blackwood Creek TAS 53 A9 55 H9
Blackwood Forest VIC 37 K12
Blackwood Nat Park QLD 8 D5 13 B14
Bladensburg Nat Park QLD 13 D9
Blair Athol QLD 8 F6
Blair Athol SA 59 E4
Blairgowrie VIC 36 J6
Blakehurst NSW 19 H4 21 C10
Blakeview SA 60 C3
Blakeville VIC 36 A2 39 E11
Blakney Creek NSW 22 K4 30 B3
Blanchetown SA 62 D5 65 H11
Bland NSW 22 H1 29 E13
Blandford NSW 23 B9
Blanket Flat NSW 22 J4 30 A3
Blaxland NSW 21 H8 23 G8
Blaxlands Ridge NSW 20 G6
Blayney NSW 22 G5
Blessington TAS 55 G11
Blewitt Springs SA 60 K2 61 D6
Bligh Park NSW 20 F7
Blighty NSW 29 J9
Blinman SA 65 B10
Bloods Creek SA 66 A4
Bloods Range (Puntitjata) NT 79 J14 90 H1
Bloomfield QLD 11 B12
Bloomsbury QLD 8 C7
Blow Clear NSW 22 E1 29 C14 29 E13
Blue Bay NSW 20 A3
Blue Lake Nat Park QLD 5 B8 7 G14
Blue Mountains Nat Park NSW 21 H9 22 H7 30 A5
Blue Mud Bay NT 87 F11
Blue Rocks TAS 55 B9
Bluewater QLD 8 A4 11 H14
Bluewater Springs Roadhouse QLD 8 A3 11 H13
Bluff QLD 9 H8
Bluff River Nature Res NSW 25 C10
Blyth SA 62 F4 65 G10
Blythdale QLD 6 E5
Boambee NSW 25 G13
Boat Harbour TAS 54 D4
Boat Harbour Beach TAS 54 C4
Boatswain Point SA 63 D12
Bobadah NSW 27 K12 29 A12
Bobbin Head NSW 19 A5 20 C6
Bobin NSW 23 B12
Bodalla NSW 30 G5
Bodallin WA 75 B8 77 J8
Bodangora NSW 22 D4
Boddington WA 72 D7 74 E4
Bogan Gate NSW 22 E1 29 C14
Bogandyera Nature Res NSW 29 K14 30 F1 43 A12
Bogantungan QLD 8 H5
Bogee NSW 22 E7
Boggabilla NSW 6 J7 24 B6
Boggabri NSW 24 H5
Boginderra Hills Nature Res NSW 22 J1 29 F13
Bogolong Creek NSW 22 H2 29 E14
Bogong VIC 43 E10
Boho VIC 42 E5
Boho South VIC 42 E5
Boigbeat VIC 40 G7
Boinka VIC 28 H2 40 E3
Boisdale VIC 43 K9 45 C10 46 E4
Bokal WA 73 C10
Bokarina QLD 4 D1
Bolgart WA 74 B4 76 J5
Bolinda VIC 39 D13 42 H1
Bolivar SA 59 B4 60 D2
Bolivia NSW 25 D10
Bollanolla Nature Res NSW 25 H12
Bollon QLD 6 H2
Bolton VIC 28 H5 40 D7
Boltons Beach Con Area TAS 53 D13
Bolwarra VIC 38 H4
Bolwarrah VIC 36 A1 39 E11
Bomaderry NSW 30 C7
Bombala NSW 30 J3
Bombo NSW 23 K8 30 B7
Bomera NSW 22 A6 24 K5
Bonalbo NSW 7 K12 25 B12
Bonang VIC 30 K2 47 A10
Bonbeach VIC 37 F8
Bondi NSW 19 F7 21 B8
Bondi Gulf Nature Res NSW 30 K3 47 A11
Bondi Junction NSW 19 F6
Bonegilla VIC 29 K12 43 B9
Boneo VIC 36 K7
Bongaree QLD 4 D4 7 F13
Bongil Bongil Nat Park NSW 25 G13
Bonnells Bay NSW 20 B1
Bonnet Bay NSW 19 J3
Bonnie Doon VIC 42 F5
Bonnie Rock WA 76 H7
Bonnie Vale WA 75 A12 77 J11
Bonny Hills NSW 23 A13
Bonnyrigg NSW 21 E9
Bonogin QLD 5 C14
Bonshaw NSW 7 K9 25 C8
Bonville NSW 25 G12
Bonython ACT 32 J3
Booborowie SA 62 E3 65 F10
Boobyalla TAS 55 C12
Booderee Nat Park ACT 30 D7
Boodie Island WA 78 E2
Bookabie SA 64 C1 68 K6
Bookaloo SA 65 C8
Bookar VIC 39 G8
Booker Bay NSW 20 B5
Bookham NSW 30 C2
Bookin QLD 10 K6 12 A6
Bool Lagoon SA 38 D1 63 B12
Boolading WA 73 D9
Boolarra VIC 44 F7 46 G1
Boolba QLD 6 H3
Boolburra QLD 9 H9
Boolcunda SA 65 D9
Booleroo Centre SA 62 F2 65 E10
Booligal NSW 29 E8
Boolite VIC 40 K7
Boomi NSW 6 J6 24 B4
Boonah QLD 5 H12 7 H12
Boonanarring Nature Res WA 74 B3 76 J5
Boonanghi Nature Res NSW 25 J11
Boonarga QLD 7 E8
Boondall QLD 3 B5 4 E7
Boondooma QLD 7 D9
Boonmoo QLD 11 D12
Boonoo Boonoo NSW 25 C10
Boonoo Boonoo Nat Park NSW 7 K11 25 B11
Boonooroo QLD 7 C13
Boorabbin WA 75 B10 77 J10
Boorabbin Nat Park WA 75 A10 77 J9
Booragoon WA 71 J3
Booral NSW 23 D11
Boorcan VIC 39 H8
Boorhaman VIC 42 C6
Boorindal NSW 27 E11
Boorndoolyanna SA 68 A5 90 K6
Boorongie North VIC 28 H4 40 E6
Booroolong Nature Res NSW 25 G9
Booroopki VIC 38 B2
Booroorban NSW 29 G8 41 D13
Boorowa NSW 22 J3 30 B2
Boort VIC 28 K6 41 J10
Boosey VIC 42 B5
Booti Booti Nat Park NSW 23 C13
Booyal QLD 7 B11
Bopeechee SA 67 H8
Boppy Mount NSW 27 H11
Borallon QLD 5 H8
Borambil NSW 22 B6
Borambola NSW 29 H14
Boraning WA 73 C8
Borda Island WA 81 B9
Borden WA 74 H7
Border Island QLD 9 B8
Border Ranges Nat Park NSW 7 J12 25 A12
Border Store NT 85 C7 86 D7
Borderdale WA 73 A12
Bordertown SA 40 K1 63 B10
Boree NSW 22 F4
Boree QLD 13 A10
Boree Creek NSW 29 H12
Boreen Point QLD 7 D13
Boro NSW 30 D4
Boronia VIC 37 D9
Boronia Heights QLD 3 K4
Boroobin QLD 4 G2
Bororen QLD 9 J11
Borrika SA 62 C7 65 J12
Borroloola NT 87 K12 89 B12
Borung VIC 41 K10
Boscabel WA 73 B11
Bossley Park NSW 21 E9
Bostobrick NSW 25 G11
Boston Island SA 64 H6
Botany NSW 19 H6 21 B9
Botany Bay NSW 19 H5 21 B9
Botany Bay Nat Park NSW 19 J6 21 B10 23 H9
Bothwell TAS 53 D9
Boucaut Bay NT 87 C9
Bouddi Nat Park NSW 20 B5 23 G10
Boulder WA 75 A12 77 J11 83 F1
Bouldercombe QLD 9 H10
Boulia QLD 12 E4
Boundain WA 73 A8
Boundary Bend VIC 28 G5 41 C8
Bountiful Island QLD 10 D4
Bourke NSW 27 E10
Bournda Nat Park NSW 30 J5
Bow NSW 22 C7
Bowden SA 58 A1
Bowelling WA 73 D10 74 F4
Bowen QLD 8 B7
Bowen Mountain NSW 20 H7
Bowen Park NSW 22 F4
Bowenvale VIC 39 C10
Bowenville QLD 7 F10
Bower SA 62 D5 65 G11
Boweya VIC 42 C6
Bowhill SA 62 D7 65 J11
Bowillia SA 62 F4 65 G9
Bowling Alley Point NSW 23 A9 25 K8
Bowling Green Bay QLD 8 A5
Bowling Green Bay Nat Park QLD 8 A6
Bowman QLD 9 F9
Bowmans SA 62 F5 65 H9
Bowna NSW 29 K13 43 A10
Bowning NSW 22 K4 30 C2
Bowral NSW 22 K7 30 B6
Bowraville NSW 25 H12
Box Hill NSW 20 F7
Box Hill VIC 35 D6 37 D9 39 F14 42 K2 44 B2
Boxwood Hill WA 75 H8
Boyacup WA 73 A13
Boyagarring Con Park WA 72 D5
Boyagin Nature Res WA 72 C6 74 D4
Boyanup WA 73 G10 74 G3
Boydtown NSW 30 K5 47 A14
Boyeo VIC 40 K3
Boyer TAS 50 A3 53 F10
Boyland QLD 5 D12
Boyne Island QLD 9 J11
Boynedale QLD 9 J11
Boyup Brook WA 73 E11 74 G4
Bracalba QLD 4 G4
Brachina SA 65 B10
Bracken Ridge QLD 3 A4 4 E6
Brackendale NSW 25 J9
Bracknell TAS 55 G9 56 K3
Bradbury NSW 21 E11
Bradbury SA 60 H4 61 B7
Braddon ACT 32 D5
Bradvale VIC 39 F9
Draefield NSW 23 A0 24 K7
Braeside VIC 35 H5 37 F8
Brahma Lodge SA 59 B5
Braidwood NSW 30 E5
Bramfield SA 64 F4
Brampton Island QLD 9 C8
Brampton Islands Nat Park QLD 9 C8
Bramston Beach QLD 11 E13

94 Brandon – Cape Howe

Brandon QLD 8 A5
Brandy Creek VIC 37 G14
Branxholm TAS 55 E12
Branxholme VIC 38 F4
Branxton NSW 23 D10
Brawlin NSW 22 K2 29 G14 30 B1
Bray Junction SA 63 C12
Braybrook VIC 35 C1
Brayfield SA 64 G6
Brayton NSW 22 K6 30 B5
Brazendale Island TAS 53 B9 55 J9
Breadalbane NSW 30 C4
Breadalbane TAS 55 G10 56 H5
Break O'Day VIC 42 H3
Breakaway Ridge Nature Res WA 75 F8
Breakfast Creek NSW 22 D6 22 J3 30 A2
Breaksea Island TAS 52 J5
Bream Creek TAS 51 B12 53 F12
Breamlea VIC 36 H3
Bredbo NSW 30 F3
Breelong NSW 22 B4
Breeza NSW 24 J6
Bremer Bay WA 75 H9
Bremer Island NT 87 C13
Brendale QLD 3 A3
Brentwood SA 62 H6 65 J8
Brentwood VIC 40 H5
Breona TAS 53 A8 55 H8
Bretti NSW 23 B11
Bretti Nature Res NSW 23 B11
Brewarrina NSW 27 D12
Brewer NSW 29 D11
Brewster VIC 39 E9
Briaba QLD 8 C6
Briagolong VIC 43 K9 45 C11 46 D4
Bribbaree NSW 22 H1 29 F14
Bribie Island QLD 4 D3 7 F13
Bribie Island Nat Park QLD 4 E3 7 F13
Bridge Creek VIC 42 F6
Bridgeman Downs QLD 3 B3
Bridgenorth TAS 55 F9 56 F4
Bridgetown WA 73 F12 74 H3
Bridgewater SA 60 H4
Bridgewater TAS 50 A5 53 F10
Bridgewater VIC 39 A11
Bridport TAS 55 D11 56 B7
Brigalow QLD 7 E9
Bright VIC 43 E9
Brighton QLD 3 A4 4 E6
Brighton SA 59 K2 60 H1 61 B5 62 F7 65 J10
Brighton TAS 53 F10
Brighton VIC 35 F3 36 E7
Brighton-Le-Sands NSW 19 H5 21 B9
Brightview QLD 5 K8
Brightwaters NSW 20 B1
Brim VIC 40 J6
Brimbago SA 63 B10
Brimboal VIC 38 D3
Brimpaen VIC 38 C5
Brindabella NSW 30 D2
Brindabella Nat Park NSW 30 D2
Brinerville NSW 25 G11
Bringalbert VIC 38 B2
Bringelly NSW 21 F10
Bringung NT 87 H8
Brinkin NT 84 A2
Brinkley SA 62 E7 65 K11
Brinkworth SA 62 F4 65 G9
Brisbane QLD 3 E4 5 E8 7 G13
Brisbane CBD QLD 2
Brisbane Forest Park QLD 3 D1 4 G7
Brisbane Ranges Nat Park VIC 36 D2 39 F12
Brisbane Water Nat Park NSW 20 C5 23 G9
Brit Brit VIC 38 E4
Britannia Creek VIC 37 C12
Brittons Swamp TAS 54 C2
Brixton QLD 8 H2 13 E11
Broad Arrow WA 77 H11 83 F1
Broad Sound QLD 9 F9
Broad Sound Island Nat Park QLD 9 E9
Broadbeach QLD 5 B13 7 H13
Broadford VIC 39 C14 42 G2
Broadmarsh TAS 53 E10
Broadmeadows SA 60 D3
Broadmeadows VIC 35 B3 36 B7
Broadmont QLD 9 H10
Broadwater NSW 7 K13 25 C14
Broadwater VIC 38 G5
Broadwater Nat Park NSW 7 K13 25 C14
Brocklehurst NSW 22 C3
Brocklesby NSW 29 J12 43 A8
Brockman WA 73 F14
Brockman Mine WA 78 F4 82 F2
Brockman Nat Park WA 74 J3
Brodribb River VIC 43 K14 47 D9
Brogo NSW 30 H5
Broke NSW 23 E9
Broken Bay NSW 20 B5 23 G9
Broken Hill NSW 26 J2 28 A2 65 C14
Bromby Islands NT 87 C12
Bromelton QLD 5 F12
Brompton SA 59 F3
Bromus WA 75 D13 83 H1
Bronte NSW 21 B9
Bronte Park TAS 52 C7 54 K7
Bronzewing VIC 28 H4 40 E6
Brookdale NSW 29 H12
Brooker SA 64 G6
Brookfield NSW 23 D11
Brookfield QLD 3 E1 5 G8
Brookfield Con Park SA 62 D5 65 H11
Brookhampton WA 73 F11
Brooking Gorge Con Park WA 79 B11 81 H8
Brooklands QLD 5 F11
Brooklyn NSW 20 C5
Brooklyn VIC 35 D1
Brooklyn Park SA 59 G3
Brooks Creek NT 85 F3 86 E4
Brooksby VIC 38 C4
Brookstead QLD 7 G10
Brookton WA 72 B5 74 D5
Brookvale NSW 19 D6 20 B7
Brookville VIC 43 H11 46 B6
Brooloo QLD 7 E12
Brooman NSW 30 E6
Broome WA 79 B8 80 H3
Broomehill WA 74 G6
Brooms Head NSW 25 E13
Brooweena QLD 7 C11
Broughton VIC 40 J2
Broughton Island NSW 23 D12
Broula NSW 22 H3
Broulee NSW 30 F6
Brovinia QLD 7 C9
Brownlow SA 62 D5 65 H11
Brownlow Hill NSW 21 F11
Browns Creek NSW 22 G4
Browns Plains QLD 3 K4 5 E10
Bruarong VIC 43 C8
Bruce ACT 32 C4
Bruce SA 62 F1 65 D9
Bruce Rock WA 74 C7 76 K7
Brucknell VIC 39 J8
Bruinbun NSW 22 F5
Brukunga SA 60 H6
Brungle NSW 30 D1
Brunswick VIC 35 C3 36 C7
Brunswick Bay WA 80 C7
Brunswick Heads NSW 7 J14 25 B14
Brunswick Junction WA 73 G9 74 F3
Bruthen VIC 43 K12 45 B14 46 D7
Bryden QLD 4 J6
Buangor VIC 39 D8
Bucasia QLD 9 D8
Buccarumbi NSW 25 E11
Buccleuch SA 63 C8 65 K12
Buchan VIC 43 J13 47 C8
Buchan South VIC 43 J13 47 C8
Bucheen Creek VIC 43 D11
Buchfelde SA 60 B3
Buckaroo NSW 22 D6
Buckenderra NSW 30 G2
Bucketty NSW 20 E1 23 F9
Buckingham SA 63 B10
Buckingham WA 73 E10
Buckland TAS 53 E12
Buckland VIC 43 E8
Buckland Junction VIC 43 F8
Buckleboo SA 64 E6
Buckley VIC 36 H1 39 H11
Buckley Swamp VIC 38 F5
Buckrabanyule VIC 41 K9
Budawang Nat Park NSW 30 E5
Buddabaddah NSW 27 J13
Buddawarka NT 87 G9
Budderoo Nat Park NSW 23 K8 30 B7
Buddigower NSW 29 E12
Buddigower Nature Res NSW 29 E12
Buddina QLD 4 D1
Buderim QLD 4 E1 7 E13
Budgee Budgee NSW 22 D6
Budgeree VIC 44 F7 46 G1
Budgerum VIC 41 H9
Budgerum East VIC 41 H10
Budgewoi NSW 20 A2 23 F10
Buenba Flat (site) VIC 43 E12
Buff Point NSW 20 A2
Buffalo VIC 44 G6
Buffalo River VIC 43 E8
Bugaldie NSW 24 J3
Bugilbone NSW 24 F2
Bugong Nat Park NSW 30 C6
Builyan QLD 9 K11
Bukalong NSW 30 J3
Bukkulla NSW 25 D8
Bulahdelah NSW 23 D12
Bulart VIC 38 E4
Buldah VIC 47 B11
Bulga NSW 23 D9
Bulgandry NSW 29 J12
Bulimba QLD 3 D4 5 E8
Bull Creek WA 71 J4
Bull Swamp VIC 37 H14
Bulla NT 86 J2 88 A2
Bulla VIC 35 A1 36 B6 39 E13 42 J1 44 A1
Bullabulling WA 75 A11 77 J10
Bullaburra NSW 21 J9
Bullagreen NSW 22 A2 24 K1 27 H14
Bullarah NSW 24 D3
Bullarook VIC 39 E11
Bullarto VIC 39 D11
Bullea Lake NSW 26 E2
Bulleen VIC 37 C8
Bullen Range Nature Res ACT 32 H1
Bullenbung NSW 29 H12
Bullengarook VIC 36 A4
Bulleringa Nat Park QLD 11 E10
Bullfinch WA 75 A8 77 J8
Bullhead Creek VIC 43 C10
Bulli NSW 21 C13 23 J8 30 B7
Bullio NSW 22 J7 30 A6
Bullioh VIC 29 K13 43 B10
Bullock Creek QLD 11 E11
Bullsbrook WA 72 F2
Bullumwaal VIC 43 J11 45 B12 46 D6
Bullyard QLD 7 A11 9 K12
Bulman NT 87 F9
Buln Buln VIC 37 F14 44 D6
Bulong WA 75 A13 77 J11 83 F1
Bulwer QLD 4 B4
Bulwer Island QLD 3 C6
Bulyee WA 74 D6
Bumbaldry NSW 22 H3
Bumberry NSW 22 F3
Bumbunga SA 62 G4 65 G9
Bunbartha VIC 42 B3
Bunburra QLD 5 H13
Bunbury WA 73 G9 74 F2
Bundaberg QLD 7 A12 9 K13
Bundalaguah VIC 45 D10 46 E4
Bundall QLD 5 B12
Bundalong VIC 42 B6
Bundanoon NSW 22 K7 30 B6
Bundarra NSW 25 F8
Bundeela NSW 22 K7 30 C6
Bundeena NSW 19 K5 21 B10 23 J9
Bundella NSW 22 A6 24 K5
Bunding VIC 36 A1
Bundjalung Nat Park NSW 25 D13
Bundook NSW 23 B11
Bundooma NT 91 H9
Bundoora VIC 35 B5 37 B8
Bundure NSW 29 H11
Bung Bong VIC 39 C9
Bunga NSW 30 H5
Bungador VIC 39 H9
Bungal VIC 36 C1 39 F11
Bungallen QLD 12 B4
Bungarby NSW 30 H3
Bungaree VIC 39 E11
Bungawalbin Nat Park NSW 7 K13 25 C13
Bungeet VIC 42 C6
Bungendore NSW 30 D4
Bungil VIC 43 B10
Bungonia NSW 30 C5
Bungowannah NSW 29 K12 43 A8
Bungulla NSW 25 C10
Bunguluke VIC 41 J9
Bungunya QLD 6 J6 24 A4
Bungwahl NSW 23 D12
Buninyong VIC 39 E10
Bunjurgen QLD 5 H13
Bunker Group QLD 9 J13
Bunnaloo NSW 29 J8 41 H13
Bunnan NSW 23 C8
Buntine WA 76 H5
Bunya NSW 23 C12
Bunya QLD 3 C2
Bunya Mountains Nat Park QLD 7 E10
Bunyan NSW 30 G3
Bunyaville State Forest Park QLD 3 C2
Bunyip VIC 37 F13 44 D5
Bunyip State Park VIC 37 E13 42 K4 44 C4
Buraja NSW 29 K11 42 A7
Burakin WA 76 H6
Burbank QLD 3 G6 5 D8
Burcher NSW 29 D13
Burdett South Nature Res WA 75 F13 83 J1
Burekup WA 73 G9
Burford Island NT 86 B5
Burges WA 72 C3
Burgooney NSW 29 D12
Burke and Wills Roadhouse QLD 10 H5
Burketown QLD 10 E3
Burleigh VIC 37 D11
Burleigh Head Nat Park QLD 5 B13
Burleigh Heads QLD 5 B13 7 H13
Burma Road Nature Res WA 76 F4
Burnbank VIC 39 D10
Burndale VIC 37 K12
Burney Island NT 87 F12
Burnie TAS 54 D5
Burning Mountain Nature Res NSW 23 B9
Burns Beach WA 72 G2
Burns Creek TAS 55 F11
Burnside SA 59 G6 60 G3 61 A6
Burnt Bridge NSW 25 J12
Burnt School Nature Res NSW 30 F4
Buronga NSW 28 F3 40 A5
Burpengary QLD 4 F5
Burra NSW 30 E3
Burra QLD 8 C2 11 K12 13 A12
Burra SA 62 E4 65 G10
Burraboi NSW 28 J7 41 F12
Burracoppin WA 74 B7 76 J7
Burraga NSW 22 H5
Burragate NSW 30 J4 47 A13
Burragorang State Rec Park NSW 21 H11
Burramine North VIC 42 A5
Burramine South VIC 42 B5
Burrandana NSW 29 J13
Burraneer NSW 19 K4
Burrapine NSW 25 H11
Burrell Creek NSW 23 B12
Burren Junction NSW 24 F3
Burrendong Dam NSW 22 D5
Burrill Lake NSW 30 E6
Burringbar NSW 25 A14
Burrinjuck NSW 30 C2
Burrinjuck Dam NSW 30 C2
Burrinjuck Nature Res NSW 30 C2
Burroin VIC 40 G5
Burrowa-Pine Mountain Nat Park VIC 29 K14 43 B12
Burrowye VIC 29 K13 43 B11
Burrum VIC 38 A7
Burrum Coast Nat Park QLD 7 A12
Burrum Heads QLD 7 B12
Burrumbeet VIC 39 E10
Burrumboot VIC 39 A13 42 D1
Burrumbuttock NSW 29 K12 43 A8
Burrup Peninsula WA 78 D4 82 C1
Burswood WA 71 F4
Burton SA 59 A4 60 D2
Burtville WA 77 F12 83 D2
Burwood NSW 19 F4 21 C9
Burwood VIC 35 E5 37 D8 39 F14 42 K2 44 C2
Burwood East VIC 35 E6
Busbys Flat NSW 25 C12
Bushfield VIC 38 H6
Bushy Park TAS 53 F9
Bushy Park VIC 43 K9 45 C10 46 E4
Busselton WA 73 J11 74 G2
Bustard Bay QLD 9 J12
Bustard Island NT 87 F12
Butcher Well North Mine WA 77 F12 83 E1
Butchers Ridge VIC 43 H13 47 B8
Bute SA 62 G4 65 G9
Butler Tanks SA 64 G6
Butru QLD 12 B4
Butterfly Gorge Nature Park NT 85 G3 86 F5
Butterleaf Nat Park NSW 25 D10
Buxton NSW 21 G13
Buxton VIC 42 H4
Buxtonville QLD 7 B12
Byabarra NSW 23 A13 25 K11
Byaduk VIC 38 G5
Byaduk North VIC 38 F5
Byawatha VIC 42 C7
Byee QLD 7 D10
Byfield QLD 9 G10
Byfield Nat Park QLD 9 G11
Byford WA 72 F4 74 D3
Bylong NSW 22 D7
Byrneside VIC 41 K14 42 C3
Byrnestown QLD 7 B10
Byrock NSW 27 F11
Byron Bay NSW 7 K14 25 B14
Bywong NSW 30 D4

C

Cabanandra NSW 47 A9
Cabanda QLD 5 J9
Cabawin QLD 7 F8
Cabbage Tree Creek VIC 47 D10
Cabbage Tree Palms Res VIC 47 D9
Caboolture QLD 4 F4 7 F12
Caboonbah QLD 4 K5
Cabramatta NSW 19 F1 21 E9
Cabramurra NSW 30 F1 43 A14
Caddens Flat VIC 38 D4
Cadell SA 62 C5 65 G12
Cadney Homestead SA 66 E3
Cadney Park SA 66 E3
Cadoux WA 74 A5 76 J6
Caiguna WA 83 H4
Cairns QLD 11 D13
Cairns Bay TAS 50 J1 53 H9
Cal Lal NSW 28 F1 40 A1 62 A5 65 G14
Calamvale QLD 3 J4 5 E9
Calca SA 64 E3
Calcifer QLD 11 D11
Calcium QLD 8 A5 11 H14
Calder TAS 54 D4
Calder Island QLD 9 C9
Caldermeade VIC 37 H12
Caldwell NSW 29 J8 41 G12
Calen QLD 9 C8
Calga NSW 20 C4
Calingiri WA 74 A4 76 J5
Calivil VIC 41 K11
Callanna SA 67 H9
Callaroy NSW 22 C7
Callawadda VIC 38 B7
Calleen NSW 29 E12
Callide QLD 9 J10
Callide Coalfields QLD 9 J10
Callington SA 60 J7 62 E7 65 J10
Callion WA 77 H10
Calliope QLD 9 J11
Caloona NSW 6 K6 24 B3
Caloundra QLD 4 D2 7 E13
Calpatanna Con Park SA 64 E3
Caltowie SA 62 F2 65 F10
Calulu VIC 43 K11 45 B12 46 D5
Calvert QLD 5 J10
Calvert VIC 38 E7
Calwell ACT 32 J4
Camballin WA 79 B10 80 H6
Cambalong NSW 30 J3
Cambarville VIC 37 A14 42 J5 44 A5
Camberwell NSW 23 D9
Camberwell VIC 35 D5 37 D8
Camboon QLD 7 A8 9 K10
Cambooya QLD 7 G10
Cambrai SA 62 D6 65 H11
Cambray WA 73 G12
Cambrian Hill VIC 39 E10
Cambridge NSW 21 G8
Cambridge TAS 50 C7 53 F11
Cambridge Gulf WA 81 C13
Camden NSW 21 F11 23 H8 30 A7
Camden South NSW 21 F11
Camels Hump Nature Res NSW 23 B11
Camena TAS 54 E6
Cameron Corner NSW QLD SA 14 K4 26 C1 67 G14
Camerons Gorge Nature Res NSW 23 B9
Camira QLD 3 J1 5 F9
Camira Creek NSW 25 D12
Camooweal QLD 10 J1 89 H14
Camooweal Caves Nat Park QLD 10 J2 89 H14
Camp Hill QLD 3 F5 5 E8
Camp Mountain QLD 3 C1 4 G7
Campania TAS 53 E11
Campbell ACT 31 B4 32 E5
Campbell Town TAS 53 B11 55 J11
Campbellfield VIC 35 B3 36 B7
Campbells Bridge VIC 38 B7
Campbells Creek VIC 39 C11
Campbells Forest VIC 39 A11
Campbelltown NSW 21 E11 23 J8 30 A7
Campbelltown SA 59 F6 60 F3
Campbelltown VIC 39 C11
Campbellville QLD 4 E2
Camperdown NSW 19 F5 21 C9
Camperdown VIC 39 H8
Campup WA 73 A13
Campwin Beach QLD 9 D8
Camurra NSW 24 D5
Canaga QLD 7 E9
Canbelego NSW 27 H11
Canberra ACT 30 D3
Canberra CBD ACT 31
Canberra City ACT 32 D5
Candelo NSW 30 J4
Canegrass WA 77 H11
Cangai NSW 25 D11
Cania Gorge Nat Park QLD 7 A9 9 K11
Caniambo VIC 42 D4
Cann River VIC 47 C11
Canna WA 76 F4
Cannawigara SA 63 B10
Cannie VIC 41 G9
Canning Vale WA 71 J5
Cannington WA 71 H5 72 F3
Cannington Mine QLD 12 C5
Cannon Creek QLD 5 H13
Cannon Hill QLD 3 E5 5 E8
Cannon Vale QLD 8 B7
Cannons Creek VIC 37 H10
Cannum VIC 40 K5
Canonba NSW 27 H13
Canowie SA 62 E3 65 F10
Canowindra NSW 22 G3
Canteen Creek (Orwaitilla) NT 89 J11 91 A11
Canterbury NSW 19 G4 21 C9
Canunda Nat Park SA 63 C13
Canungra QLD 5 D13 7 H13
Canyonleigh NSW 22 K6 30 B5
Cap Island Con Park SA 64 G4
Capalaba QLD 3 G7 5 D8 7 G13
Capalaba West QLD 3 F7
Capamauro Nature Res WA 76 G4
Caparra NSW 23 B12
Cape Adieu SA 68 K5
Cape Arid WA 83 J2
Cape Arid Nat Park WA 83 J2
Cape Arnhem NT 87 D13
Cape Barren Island TAS 55 A14
Cape Barrow NT 87 F11
Cape Baskerville WA 79 A8 80 F3
Cape Bauer SA 64 E3
Cape Beatrice NT 87 G13
Cape Bedford QLD 11 A12 16 K7
Cape Bernier WA 81 A12
Cape Borda WA 79 A9 80 F4
Cape Bossut WA 79 C8 80 J2
Cape Bougainville WA 81 A10
Cape Bouvard WA 72 H6 74 E2
Cape Bowling Green QLD 8 A6
Cape Brewster WA 80 C7
Cape Bridgewater VIC 38 J3
Cape Byron NSW 7 J14 25 B14
Cape Carnot SA 64 J5
Cape Clear VIC 39 F10
Cape Cleveland QLD 8 A5
Cape Clinton QLD 9 F11
Cape Cockburn NT 86 B6
Cape Conran Coastal Park VIC 47 D10
Cape Cossigny WA 78 D5 82 B3
Cape Crawford NT 89 C11
Cape Croker NT 86 A6
Cape Cuvier WA 78 H1
Cape de Couedic SA 63 K9
Cape Degerando TAS 55 K14
Cape Direction QLD 16 F4
Cape Dombey NT 86 F2
Cape Don NT 86 B5
Cape Dussejour WA 81 C13
Cape Farewell TAS 54 A6
Cape Farquhar WA 78 H1
Cape Flattery QLD 11 A12 16 J7
Cape Ford NT 86 E2
Cape Fourcroy NT 86 C2
Cape Freycinet WA 73 K13 74 H1
Cape Gambier NT 85 B2 86 C4
Cape Gantheaume SA 63 H9
Cape Gantheaume Con Park SA 63 H9
Cape Grafton QLD 11 D13
Cape Grenville QLD 16 D3
Cape Grey NT 87 E12
Cape Grim TAS 54 B1
Cape Hamelin WA 73 K14
Cape Hart Con Park SA 63 G9
Cape Helvetius NT 86 C2
Cape Hillsborough Nat Park QLD 9 C8
Cape Hotham NT 85 B3 86 C4
Cape Howe NSW VIC 30 K5 47 C14

Cape Jaubert – Coolamon 95

Cape Jaubert WA 79 C8 80 K2
Cape Jervis SA 61 K1 63 G8 65 K9
Cape Keerweer QLD 16 G1
Cape Keith NT 85 A3 86 B4
Cape Keraudren TAS 54 A1
Cape Keraudren WA 78 D6 82 A6
Cape Kimberley QLD 11 C12
Cape Knob WA 75 J9
Cape Lambert WA 78 D4 82 C2
Cape Latouche Treville WA 79 B8 80 J2
Cape Le Grand WA 75 H13 83 J1
Cape Le Grand Nat Park WA 75 G14 83 J1
Cape Leeuwin WA 73 J14 74 J2
Cape Leseur WA 76 B1 78 K1
Cape Leveque WA 80 E4
Cape Liptrap VIC 44 J5
Cape Liptrap Coastal Park VIC 44 H5
Cape Londonderry WA 81 A11
Cape Manifold QLD 9 G11
Cape Melville QLD 16 H6
Cape Melville Nat Park QLD 16 J5
Cape Missiessy WA 79 C8 80 K2
Cape Naturaliste TAS 55 C14
Cape Naturaliste WA 73 K10 74 G1
Cape Nelson VIC 38 J3
Cape Nelson State Park VIC 38 J3
Cape Otway VIC 39 K9
Cape Palmerston QLD 9 E9
Cape Palmerston Nat Park QLD 9 E9
Cape Pasley WA 83 J2
Cape Paterson VIC 44 G4
Cape Peron North WA 76 A1 78 J1
Cape Pillar TAS 51 K14 53 H13
Cape Pond WA 81 B8
Cape Portland TAS 55 C13
Cape Range Nat Park WA 78 F1
Cape Richards QLD 11 F13
Cape Riche WA 75 J8
Cape River QLD 8 C3 11 K12
Cape Rodstock SA 64 F3
Cape Ronsard WA 78 J1
Cape Ruthieres WA 80 A12
Cape Schanck VIC 36 K7 39 J13 44 F1
Cape Scott NT 86 F2
Cape Shield NT 87 E12
Cape Sidmouth QLD 16 G4
Cape Sorell TAS 54 K3
Cape St Cricq WA 76 A1 78 J1
Cape St Lambert WA 81 B12
Cape Stewart NT 87 C10
Cape Talbot WA 81 A11
Cape Thouin WA 78 D5 82 B4
Cape Torrens Con Park SA 63 K8
Cape Tribulation QLD 11 B12
Cape Upstart QLD 8 A6
Cape Upstart Nat Park QLD 8 A6
Cape Van Diemen NT 86 B3
Cape Van Diemen QLD 10 C4
Cape Vancouver WA 74 K7
Cape Vanderlin NT 87 J13 89 A13
Cape Voltaire WA 81 B9
Cape Wellington VIC 45 K8 46 K2
Cape Wessel NT 87 A13
Cape Weymouth QLD 16 E4
Cape Wickham TAS 54 A6
Cape Wilberforce NT 87 C12
Cape York QLD 16 B2
Cape York Peninsula QLD 16 F2
Capel WA 73 H10 74 G2
Capella QLD 8 G6
Capels Crossing VIC 41 G11
Capercup WA 73 C10
Capertee NSW 22 F6
Capital Hill ACT 31 D2 32 E5
Capoompeta Nat Park NSW 25 D10
Capricorn Coast Nat Park QLD 9 G11
Capricorn Group QLD 9 H12
Capricorn Roadhouse WA 78 G6 82 H6
Capricornia Cays Nat Park QLD 9 H13
Captain Billy Landing QLD 16 D3
Captains Creek Nature Res NSW 25 B11
Captains Flat NSW 30 E4
Carabost NSW 29 J14
Caragabal NSW 22 H1 29 E14
Caralue SA 64 F6
Caramut VIC 38 G6
Caranbiri Con Res NT 87 K11 89 B12
Carapooee VIC 39 B9
Carapook VIC 38 E3
Caravan Head NSW 19 J4
Carawa SA 64 D3
Carboor VIC 42 E7
Carbrook QLD 5 C9
Carbunup River WA 73 J11
Carcoar NSW 22 G4
Carcuma Con Park SA 63 C8 65 K12
Cardinia VIC 37 G11
Cardross VIC 28 F3 40 B5
Cardwell QLD 11 F13
Careunga Nature Res NSW 24 C5
Carey Gully SA 60 G4
Cargerie VIC 39 F11
Cargo NSW 22 F4
Carina QLD 3 F5
Carina VIC 28 H2 40 F2
Carina Heights QLD 3 F5
Carinda NSW 27 F14
Carindale QLD 3 F6 5 E8
Carine WA 71 D2
Caringbah NSW 19 J4 21 D10
Carisbrook VIC 39 C10
Carlecatup WA 73 A11
Carlingford NSW 19 D3 21 D8
Carlisle WA 71 G5
Carlisle Island Nat Park QLD 9 C8
Carlisle River VIC 39 J9
Carlisle State Park VIC 39 J9
Carlotta WA 73 G13
Carlsruhe VIC 39 D12
Carlton TAS 51 C10 53 F11
Carlton VIC 34 A3 35 D3
Carlyam Nature Res WA 76 G6
Carmila QLD 9 E9
Carmila Beach QLD 9 E9
Carnamah WA 76 G5
Carnarvon WA 76 A2 78 J1
Carnarvon Nat Park QLD 6 A4 8 K6 13 H14
Carnes SA 66 J4
Carnes Hill NSW 21 E10
Carngham VIC 39 E10
Caroda NSW 24 F6
Caroona NSW 22 A7 24 K6
Carpa SA 62 K4 64 G7
Carpendeit VIC 39 H9
Carpenter Rocks SA 63 C14
Carrai Nat Park NSW 25 H10
Carrajung VIC 45 F9 46 G3
Carramar NSW 21 D9
Carranballac VIC 39 F8
Carrara QLD 5 B13
Carrathool NSW 29 F9
Carr-Boyd WA 77 H11 83 E1
Carrick TAS 55 G9 56 H4
Carrickalinga SA 61 G3 63 G8 65 K9
Carrieton SA 62 F1 65 D10
Carroll NSW 24 J6
Carroll Gap NSW 24 H6
Carrolup WA 73 A11
Carrow Brook NSW 23 C9
Carrum VIC 35 J5 37 F8 39 G14 44 D2
Carrum Downs VIC 35 J6 37 F9
Carseldine QLD 3 B4 4 E7
Cartwright NSW 21 E9
Carwarp VIC 28 G3 40 B5
Cascade WA 75 F12
Cascade Nat Park NSW 25 G12
Casey ACT 32 A4
Cashmere QLD 3 A1 4 F6
Cashmore VIC 38 H3
Casino NSW 7 K12 25 C13
Cassilis NSW 22 B6
Cassilis VIC 43 G11 46 B6
Cassini Island WA 81 A9
Castambul SA 60 F4
Castella VIC 37 A11
Casterton VIC 38 E3 63 A13
Castle Forbes Bay TAS 50 H1 53 H9
Castle Hill NSW 19 C2 21 D8
Castle Rock NSW 23 C8
Castle Tower Nat Park QLD 9 J11
Castleburn VIC 43 J9 45 A11 46 C4
Castlecrag NSW 19 D6
Castlemaine VIC 39 C11
Castlereagh NSW 21 G8
Castlereagh Bay NT 87 C10
Castlereagh Nature Res NSW 21 G8
Castleton QLD 11 G10
Casuarina NT 84 A3
Casula NSW 21 E10
Cataby WA 74 A2 76 J4
Catamaran TAS 53 K9
Catani VIC 37 G12 44 E4
Cathcart NSW 30 J4
Cathcart VIC 38 D7
Cathedral Beach QLD 7 B13
Cathedral Range State Park VIC 42 H5
Cathedral Rock Nat Park NSW 25 G10
Catherine Field NSW 21 F10
Catherine Hill Bay NSW 20 A1
Cathkin VIC 42 G4
Cathundral NSW 22 B1 27 J14
Cattai NSW 20 F6
Cattai Nat Park NSW 20 F6 23 G9
Catumnal VIC 41 J10
Caulfield VIC 35 E5 37 D8
Cavan NSW 30 C3
Cavan SA 59 D4 60 E2
Cave Hill Nature Res WA 75 B12 77 K11
Caveat VIC 42 F4
Cavendish VIC 38 E5
Caversham WA 71 D6
Caveside TAS 54 G7
Cawarral QLD 9 G10
Cawdor NSW 21 F11
Cawndilla Lake NSW 28 B3
Cawongla NSW 25 B13
Cecil Park NSW 21 E9
Cecil Plains QLD 7 G9
Cedar Bay Nat Park QLD 11 B12
Cedar Brush NSW 20 D2
Cedar Creek QLD 4 G6 5 D11
Cedar Grove QLD 5 E11
Cedar Point NSW 25 B13
Cedarton QLD 4 G2
Ceduna SA 64 C2 68 K7
Cement Creek VIC 37 C13
Central Castra TAS 54 E6
Central Mangrove NSW 20 D3
Central McDonald NSW 20 F4
Central Mount Wedge NT 90 D5
Central Plateau Con Area TAS 52 A7 53 A9 54 H7
Central Tilba NSW 30 G5
Centre Bore SA 68 B5
Centre Island NT 87 J13 89 A13
Ceratodus QLD 7 B9
Ceres NSW 22 C2
Ceres VIC 36 G2 39 G12
Cervantes WA 76 H4
Cessnock NSW 23 E10
Chadinga Con Res SA 64 C1 68 K6
Chadstone VIC 35 E5
Chaelundi Nat Park NSW 25 F11
Chain of Lagoons TAS 55 G14
Chain of Ponds SA 60 E5
Chain Valley Bay NSW 20 A1
Chakola NSW 30 G3
Chalky Island TAS 55 B8
Chambers Bay NT 85 B4 86 C5
Chambers Flat QLD 5 E10
Chambers Pillar Historical Res NT 91 H8
Champagny Island WA 80 C6
Chandada SA 64 E4
Chandler QLD 3 F7 5 D8
Chandler SA 66 C2 68 B7
Chandlers Creek VIC 30 K3 47 B11
Channar Mine WA 78 G5 82 G3
Channel Island NT 85 C2
Chapel Hill QLD 3 F2 5 F8
Chapman ACT 32 G2
Chappell Islands TAS 55 C8
Chapple Vale VIC 39 J9
Charam VIC 38 C3
Charbon NSW 22 E6
Charles Darwin Nat Park NT 84 D3
Charleston SA 60 G5
Charleston Con Park SA 60 G6
Charleville QLD 13 K13 15 D14
Charleyong NSW 30 D5
Charleys Creek VIC 39 J9
Charlotte Pass NSW 30 H1 43 D14
Charlton VIC 41 K9
Charlwood QLD 5 J13
Charmhaven NSW 20 B2
Charnwood ACT 32 B2
Charra SA 64 C2 68 K7
Charters Towers QLD 8 B4 11 J13
Chasm Island NT 87 F12
Chatsbury NSW 22 K6 30 B5
Chatswood NSW 19 D5 21 C8
Chatswood West NSW 19 D5
Chatsworth NSW 25 D13
Chatsworth VIC 38 F7
Cheadanup Nature Res WA 75 F11
Cheepie QLD 15 E11
Chelmer QLD 3 F3
Chelsea VIC 35 H5 37 F8
Cheltenham NSW 19 C3 21 D8
Cheltenham SA 59 E2
Cheltenham VIC 35 G4 37 E8
Cherbourg QLD 7 D11
Chermside QLD 3 C4 4 E7
Chermside West QLD 3 C3
Cherry Gardens SA 60 H3 61 C7
Cherry Tree Hill NSW 25 D8
Cherry Tree Pool WA 73 A11
Cherrybrook NSW 19 C3 20 D7
Cherrypool VIC 38 C5
Cherryville SA 60 F4
Cheshunt VIC 42 E7
Chester Hill NSW 21 D9
Chesterton Range Nat Park QLD 6 D2
Chetwynd VIC 38 D3
Cheviot VIC 42 G4
Cheviot Island QLD 9 E10
Chewton VIC 39 C12
Cheyne Bay WA 75 J8
Cheyne Beach WA 74 J7
Cheynes Bridge VIC 43 K8 45 B9 46 D3
Chichester NSW 23 C10
Chiddarcooping Nature Res WA 74 A7 77 J8
Chidlow WA 72 E3
Chifley ACT 32 F3
Chifley NSW 21 B9
Chifley WA 77 J12 83 F2
Childers QLD 7 B11
Childers VIC 44 E6 46 F1
Childowlah NSW 30 C2
Chillagoe QLD 11 D11
Chillagoe-Mungana Caves Nat Park QLD 11 D11
Chilli Beach QLD 16 E4
Chillingham NSW 25 A13
Chillingollah VIC 28 H5 41 E8
Chiltern VIC 29 K12 43 B8
Chiltern Box-Ironbark Nat Park VIC 29 K12 43 B8
Chinaman Creek SA 62 G1 65 E9
Chinaman Flat VIC 40 H3
Chinaman Island VIC 37 H10
Chinamans Wells SA 63 D10
Chinbi QLD 13 B10
Chinchilla QLD 7 E8
Chinderah NSW 25 A14
Chinkapook VIC 28 H5 40 E7
Chinocup Nature Res WA 74 F7
Chipping Norton NSW 21 D9
Chisholm ACT 32 J4
Chittaway Point NSW 20 B3
Chorregon QLD 13 D9
Chowerup WA 73 C13
Chowilla Reg Res SA 28 E1 62 A4 65 G13
Christies Beach SA 60 J1 61 C5
Christmas Creek QLD 5 F14
Christmas Hills TAS 54 C2
Christmas Hills VIC 37 B10
Christmas Island TAS 54 A6
Chudleigh TAS 54 G7
Chum Creek VIC 37 B11
Church Point NSW 19 A7 20 B6
Churchill VIC 45 E8 46 G2
Churchill Island VIC 37 K10
Churchill Nat Park VIC 37 E9 44 C3
Chute VIC 39 D9
Canberra City ACT 31 A3 32 D5
City Beach WA 71 F2
Clackline WA 72 D2 74 C4 76 K5
Clairview QLD 9 F9
Clandulla NSW 22 E6
Clapham SA 59 J4
Clare QLD 8 B5
Clare SA 62 F4 65 G10
Claremont TAS 50 B5 53 F10
Claremont WA 71 G2
Claremont Isles Nat Park QLD 16 G4
Clarence Gardens SA 59 H3
Clarence Point TAS 56 C2
Clarence Town NSW 23 D11
Clarendon NSW 20 G7
Clarendon SA 60 J2 61 C6 62 F7 65 J10
Clarendon TAS 55 G10 56 K6
Clarendon VIC 39 F11
Clareville NSW 20 B6
Clarina QLD 10 E6
Clarke Island TAS 55 B13
Clarkefield VIC 39 E13 42 H1
Clarkes Hill Nature Res NSW 30 F1 43 A13
Claude Road TAS 54 F7
Claverton QLD 15 F13
Clayfield QLD 3 D4
Claymore WA 73 G11
Clayton SA 63 E8 65 K10
Clayton VIC 35 F5 37 E8
Clear Island Waters QLD 5 B13
Clear Lake VIC 38 C4
Clear Mountain QLD 3 A1
Clear Ridge NSW 29 E13
Clearview SA 59 E4
Cleland Con Park SA 59 H6 60 G3 61 A7
Clematis VIC 37 E11
Clermont QLD 8 G6
Cleve SA 62 K4 64 G7
Cleveland QLD 5 C8
Cleveland TAS 53 A11 55 H11
Clifton NSW 21 C12
Clifton QLD 7 H10
Clifton Beach QLD 11 D13
Clifton Beach TAS 51 E8 53 G11
Clifton Creek VIC 43 K11 45 B13 46 D6
Clifton Gardens NSW 19 E6
Clifton Springs VIC 36 G4 39 G13
Clinton SA 62 G5 65 H9
Clinton Centre SA 62 G5 65 H9
Cloncurry QLD 10 K5 12 A5
Clonmel Island VIC 45 H9 46 H3
Clontarf NSW 19 E6 21 B8
Clouds Creek NSW 25 F11
Clovelly NSW 21 B9
Clovelly Park SA 59 J3
Cloverdale WA 71 G6
Cluan TAS 55 G9 56 J3
Club Terrace VIC 47 C10
Clunes NSW 25 B14
Clunes VIC 39 D10
Clybucca NSW 25 J12
Clyde VIC 37 G10 44 D3
Clyde River Nat Park NSW 30 E5
Clydebank VIC 45 D11 46 E4
Coal Creek VIC 37 K14
Coalcliff NSW 21 C12
Coaldale NSW 25 D12
Coalseam Con Park WA 76 F4
Coalstoun Lakes QLD 7 C11
Cobains VIC 45 D11 46 E4
Cobaki NSW 5 A14
Cobar NSW 27 H10
Cobargo NSW 30 G5
Cobark NSW 23 B10
Cobaw VIC 39 D13 42 G1
Cobbadah NSW 24 F7
Cobba-da-mana QLD 7 J9 25 A8
Cobbannah VIC 43 J10 45 A11 46 C4
Cobbity NSW 21 F11
Cobbora NSW 22 C5
Cobby Cobby Island QLD 5 B10
Cobden VIC 39 H8
Cobdogla SA 62 B5 65 H12
Cobera SA 62 B6 65 J12
Coboco NSW 22 B3
Cobourg Marine Park NT 85 A4 86 B5
Cobourg Peninsula NT 86 B5
Cobram VIC 29 K10 42 A4
Cobrico VIC 39 H8
Cobungra VIC 43 G10 46 A5
Coburg VIC 35 C3 36 C7 39 F14 42 K2 44 B1
Cocamba VIC 40 E7
Cocata Con Park SA 64 F5
Cocata Con Res SA 64 F5
Cochranes Creek VIC 39 B9
Cockaleechie SA 64 G6
Cockatoo VIC 37 E11 42 K4 44 C4
Cockatoo Island WA 80 E5
Cockatoo Tank WA 75 B9 77 K9
Cockatoo Valley SA 60 C5
Cockburn SA 26 K1 28 A1 65 D14
Cockermouth Island QLD 9 C9
Cockle Creek TAS 53 K9
Cocklebiddy Motel WA 83 G4
Coconut Grove NT 84 B2
Cocoparra Nat Park NSW 29 F11
Cocoparra Nature Res NSW 29 E11
Codrington VIC 38 H5
Coen QLD 16 H3
Coffin Bay SA 64 H5
Coffin Bay Nat Park SA 64 H5
Coffs Harbour NSW 25 G13
Coghills Creek VIC 39 D10
Cohuna VIC 28 K7 41 H11
Coila Creek NSW 30 F5
Cokum VIC 41 G9
Colac VIC 39 H10
Colbinabbin VIC 39 A13 42 D1
Coldstream VIC 37 C10 42 K3 44 B3
Coleambally NSW 29 G10
Colebee NSW 21 F8
Colebrook TAS 53 E10
Coledale NSW 21 C13 23 J8
Coleraine VIC 38 E4
Coles Bay TAS 53 C14 55 K14
Coleyville QLD 5 J11
Colignan VIC 28 G4 40 B5
Colinroobie NSW 29 F12
Colinton NSW 30 F3
Collarenebri NSW 24 D2
Collaroy NSW 19 C7 20 B7
Collector NSW 30 C4
Collerina NSW 27 D12
Colley SA 64 E4
Collie NSW 22 A2
Collie WA 73 E9 74 F3
Collie Cardiff WA 73 E10
Collier Bay WA 80 E6
Collier Range Nat Park WA 78 H6 82 K5
Collingullie NSW 29 H12
Collingwood VIC 35 D4 37 D8
Collins WA 73 F14
Collins Cap TAS 50 C3 53 F10
Collins Island QLD 9 F10
Collinsvale TAS 50 C4 53 F10
Collinsville QLD 8 C6
Colly Blue NSW 22 A7 24 K5
Colo NSW 20 G5
Colo Heights NSW 20 H5 23 F8
Colton QLD 7 B12
Colton SA 64 F4
Columboola QLD 7 E8
Colyton NSW 21 F8
Comara NSW 25 H11
Comaum SA 38 D1 63 A12
Combaning NSW 22 J1 29 F14
Combara NSW 24 J1
Combienbar VIC 47 C11
Combo Waterhole Con Park QLD 12 B7
Combogolong NSW 24 G1
Comboyne NSW 23 A12
Come-By-Chance NSW 24 G1
Comerong Island Nature Res NSW 30 C7
Comet QLD 8 H7
Comet Vale WA 77 G11
Comleroy Road NSW 20 H6
Commodore Heights NSW 20 B5
Como NSW 19 J3 21 C10
Como WA 71 H4
Conara TAS 53 A11 55 H11
Conargo NSW 29 H9 41 F14
Concord NSW 19 E4 21 C8
Concordia SA 60 B4
Condah VIC 38 G4
Condamine QLD 6 E7
Condell Park NSW 21 D9
Conder ACT 32 K4
Condingup WA 75 G14 83 J2
Condobolin NSW 29 C13
Condong NSW 25 A14
Condowie SA 62 F4 65 G9
Congelin WA 72 C7
Congo NSW 30 F6
Congupna VIC 42 C3
Conimbla NSW 22 G3
Conimbla Nat Park NSW 22 H3
Coningham TAS 50 G5
Coniston NSW 21 C14
Conjola NSW 30 D6
Conjola Nat Park NSW 30 D7
Conmurra SA 63 C12
Connells Lagoon Con Res NT 89 F12
Connells Point NSW 19 H4
Connemurra NSW 22 A6 24 K5
Connewarre VIC 36 H3
Connewirrecoo VIC 38 D3
Conoble NSW 29 C8
Conondale QLD 4 H1 7 E12
Conondale Nat Park QLD 4 J1 7 E12
Contine WA 72 B7
Conway Beach QLD 9 C8
Conway Nat Park QLD 9 C8
Coober Pedy SA 66 G4
Coobowie SA 62 H7 65 J8
Coochiemudlo Island QLD 5 C9
Coochin Creek QLD 4 E3
Coodanup WA 72 G6
Cooee TAS 54 D5
Coogee NSW 19 G6 21 B9
Coojar VIC 38 D4
Cook ACT 32 D3
Cook SA 68 H3
Cookamidgera NSW 22 F2
Cookardinia NSW 29 J13
Cooke Plains SA 63 D8 65 K11
Cookernup WA 73 G8
Cooks Gap NSW 22 C6
Cooktown QLD 11 A12 16 K7
Coolabah NSW 27 G12
Coolabunia QLD 7 E11
Coolac NSW 29 G14 30 C1
Cooladdi QLD 15 E12
Coolah NSW 22 B6
Coolah Tops Nat Park NSW 22 B7
Coolamon NSW 29 G13

96 Coolana – Doughboy

Coolana QLD 5 J8
Coolangatta QLD 5 A14 7 H13 25 A14
Coolaroo VIC 35 A2 36 B7
Coolatai NSW 24 D7
Coolbaggie Nature Res NSW 22 B4
Coolbinia WA 71 E4
Coolgardie WA 75 A12 77 J10
Coolimba WA 76 G3
Coolmunda Dam QLD 7 J9 25 A8
Coolongolook NSW 23 C12
Cooltong SA 28 F1 62 B5 65 G13
Coolum Beach QLD 7 E13
Coolumbooka Nature Res NSW 30 J3 47 A12
Coolup WA 72 G7 74 E3
Cooma NSW 30 G3
Cooma VIC 41 K14 42 C2
Coomallo Nature Res WA 76 H4
Coomandook SA 63 D8 65 K11
Coomba NSW 23 C12
Coombabah QLD 5 B12
Coombah NSW 28 C2
Coomera QLD 5 C11 7 H13
Coomera Island QLD 5 B11
Coominya QLD 4 K7 7 G12
Coonabarabran NSW 24 J3
Coonalpyn SA 63 C9
Coonamble NSW 24 H1
Coonana WA 77 J13 83 F2
Coonawarra SA 38 D1 63 B12
Coondle WA 72 D1
Coongie Lake SA 14 F3 67 D13
Coongoola QLD 15 G13
Coonooer Bridge VIC 39 A9 41 K9
Coopernook NSW 23 B13
Coopers Creek VIC 45 C8 46 E2
Coopers Plains QLD 3 G4
Cooplacurripa NSW 23 A11
Coopracambra Nat Park VIC 30 K3 47 B12
Coorabakh Nat Park NSW 23 B12
Coorabie SA 68 K5
Cooran QLD 7 D12
Cooranbong NSW 20 C1 23 F10
Cooranga North QLD 7 E10
Cooranup WA 73 C13
Cooriemungle VIC 39 J8
Coornartha Nature Res NSW 30 G3
Coorong Nat Park SA 63 D9
Coorow WA 76 G5
Cooroy QLD 7 E12
Coorparoo QLD 3 F4
Cootamundra NSW 22 K2 29 G14 30 B1
Coothalla QLD 15 E13
Cooyal NSW 22 D6
Cooyar QLD 7 F11
Copacabana NSW 20 B4
Cope Cope VIC 41 K8
Copeton Dam NSW 25 E8
Copeville SA 62 C6 65 J12
Copley SA 65 A10 67 K10
Copmanhurst NSW 25 E12
Coppabella QLD 8 E7
Copperfield QLD 8 G6
Copperfield Mining Centre WA 77 F10
Copperhannia Nature Res NSW 22 H4
Copping TAS 51 B12 53 F12
Cora Lynn VIC 37 G12 44 D4
Corack VIC 41 J8
Corack East VIC 41 J8
Corackerup Nature Res WA 74 H7
Coragulac VIC 39 H9
Coraki NSW 7 K13 25 C13
Coral Bay WA 78 G1
Coral Coast QLD 7 A12 9 K13
Coral Sea QLD 11 A14
Coramba NSW 25 G12
Cordalba QLD 7 B11
Cordering WA 73 C10
Coree NSW 29 J9
Coreen NSW 29 J11
Corella Creek NT 89 E11
Corfield QLD 13 C9
Coridhap VIC 39 F10
Corinda QLD 3 G3
Corindi Beach NSW 25 F13
Corinella VIC 37 K11 44 F3
Corinna TAS 54 G2
Corio VIC 36 F3
Cornella VIC 39 A13 42 E1
Corner Inlet VIC 44 H7
Cornucopia VIC 37 F12
Cornwall TAS 55 G13
Cornwallis NSW 20 G7
Corny Point SA 62 J7 64 J7
Corobimilla NSW 29 G11
Coromandel East SA 59 K5
Coromandel Valley SA 59 K4 60 H3 61 B6
Coromby VIC 38 A6
Coronation Beach WA 76 F3
Coronation Islands WA 80 C7
Coronet Bay VIC 37 K11
Corop VIC 41 K13 42 D1
Cororooke VIC 39 H9
Corowa NSW 29 K11 42 A7
Corridgery NSW 22 F1 29 D14
Corrigin WA 74 D6
Corrimal NSW 21 C14 23 J8 30 B7
Corroboree Park Inn NT 85 D3 86 D4
Corroboree Rock Con Res NT 91 F9
Corrowong NSW 30 J2
Corryong VIC 29 K14 43 C12
Cosgrove VIC 42 C4
Cosmo Newberry WA 77 E12 83 C2
Cossack WA 78 E4 82 C2
Costerfield VIC 39 B13 42 F1
Cottage Point NSW 20 C6
Cottan-Bimbang Nat Park NSW 23 A12 25 K10
Cottesloe WA 71 G1
Cottles Bridge VIC 37 B9
Cougal NSW 25 A13
Coulomb Point Nature Res WA 79 A8 80 G3
Coulson QLD 5 H12
Coulston Park QLD 9 E8
Coulta SA 64 H5
Countegany NSW 30 G4
Couta Rocks TAS 54 E1
Coutts Crossing NSW 25 E12
Cowabbie West NSW 29 F12
Cowan NSW 20 D6
Cowan Cowan QLD 4 B5
Cowangie VIC 28 H2 40 E2 65 K14
Cowaramup WA 73 J12 74 G2
Coward Springs SA 66 H7
Cowcowing Lakes WA 74 A5 76 J6
Cowell SA 62 J4 64 G7
Cowes VIC 37 K9 44 F3
Cowley QLD 11 E13
Cowper NSW 25 E13
Cowra NSW 22 H3
Cowwarr VIC 45 D9 46 E3
Cox Peninsula NT 85 C1 86 D3
Cox Scrub Con Park SA 61 F7
Crab Island QLD 16 C1
Crabtree TAS 50 E2 53 G9
Crace ACT 32 B5
Cracow QLD 7 B8
Cradle Mountain - Lake St Clair Nat Park TAS 52 A5 54 H5
Cradle Valley TAS 54 G5
Cradoc TAS 50 H2 53 H9
Cradock SA 65 C10
Crafers SA 59 J6 60 G3 61 B7
Crafers West SA 59 J6
Craiggiemore WA 77 F12 83 D2
Craigie NSW 30 J3 47 A11
Craigie WA 71 B2
Craigieburn VIC 36 B7 39 E14 42 J2 44 A1
Craiglie QLD 11 C12
Cramenton VIC 28 G4 40 D6
Cramps TAS 53 A9 55 H9
Cramsie QLD 8 H1 13 E10
Cranbourne VIC 35 K7 37 G9 44 D3
Cranbrook TAS 53 B13 55 J13
Cranbrook WA 74 H6
Cranebrook NSW 21 G8
Craneford SA 60 C7
Craven NSW 23 C11
Cravensville VIC 43 C11
Crawley WA 71 G3
Crayfish Creek TAS 54 C4
Creek Junction VIC 42 E5
Creek View VIC 39 A13 42 D1
Cremorne NSW 19 E6 21 B8
Cremorne TAS 51 E8 53 G11
Crescent Head NSW 25 J12
Cressy TAS 55 G9 56 K5
Cressy VIC 39 G10
Crestmead QLD 3 K5 5 E10
Crestwood NSW 32 F7
Creswick VIC 39 D11
Crib Point VIC 37 J9
Croajingolong Nat Park VIC 47 D12
Croftby QLD 5 J14
Croker Island NT 88 B6
Cromer Con Park SA 60 E6
Cronulla NSW 19 K5 21 B10
Crooble NSW 24 C6
Crooked River VIC 43 H9 46 B4
Crookwell NSW 22 K5 30 B4
Croppa Creek NSW 24 C6
Cross SA 60 F2
Crossdale QLD 4 J5
Crossman WA 72 D7
Crow Mountain NSW 24 G7
Crowdy Bay Nat Park NSW 23 B13
Crowes VIC 39 K9
Crowlands VIC 39 C8
Crows Nest NSW 19 E5
Crows Nest QLD 7 F11
Crows Nest Nat Park QLD 7 F11
Croxton East VIC 38 F5
Croydon QLD 10 F7
Croydon SA 59 F3 60 F2
Croydon VIC 37 C10 42 K3 44 B3
Crusoe Island QLD 5 B10
Crymelon VIC 40 J5
Cryon NSW 24 F2
Crystal Brook SA 62 G3 65 F9
CSA Mine NSW 27 H10
Cuballing WA 72 A7 74 E5
Cubbaroo NSW 24 F3
Cuckoo TAS 55 E11
Cudal NSW 22 F3
Cudgee VIC 38 H7
Cudgegong NSW 22 E6
Cudgen NSW 25 A14
Cudgera Creek NSW 25 A14
Cudgewa VIC 29 K14 43 B12
Cudgewa North VIC 43 B12
Cudlee Creek SA 60 F5
Cudlee Creek Con Park SA 60 F5
Cudmirrah NSW 30 D7
Cudmore Nat Park QLD 8 G4 13 D13
Cue WA 76 D7
Culbin WA 73 C9
Culburra NSW 30 C7
Culburra SA 63 C9
Culcairn NSW 29 J12
Culgoa VIC 28 J5 41 G8
Culgoa Floodplain Nat Park QLD 6 K1 27 B12
Culgoa Nat Park NSW 6 K1 27 C12
Culgoora NSW 24 F4
Culham WA 72 D1
Cullacabardee WA 71 C4
Cullen NT 85 G4 86 F5
Cullen Bullen NSW 22 F6
Cullendulla NSW 30 E6
Cullendulla Creek Nature Res NSW 30 E5
Cullerin NSW 30 C4
Cullulleraine VIC 28 F2 40 B3 65 H14
Cumborah NSW 27 D14
Cummins SA 64 H5
Cumnock NSW 22 E3
Cundare VIC 39 G10
Cundeelee WA 77 J13 83 F2
Cunderdin WA 72 A2 74 C5 76 K6
Cundinup WA 73 G12
Cungena SA 64 D4
Cunliffe SA 62 H5 65 G9
Cunnamulla QLD 15 H13
Cunnawarra Nat Park NSW 25 H10
Cunningham SA 62 H5 65 H9
Cunningham Islands NT 87 C12
Cunninyeuk NSW 28 H7 41 E10
Cuprona TAS 54 D6
Curacoa Island QLD 11 G14
Curban NSW 22 A3 24 K2
Curdie Vale VIC 38 J7
Curdimurka SA 67 H8
Curl Curl NSW 19 D7 20 B7
Curlew Island QLD 9 E9
Curlewis NSW 24 J6
Curlewis VIC 36 G4
Curlwaa NSW 28 F3 40 A4
Currabubula NSW 24 J6
Curramulka SA 62 H6 65 J8
Currarong NSW 30 D7
Currawang NSW 30 C4
Currawarna NSW 29 H12
Currawinya Nat Park QLD 15 J10 26 B7
Currency Creek SA 63 F8 65 K10
Currie TAS 54 B6
Curries VIC 38 H3
Currimundi QLD 4 D2
Currumbin QLD 5 A14
Currumbin Valley QLD 5 B14
Currumbin Waters QLD 5 B14
Curtin ACT 32 F3
Curtin WA 75 A13 77 J11 83 F1
Curtin Airport WA 80 G6
Curtin Springs NT 90 J5
Curtis Island QLD 9 H11
Curtis Island Nat Park QLD 9 H11
Curyo VIC 28 K5 40 H7
Cuttabri NSW 24 G3
Cuumbean Nature Res NSW 30 D4
Cygnet TAS 50 H3 53 H9
Cygnet River SA 63 H8 65 K8
Cynthia QLD 7 B9

D

D'Aguilar QLD 4 G3
D'Aguilar Nat Park QLD 4 G6 7 F12
D'Entrecasteaux Nat Park WA 73 G14 74 J3
Daandine QLD 7 F9
Dadswells Bridge VIC 38 B6
Daguragu NT 88 D3
Dahlen VIC 38 A5
Daintree QLD 11 C12
Daintree Nat Park QLD 11 C12
Daisy Dell TAS 54 G6
Daisy Hill QLD 3 J7 5 D9
Daisy Hill State Forest QLD 3 J7
Dajarra QLD 12 C3
Dakabin QLD 4 F5
Dalbeg QLD 8 B5
Dalby QLD 7 F9
Dale Bridge WA 72 C4
Dale Con Park WA 72 E4 74 D4
Dales Creek VIC 36 A2
Dalgety NSW 30 H2
Dalkeith WA 71 H2
Dallarnil QLD 7 B11
Dalma QLD 9 H10
Dalmeny NSW 30 G5
Dalmore VIC 37 G11
Dalmorton NSW 25 F11
Dalrymple Nat Park QLD 8 B4 11 J13
Dalton NSW 22 K4 30 C3
Dalwallinu WA 76 H5
Daly River NT 85 G1 86 F3
Daly Waters NT 86 K7 88 B7
Dalyston VIC 44 G4
Dampier WA 78 E4 82 C1
Dananbilla Nature Res NSW 22 J3 30 A2
Dandaloo NSW 22 C1 27 K13 29 A13
Dandaragan WA 74 A2 76 J4
Dandenong VIC 35 G7 37 E9 44 C2
Dandenong North VIC 35 G7
Dandenong Ranges Nat Park VIC 37 D10 42 K3 44 C3
Dandenong South VIC 35 H7
Dandongadale VIC 43 E8
Dangarfield NSW 23 C9
Dangarsleigh NSW 25 H9
Dangelong Nature Res NSW 30 G4
Danggali Con Park SA 28 D1 62 A3 65 F13
Dangin WA 72 A4 74 D5 76 K6
Danyo VIC 28 H2 40 F2
Dapper Nature Res NSW 22 C5
Dapto NSW 23 K8 30 B7
Daradgee QLD 11 E13
Darawank Nature Res NSW 23 C12
Darbalara NSW 29 H14 30 C1
Darbys Falls NSW 22 H4
Darch Island NT 86 B6
Dardadine WA 73 C9
Dardanup WA 73 G10 74 F3
Dareton NSW 28 F3 40 A4
Dargo VIC 43 H10 46 C4
Dark Corner NSW 22 F6
Darkan WA 73 C9 74 F4
Darke Peak SA 64 F6
Darkes Forest NSW 21 D12
Darkwood NSW 25 G12
Darley VIC 36 B3
Darling Harbour NSW 18 C1
Darling Point NSW 19 F6
Darlinghurst NSW 18 D3 19 F6
Darlington QLD 5 E14
Darlington SA 59 K3
Darlington TAS 53 E13
Darlington VIC 39 G8
Darlington Point NSW 29 G10
Darnick NSW 28 C6
Darnum VIC 44 E6
Daroobalgie NSW 22 F2 29 D14
Darr QLD 8 G1 13 E10
Darra QLD 3 G2
Darradup WA 73 H13
Darraweit Guim VIC 39 D14 42 H1
Darriman VIC 45 F10 46 G3
Dartmoor VIC 38 G3 63 A14
Dartmouth QLD 8 H2 13 E11
Dartmouth VIC 43 D11
Darwin NT 85 C1 86 D3
Darwin CBD NT 84
Dattening WA 72 C6
Davenport Range Nat Park NT 89 J10 91 A10
Daveyston SA 60 A5
Davidson NSW 19 C5 20 C7
Davies Creek Nat Park QLD 11 D12
Davies Plain VIC 43 E13
Davis Creek NSW 23 C9
Davistown NSW 20 B4
Davyhurst WA 77 H10
Daw Island WA 83 J3
Dawes Point NSW 18 A2
Dawesley SA 60 H6
Dawesville WA 72 G6
Dawson SA 62 E2 65 E10
Dawsons Hill NSW 23 C9
Dayboro QLD 4 G5 7 F12
Daydream Island QLD 9 B8
Daylesford VIC 39 D11
Daymar QLD 6 J5 24 B3
Daysdale NSW 29 J11
Daytrap VIC 28 H5 40 E7
Daytrap Corner VIC 28 H5 40 F7
De La Poer Range Nature Res WA 77 D12 83 C2
De Salis NSW 32 G7
De Witt Island TAS 52 K7
Dead Horse Gap NSW 30 H1 43 D13
Deagon QLD 3 A5
Deakin ACT 31 D1 32 F4
Deakin WA 68 H1 83 F7
Dean VIC 39 E11
Dean Park NSW 21 F8
Deanmill WA 73 F13 74 H3
Deans Marsh VIC 39 H11
Deception Bay QLD 4 E5 7 F13
Deddington TAS 55 G11
Dederang VIC 43 D9
Dee Why NSW 19 C7 20 B7
Deeford QLD 9 J10
Deep Creek Con Park SA 61 K2 63 G8 65 K9
Deep Lead VIC 38 C7
Deepwater NSW 25 D10
Deepwater Nat Park QLD 9 J12
Deer Park VIC 36 C6 39 F13 42 K1
Deer Vale NSW 25 G11
Deeragun QLD 8 A4 11 H14
Deeral QLD 11 D13
Delamere SA 61 J2 63 G8 65 K9
Delaneys Creek QLD 4 G4
Delatite VIC 42 G6 46 A1
Delegate NSW 30 J3 47 A10
Delegate River VIC 30 J2 47 A10
Delfin Island SA 59 E1
Dellicknora VIC 47 A10
Dellyanine WA 73 B10
Deloraine TAS 55 F8 56 H1
Delungra NSW 24 E7
Demon Nature Res NSW 25 C11
Denham WA 76 B1 78 K1
Denham Group Nat Park QLD 16 C3
Denham Island QLD 10 D3
Denham Sound WA 76 B1
Denial Bay SA 64 C2 68 K7
Denicull Creek VIC 38 D7
Deniliquin NSW 29 J9 41 G14
Denman NSW 23 D8
Denman SA 68 H2
Denmark WA 74 K5
Dennes Point TAS 50 G6 53 G10
Dennington VIC 38 H6
Deptford VIC 43 J11 45 A13 46 C6
Depuch Island WA 78 E4 82 C3
Derby TAS 55 E12
Derby VIC 39 A11
Derby WA 79 A10 80 G5
Dereel VIC 39 F10
Dergholm VIC 38 D2 63 A13
Dergholm State Park VIC 38 D2 63 A12
Dering VIC 40 F5
Deringulla NSW 22 A5 24 K4
Dernancourt SA 59 E6
Deroora QLD 8 H2 13 F11
Derrinallum VIC 39 G8
Derriwong NSW 29 C13
Derwent Bridge TAS 52 C6 54 K6
Desault Bay WA 79 C8 80 K2
Desdemona WA 77 F11 83 E1
Detpa VIC 40 J4
Deua Nat Park NSW 30 F5
Devenish VIC 42 C5
Devils Marbles Con Res NT 89 J9 91 A9
Devoit TAS 55 E9 56 E3
Devon VIC 45 G9 46 H2
Devon Meadows VIC 37 G10
Devoncourt QLD 12 B4
Devonian Reef Con Park WA 79 B11 81 H8
Devonport TAS 54 E7
Dewars Pool WA 72 E1
Dhalinybuy NT 87 D12
Dharawal Nature Res NSW 21 D12
Dharawal State Rec Area NSW 21 D12
Dharug Nat Park NSW 20 E4 23 G9
Diamantina Nat Park QLD 12 F6
Diamond Creek VIC 35 A6 37 B9 39 E14 42 J2 44 B2
Dianella WA 71 D4
Diapur VIC 40 K3
Dickson ACT 32 C5
Dicky Beach QLD 4 D2
Didleum Plains TAS 55 F11
Digby VIC 38 F3
Digby Island QLD 9 D9
Diggers Rest VIC 36 B5 39 E13 42 J1
Dillalah Ridge QLD 15 E13
Dillcar QLD 13 D9
Dillon Bay WA 75 J9
Dilpurra NSW 28 H6 41 E10
Dilston TAS 55 F9 56 F4
Dimboola VIC 38 A5 40 K5
Dimbulah QLD 11 D12
Dingee VIC 41 K12
Dingley Village VIC 35 G5 37 E8
Dingo QLD 9 H8
Dingup WA 73 E13
Dingwall VIC 28 K6 41 H10
Dinmore QLD 5 G9
Dinner Plain VIC 43 F10 46 A5
Dinninup WA 73 D11 74 G4
Dinoga NSW 24 F7
Dinyarrak VIC 40 K2
Dipperu Nat Park QLD 8 E7
Direk SA 59 A4 60 D2
Dirk Hartog Island WA 76 B1 78 K1
Dirnaseer NSW 22 K1 29 G14
Dirranbandi QLD 6 J4 24 A1
Disaster Bay NSW 30 K5 47 B14
Discovery Bay VIC 38 H2
Discovery Bay Coastal Park VIC 38 H2 63 A14
Diwarra NSW 28 B4
Dixie VIC 39 H8
Dixons Creek VIC 37 B11 42 J3 44 A3
Djugerari WA 79 C11 81 K8
Djukbinj Nat Park NT 85 C3 86 D4
Dobbyn QLD 10 J4
Docker VIC 42 D7
Docker River (Kaltukatjara) NT 79 J14 83 A7
Doctors Flat VIC 43 H12 46 B6
Dodges Ferry TAS 51 C9 53 F11
Dolphin Island WA 78 D4 82 C2
Dolphin Island Nature Res WA 78 D3 82 B1
Don TAS 54 E7
Don Valley VIC 37 C12
Donald VIC 41 K8
Donalds Well SA 68 A5 90 K6
Doncaster VIC 35 C6 37 C9
Dongara WA 76 G3
Donnelly River WA 73 F13
Donnybrook QLD 4 E4
Donnybrook VIC 36 A7
Donnybrook WA 73 G10 74 G3
Doo Town TAS 51 F13
Dooboobetic VIC 41 K8
Doodenanning WA 72 B3
Doodlakine WA 74 C6 76 K7
Dooen VIC 38 A5
Dookie VIC 42 C4
Doolandella QLD 3 J3
Doomadgee QLD 10 F2
Doomben QLD 3 D5 4 E7
Doonside NSW 21 E8
Dooragan Nat Park NSW 23 B13
Dooralong NSW 20 C2
Doreen NSW 24 F4
Doreen VIC 37 B9 39 E14 42 J2 44 A2
Dorodong VIC 38 D2
Dorre Island WA 76 A1 78 J1
Dorrigo NSW 25 G12
Dorrigo Nat Park NSW 25 G12
Dorset Vale SA 60 J3 61 C7
Double Bridges (site) VIC 43 J12 45 A14 46 C7
Double Sandy Point Coastal Res TAS 55 D10 56 A7
Doubtful Islands Bay WA 75 H9
Doughboy NSW 30 D4

Douglas – Forty Mile Scrub 97

Douglas VIC 38 C4
Douglas-Apsley Nat Park TAS 53 A13 55 H13
Douglas Park NSW 21 E12
Douglas River TAS 53 A14 55 H14
Dover TAS 53 J9
Dover Heights NSW 19 F7 21 B8
Doveton VIC 35 G7
Dowerin WA 74 B5 76 J6
Downer ACT 32 C5
Downfall Nature Res NSW 29 J14
Downside NSW 29 H13
Doyalson NSW 20 B1 23 F10
Dragon Rocks Nature Res WA 75 E8
Dragon Tree Soak Nature Res WA 79 D9
Drake NSW 25 C11
Dreeite VIC 39 H9
Drewvale QLD 3 J4
Driffield VIC 44 E7 46 F1
Drik Drik VIC 38 G3
Drillham QLD 6 E7
Dripstone NSW 22 D4
Dromana VIC 36 J7 39 H14 44 E1
Dromedary TAS 50 A4 53 F10
Dronfield QLD 12 B4
Drouin VIC 37 G14 44 D5
Drouin South VIC 37 G14 44 D5
Drouin West VIC 37 F14
Drovers Cave Nat Park WA 76 H3
Drumborg VIC 38 G3
Drummond QLD 8 H5
Drummoyne NSW 19 E5 21 C8
Drung Drung VIC 38 B6
Dry Creek SA 59 D4
Dry Creek VIC 42 F5
Dryander Nat Park QLD 8 B7
Drysdale VIC 36 G4 39 G13
Drysdale Island NT 87 B11
Drysdale River Nat Park WA 81 C11
Duaringa QLD 9 H9
Dubbo NSW 22 C3
Dubelling WA 72 A4
Dublin SA 62 F5 65 H9
Duchess QLD 12 B4
Duck Island VIC 36 H5
Duddo VIC 28 H2 40 E2
Dudinin WA 74 E6
Dudley VIC 44 G4
Dudley Con Park SA 63 G9
Dudley Park SA 59 E4
Duff Creek SA 66 F6
Duffholme VIC 38 B4
Duffy ACT 32 F2
Duffys Forest NSW 19 B5 20 C6
Duke Islands QLD 9 E10
Duke of Orleans Bay WA 83 J2
Dulacca QLD 6 E7
Dularcha Nat Park QLD 4 F2
Dulbolla QLD 5 F14
Dulbydilla QLD 6 D2
Dulcie Ranges Nat Park NT 91 D11
Dululu QLD 9 H10
Dulwich SA 59 G5
Dumaresq NSW 25 G9
Dumbalk VIC 44 G6 46 H1
Dumbalk North VIC 44 G7 46 G1
Dumberning WA 73 B8
Dumbleyung WA 74 F6
Dumbleyung Lake Nature Res WA 74 F6
Dumosa VIC 28 K5 41 H8
Dunalley TAS 51 D12 53 F12
Duncraig WA 71 C2
Dundas NSW 21 D8
Dundas QLD 4 J6
Dundas TAS 52 A4 54 H4
Dundas Nature Res WA 75 D14 83 H1
Dundas Valley NSW 19 D3
Dundee NSW 25 E10
Dundee Beach NT 86 D3
Dundonnell VIC 39 F8
Dundurrabin NSW 25 G11
Dunedoo NSW 22 B5
Dunggir Nat Park NSW 25 H12
Dungog NSW 23 D11
Dungowan NSW 25 J8
Dunk Island QLD 11 F13
Dunkeld NSW 22 F5
Dunkeld QLD 6 E3
Dunkeld VIC 38 E6
Dunlop ACT 32 B2
Dunluce QLD 13 A10
Dunmarra NT 88 C7
Dunmore NSW 22 D2 29 B14
Dunn Rock Nature Res WA 75 F9
Dunnstown VIC 39 E11
Dunolly VIC 39 B10
Dunoon NSW 25 B13
Dunorlan TAS 54 F7
Dunrobbin Bridge TAS 53 E8
Dunrobin VIC 38 E3
Dunsborough WA 73 J11 74 G1
Dunwich QLD 5 B8 7 G13
Durack QLD 3 H3
Dural NSW 19 B3 20 D7
Duramana NSW 22 F5
Duranillin WA 73 C10 74 G4
Durdidwarrah VIC 36 D1 39 F11
Durham QLD 11 F9
Durham Lead VIC 39 F10
Durham Ox VIC 28 K7 41 J10
Duri NSW 24 J7
Durong South QLD 7 D9
Durras NSW 30 E6
Durundur QLD 4 G3
Dutton SA 62 E5 65 H11
Dutton Park QLD 3 F4
Duverney VIC 39 G9
Dwarda WA 72 C7 74 E4
Dwellingup WA 72 F7 74 E3
Dwyers NSW 27 F11
Dykehead QLD 7 C9
Dynnyrne TAS 49 D1
Dysart QLD 8 F7
Dysart TAS 53 E10

E

Eagle Bay WA 73 K10 74 G1
Eagle Bore SA 68 A5 90 K5
Eagle Farm QLD 3 D5
Eagle Heights QLD 5 D12
Eagle on the Hill SA 59 H6
Eagle Point VIC 43 K11 45 C13 46 E6
Eagle Vale NSW 21 E11
Eagleby QLD 5 D10
Eaglehawk VIC 39 A12
Eaglehawk Neck TAS 51 F13 53 G13
Eaglevale VIC 43 H9 46 B4
Earlston VIC 42 D4
Earlwood NSW 21 C9
East Brisbane QLD 3 E4
East Fremantle WA 71 H2
East Gosford NSW 20 B4
East Guyong NSW 22 F5
East Haydon QLD 10 F6
East Hills NSW 19 H2 21 D10
East Islands QLD 16 C3
East Kangaroo Island TAS 55 C8
East Killara NSW 19 D5
East Kurrajong NSW 20 G6
East Lynne NSW 30 E6
East Melbourne VIC 34 C4
East Palmerston QLD 11 E13
East Perth WA 70 B4 71 F4
East Point NT 84 C1
East Ryde NSW 19 E4
East Sassafras TAS 55 E8
East Strait Island QLD 16 B2
East Vernon Island NT 85 B2 86 C4
East Victoria Park WA 71 G5
Eastbrook WA 73 F14
Easter Group WA 76 F2
Eastern Creek NSW 21 E8
Eastern Group WA 83 J3
Eastern View VIC 39 J11
Eastwood NSW 19 D3 21 D8
Eastwood SA 58 D3
Eaton WA 73 G9
Eatons Hill QLD 3 B2
Eba Island SA 64 E3
Ebenezer NSW 20 F6
Ebor NSW 25 G11
Eccleston NSW 23 C10
Echo Hill SA 66 B1 68 B6
Echuca VIC 29 K8 41 J13 42 B1
Echunga SA 60 J4 62 E7 65 J10
Ecklin South VIC 39 H8
Eddington QLD 10 K7 12 A6
Eddington VIC 39 B10
Eden NSW 30 J5 47 A14
Eden Hill WA 71 E5
Eden Hills SA 59 K4 60 H2 61 B6
Eden Island QLD 5 B10
Eden Valley SA 60 C7 62 E6 65 H11
Edenhope VIC 38 C2 63 A12
Edensor Park NSW 21 E9
Edgecliff NSW 21 B8
Edgeroi NSW 24 F5
Edgewater WA 71 A2
Edi VIC 42 E7
Edillilie SA 64 H5
Edith NSW 22 H6
Edith Creek TAS 54 D2
Edithburgh SA 62 H7 65 J8
Edithvale VIC 35 H5 37 F8 39 G14 44 D2
Edjudina Mine WA 77 G12 83 E2
Edmondson Park NSW 21 E10
Edmonton QLD 11 D13
Edmund Kennedy Nat Park QLD 11 F13
Edrom NSW 30 K5 47 A14
Edungalba QLD 9 H9
Edward Island NT 87 G11
Edwards Creek SA 66 F6
Edwardstown SA 59 J3
Egan Peaks Nature Res NSW 30 J4 47 A13
Egg Island TAS 50 G2
Egg Lagoon TAS 54 A6
Eidsvold QLD 7 B9
Eight Mile Plains QLD 3 H5 5 E9
Eildon VIC 42 G5
Einasleigh QLD 11 G10
El Alamein SA 62 H1 65 D8
El Arish QLD 11 E13
Elaine VIC 39 F11
Elalie QLD 9 E9
Elands NSW 23 B12
Elanora Heights NSW 19 B7 20 B7
Elbow Hill SA 62 K4 64 G7
Elcho Island NT 87 C11
Elcombe NSW 24 E6
Elderslie TAS 53 E9
Eldon TAS 53 E11
Eldorado VIC 42 C7
Electrona TAS 50 G5 53 G10
Elgin WA 73 H10
Elgin Vale QLD 7 D11
Elimbah QLD 4 F4
Elizabeth SA 59 A5 60 D3 62 F6 65 J10
Elizabeth East SA 59 A6
Elizabeth Grove SA 59 A6
Elizabeth Island VIC 37 K10
Elizabeth Town TAS 55 F8
Ella Bay Nat Park QLD 11 E13
Ellam VIC 40 J5
Ellenborough NSW 23 A12 25 K11
Ellenbrook WA 71 B6
Ellendale TAS 53 E8
Ellerslie NSW 28 E3
Ellerslie VIC 38 G7
Ellerslie Nature Res NSW 29 H14
Ellerston NSW 23 B10
Ellery Creek Nature Park NT 90 F7
Elliminyt VIC 39 H10
Ellinbank VIC 37 H14 44 E6
Elliot Price Con Park SA 67 F8
Elliott NT 89 D8
Elliott QLD 7 A12 9 K13
Elliott TAS 54 D5
Elliott Heads QLD 7 A12 9 K13
Elliston SA 64 F4
Elmhurst VIC 39 C9
Elmore VIC 39 A13 41 K13 42 D1
Elong Elong NSW 22 C4
Elphinstone QLD 8 D7
Elphinstone VIC 39 C12
Elsey Nat Park NT 86 H7
Elsmore NSW 25 E8
Eltham NSW 25 B14
Eltham VIC 35 B6 37 C9 39 F14 42 J2 44 B2
Elura Mine NSW 27 G10
Elwood VIC 35 E3
Emerald QLD 8 H7
Emerald VIC 37 E11 42 K3 44 C3
Emerald Hill NSW 24 H5
Emerald Springs NT 85 G4 86 F5
Emily and Jessie Gaps Nature Park NT 91 F8
Emita TAS 55 B8
Emmaville NSW 25 D9
Emmdale NSW 26 J7
Emmet QLD 8 K1 13 G11
Empire Bay NSW 20 B5
Empire Vale NSW 25 C14
Emu VIC 39 B9
Emu Bay SA 63 H8 65 K8
Emu Downs SA 62 E4 65 G10
Emu Flat VIC 39 C13 42 G1
Emu Junction SA 68 E5
Emu Park QLD 9 G11
Emu Plains NSW 21 G8
Emuford QLD 11 E12
Endeavour River Nat Park QLD 11 A12 16 K7
Enderby Island WA 78 E3 82 C1
Endyalgout Island NT 85 A6 86 C6
Eneabba WA 76 G4
Enfield NSW 19 F4 21 C9
Enfield SA 59 E4 60 F2
Enfield VIC 39 F10
Enfield State Park VIC 39 F10
Engadine NSW 19 K2 21 C10
Engawala NT 91 D9
Englefield VIC 38 D4
English Town TAS 55 G11
Enmore NSW 21 C9 25 H9
Enngonia NSW 27 C10
Enoggera QLD 3 D3
Ensay VIC 43 H12 46 B7
Ensay North VIC 43 H12 46 B7
Ensay South VIC 43 H12 46 B6
Eppalock VIC 39 B12
Epping NSW 19 D3 21 D8
Epping VIC 35 A4 37 B8 39 E14 42 J2 44 A2
Epping Forest TAS 53 A11 55 H10
Epping Forest Nat Park QLD 8 F4 13 C14
Epsom QLD 9 D8
Epsom VIC 39 A12
Ercildoun VIC 39 D10
Eribung NSW 22 D1 29 B14
Eric Bonython Con Park SA 61 K3
Erica VIC 44 C7 46 E1
Ergolia NSW 29 E11
Erikin WA 74 C6 76 K7
Erina NSW 20 B4
Erindale SA 59 G6
Erldunda NT 90 H7
Ermington NSW 19 E3 21 D8
Ernabella (Pukatja) SA 68 A5
Ernest QLD 5 B12
Ernest Henry Mine QLD 10 K5
Eromanga QLD 15 E8
Erriba TAS 54 F6
Erringibba Nat Park QLD 6 F7
Errinundra VIC 47 B10
Errinundra Nat Park VIC 30 K2 47 B10
Errolls WA 77 D8
Erskine Island QLD 9 H12
Erskine Park NSW 21 F9
Erskineville NSW 21 B9
Esk QLD 4 K6 7 F11
Eskdale VIC 43 D10
Esmond VIC 29 K11 42 B6
Esperance WA 75 G13 83 J1
Esperance Bay WA 75 G13 83 J1
Essendon VIC 35 C2 36 C7
Estcourt VIC 37 E12
Eton QLD 9 D8
Ettalong Beach NSW 20 B5
Ettrick NSW 7 J12 25 B12
Etty Bay QLD 11 E13
Euabalong NSW 29 C11
Euabalong West NSW 29 C11
Eubenangee Swamp Nat Park QLD 11 E13
Eucla WA 68 K1 83 G7
Eucla Nat Park WA 68 K1 83 G7
Eucumbene Cove NSW 30 G2
Euchareena NSW 22 E4
Eurimbula Nat Park QLD 9 J12
Euroa VIC 42 E4
Eurobin VIC 43 E9
Eurobodalla NSW 30 G5
Eurobodalla Nat Park NSW 30 F6
Eurong QLD 7 B13
Eurongilly NSW 29 G14
Eudlo QLD 4 F1
Eudlo Creek Nat Park QLD 4 F1
Eudunda SA 62 E5 65 H11
Eugenana TAS 54 E7
Eugowra NSW 22 F3
Eulo QLD 15 H11
Eumundi QLD 7 E13
Eumungerie NSW 22 B3
Eungai NSW 25 H12
Eungella QLD 8 D7
Eungella Nat Park QLD 8 C7
Eurack VIC 39 G10
Eurambeen VIC 39 D9
Euramo QLD 11 F13
Eurelia SA 62 F1 65 D10
Eurilla Con Park SA 60 G3 61 A7
Euston NSW 28 G4 40 C7
Evandale TAS 55 G10 56 J6
Evans Crown Nature Res NSW 22 G6
Evans Head NSW 7 K13 25 C14
Evans Island SA 64 D2
Evansford VIC 39 D10
Evanston SA 60 C4
Evanston WA 77 G9
Evatt ACT 32 B3
Everard Junction WA 79 J11 83 A4
Everett Island NT 87 C12
Eversley VIC 39 D8
Everton VIC 42 C7
Everton Hills QLD 3 C2
Everton Park QLD 3 C3 4 E7
Ewaninga Rock Carvings Con Res NT 91 F8
Ewens Ponds SA 38 G1
Exeter NSW 22 K7 30 B6
Exeter TAS 55 E9 56 E3
Exford VIC 36 C4
Exmouth WA 78 F1
Exmouth Gulf WA 78 F2
Expedition Nat Park QLD 6 B5 9 K8
Exton TAS 55 G8 56 H1
Eyre Island SA 64 D2
Eyre Peninsula SA 62 K3 64 E5

F

Fadden ACT 32 H4
Failford NSW 23 C12
Fair Cape QLD 16 E3
Fairbank VIC 37 K14
Fairfax Islands QLD 9 J13
Fairfield NSW 19 F1 21 D9
Fairfield West NSW 19 F1
Fairhaven VIC 36 K1 37 J10 39 J11 47 C13
Fairholme NSW 29 D13
Fairley VIC 41 G10
Fairneyview QLD 5 H8
Fairview Con Park SA 63 B11
Fairview Park SA 59 C7
Fairy Hill NSW 25 B13
Fairy Meadow NSW 21 C14
Fairyland Mine WA 77 E10
Falcon WA 72 H6 74 E2
Falls Creek NSW 30 C7
Falls Creek Alpine Village VIC 43 F10
Falmouth TAS 55 G14
False Cape Bossut WA 79 B8 80 J2
Family Islands Nat Park QLD 11 F13
Fannie Bay NT 84 D1
Fantome Island QLD 11 G14
Faraday VIC 39 C12
Farina SA 67 J10
Farleigh QLD 9 D8
Farnham NSW 22 E4
Farrar WA 73 B12
Farrell Flat SA 62 E4 65 G10
Farrer ACT 32 G4
Fassifern QLD 5 J12
Faulconbridge NSW 21 H8
Faulkland NSW 23 C11
Faure Island WA 76 B2 78 K2
Fawcett VIC 42 G4
Fawkner VIC 35 B3
Federal NSW 25 B14
Feilton TAS 50 B1
Felixstow SA 59 F5
Feluga QLD 11 E13
Fentonbury TAS 53 E8
Fentons Creek VIC 39 A9
Ferguson SA 64 A4 66 K4
Ferguson VIC 39 J9
Fern Tree TAS 50 D5 53 G10
Fernances NSW 20 F3
Fernbank VIC 43 K10 45 C12 46 E5
Fernbrook WA 73 F9
Ferndale NSW 29 J12
Ferndale VIC 37 J14
Ferndale WA 71 H5
Ferndene TAS 54 E6
Fernihurst VIC 41 J10
Fernlees QLD 8 H7
Fernshaw VIC 37 B12
Ferntree Gully VIC 37 D10
Fernvale QLD 5 H8
Ferny Glen QLD 5 D13
Ferny Grove QLD 3 C1 4 F7
Ferny Hills QLD 3 C2
Ferryden Park SA 59 E3
Fiddletown NSW 20 D6
Field Island NT 85 B5 86 C6
Fiery Flat VIC 41 K10
Fifield NSW 29 B13
Fig Tree NSW 21 D14
Fig Tree Pocket QLD 3 F2
Finch Hatton QLD 8 D7
Findon SA 59 F2 60 F1
Fine Flower NSW 25 D12
Fingal NSW 5 A14 25 A14
Fingal TAS 55 G13
Finger Post NSW 22 D4
Finke (Apatula) NT 91 J9
Finke Bay NT 85 B4 86 C5
Finke Gorge Nat Park NT 90 G7
Finley NSW 29 J10
Finniss SA 63 E8 65 K10
Finniss Con Park SA 61 F7
Fish Creek VIC 44 H6
Fish Point VIC 41 F10
Fish River Res NT 85 J2 86 G3
Fisher ACT 32 G3
Fisher SA 68 H4
Fisherman Islands QLD 3 C7 4 D7
Fishermens Bend VIC 35 D2
Fiskville VIC 36 B2
Fitzgerald TAS 53 F8
Fitzgerald WA 75 G9
Fitzgerald River Nat Park WA 75 H9
Fitzgibbon QLD 3 B4
Fitzroy SA 58 A2 59 F4
Fitzroy VIC 34 A4 35 D3
Fitzroy Crossing WA 79 B11 81 J8
Fitzroy Falls NSW 22 K7 30 B6
Fitzroy Island QLD 11 D13
Fitzroy Island Nat Park QLD 11 D13
Five Day Creek NSW 25 H11
Five Ways NSW 27 J12 29 A12
Fiveways VIC 37 G10
Flaggy Rock QLD 9 E9
Flagstaff Hill SA 59 K4 60 H2 61 B6
Flat Rocks WA 73 A12
Flat Witch Island TAS 52 K7
Flaxley SA 60 J5
Flaxton QLD 4 F1
Fleurieu Peninsula SA 61 J3 63 F8
Flinders QLD 5 H11
Flinders VIC 37 K8 39 J14 44 F2
Flinders Bay WA 73 J14 74 J2
Flinders Chase Nat Park SA 63 K9
Flinders Group Nat Park QLD 16 H5
Flinders Island QLD 16 H5
Flinders Island SA 64 G3
Flinders Island TAS 55 B9
Flinders Park SA 59 F3
Flinders Ranges Nat Park SA 65 B10
Flintstone TAS 53 B9 55 J9
Flora River Nature Park NT 85 J4 86 H5
Floreat WA 71 F2
Florey ACT 32 B3
Florida NSW 27 H11
Florida WA 72 H6
Florieton SA 62 D4 65 G11
Flowerdale TAS 54 D5
Flowerdale VIC 42 H3
Flowerpot TAS 50 J5 53 H10
Flowery Gully TAS 55 E9 56 E2
Fluorspar QLD 11 D11
Flynn ACT 32 B3
Fog Bay NT 86 D2
Foleyvale QLD 9 H9
Footscray VIC 35 D2 36 C6
Forbes NSW 22 F2 29 D14
Forcett TAS 51 B10 53 F11
Forde ACT 32 A5
Fords Bridge NSW 27 D9
Forest TAS 54 C3
Forest Den Nat Park QLD 8 E2 13 C12
Forest Glen NSW 20 E6
Forest Lake QLD 3 J2 5 F9
Forest Range SA 60 G4
Forest Reefs NSW 22 G4
Forestdale QLD 3 K3 5 E9
Forester TAS 55 D12
Foresters Beach NSW 20 B4
Forestier Peninsula TAS 51 D13 53 G13
Forestville NSW 19 D6 20 C7
Forge Creek VIC 43 K11 45 C13 46 E6
Forrest ACT 31 D2 32 E5
Forrest VIC 39 J10
Forrest WA 83 F6
Forrest Beach QLD 11 G14
Forrest Lakes WA 68 F1 83 E7
Forrestfield WA 71 G7
Forreston SA 60 E5
Forsayth QLD 11 G9
Forster NSW 23 C12
Forsyth Island QLD 10 D3
Forsyth Island TAS 55 A14
Forsyth Islands QLD 10 D3
Fort Glanville Con Park SA 60 F1
Fort Lytton Nat Park QLD 3 D6 4 D7
Fortescue River Roadhouse WA 78 E3 82 D1
Forth TAS 54 E7
Fortis Creek Nat Park NSW 25 D12
Fortitude Valley QLD 2 A3 3 E4
Forty Mile Scrub Nat Park QLD 11 F11

98 Foster – Guildford

Foster VIC 44 G7 46 H1
Fosterton NSW 23 D11
Fosterville VIC 39 A12
Four Mile Creek TAS 55 G14
Fowlers Bay SA 68 K6
Fowlers Gap NSW 26 G2
Foxdale QLD 8 C7
Foxhow VIC 39 G9
Framlingham VIC 38 H7
Frampton NSW 22 K1 29 G14
Frances SA 38 B1 63 A11
Francois Peron Nat Park WA 76 B2 78 K1
Frank Hann Nat Park WA 75 E10
Frankford TAS 55 F8 56 F2
Frankland WA 73 B14 74 H5
Franklin ACT 32 B5
Franklin - Gordon Wild Rivers Nat Park TAS 52 D5 54 K5
Franklin TAS 50 G1 53 H9
Franklin Harbor Con Park SA 62 J4 64 G7
Franklin Island SA 64 D2
Franklin Vale QLD 5 K10
Franklinford VIC 39 D11
Frankston VIC 35 K5 37 G8 39 G14 44 D2
Frankton SA 62 E5 65 H11
Fraser ACT 32 A3
Fraser Island QLD 7 B13
Freeling SA 62 E5 65 H10
Freemans Reach NSW 20 F6
Freemans Waterhole NSW 23 E10
Freemantle Nature Res NSW 22 F5
Freeth Junction SA 66 B6 91 K11
Fregon (Kaltjiti) SA 68 B5
Fremantle WA 71 J1 72 G4 74 D2 76 K4
French Island VIC 37 J10 44 E3
French Island Nat Park VIC 37 J10 44 E3
French Park NSW 29 H12
Frenchmans VIC 39 C8
Frenchs Forest NSW 19 C6 20 B7
Freshwater Creek VIC 36 H2 39 H12
Freshwater Nat Park QLD 4 F5
Frewhurst QLD 11 F11
Freycinet Nat Park TAS 53 C14 55 K14
Freycinet Peninsula TAS 53 C14
Friday Island QLD 16 B1
Frogmore NSW 22 J4 30 A3
Fulham SA 59 G2 60 F1
Fulham Gardens SA 59 F2
Fulham Island TAS 51 D11
Fulham Vale QLD 4 K4
Fullarton SA 59 H5 60 G2 61 A6
Fullerton NSW 22 J5 30 A4
Fumina VIC 42 K6 44 C6 46 E1
Furner SA 63 C13
Furracabad NSW 25 E9
Fyans Creek VIC 38 C6
Fyansford VIC 36 G2
Fyshwick ACT 32 F6

G

Gabba Island QLD 16 A2
Gabo Island VIC 47 C14
Gaffneys Creek VIC 42 H6 46 C1
Gagebrook TAS 50 A5 53 F10
Gagudju Cooinda Lodge NT 85 D6 86 D6
Gailes QLD 3 J1 5 F9
Gairdner WA 75 H8
Galah VIC 28 H4 40 E5
Galaquil VIC 40 J6
Galaquil East VIC 40 J6
Gale ACT 32 H7
Galga SA 62 C6 65 J12
Galiwinku NT 87 C11
Galong NSW 22 K3 30 B2
Galore NSW 29 H12
Galston NSW 19 A3 20 D7
Gama VIC 40 G6
Gammon Ranges Nat Park SA 65 A11 67 K11
Gan Gan NT 87 E11
Ganmain NSW 29 G12
Gannawarra VIC 28 J7 41 G11
Gapsted VIC 43 D8
Gapuwiyak NT 87 D11
Garah NSW 6 K6 24 C4
Garden Island SA 59 C2 60 E2
Garden Island TAS 50 K3
Garden Island WA 72 G4 74 D2
Garden Island Creek TAS 50 K3 53 H10
Gardens Of Stone Nat Park NSW 22 F7
Gardners Bay TAS 50 J3 53 H10
Garema NSW 22 G1 29 D14
Garfield VIC 37 F13 44 D4
Garfield North VIC 37 F12
Gargett QLD 9 D8
Garie NSW 21 C11 23 J9
Garigal Nat Park NSW 19 C5 23 H9
Garland NSW 22 G4
Garnpung Lake NSW 28 D5
Garra NSW 22 F3
Garran ACT 32 F4
Garrawilla NSW 24 J4
Garrthalala NT 87 D12
Garvoc VIC 38 H7
Gary Junction WA 79 F11
Gascoyne Junction WA 76 A3 78 J2
Gatton QLD 7 G11
Gatum VIC 38 D4
Gaven QLD 5 C12
Gawler SA 60 B4 62 E6 65 H10
Gawler TAS 54 E6
Gawler Ranges Con Res SA 64 D4
Gawler Ranges Nat Park SA 64 D5
Gayndah QLD 7 C10
Gaythorne QLD 3 D3
Gazette VIC 38 G5
Gecko Mine NT 89 G8
Geebung QLD 3 C4
Geehi NSW 30 G1 43 C13
Geelong VIC 36 G3 39 G12
Geera QLD 8 H3 13 F12
Geeralying WA 73 B8
Geeveston TAS 50 J1 53 H9
Geikie Gorge Nat Park WA 79 B12 81 H9
Gelantipy VIC 43 G13 47 A8
Gellibrand VIC 39 J10
Gembrook VIC 37 E12 44 C4
Gemoka QLD 11 K9 13 A8
Genoa VIC 47 C13
Geoffrey Bay WA 79 C8 80 K2
Geographe Bay WA 73 J10 74 G2
George Fisher Mine QLD 10 K3 12 A3
George Town TAS 55 D9 56 C2
Georges Creek Nature Res NSW 25 H10
Georges Hall NSW 21 D9
Georges Junction NSW 25 H10
Georges Plains NSW 22 G5
Georges River Nat Park NSW 19 H2
Georgetown QLD 11 F9
Georgetown SA 62 F3 65 F10
Georgica NSW 25 B13
Gepps Cross SA 60 F2 59 D4
Geraldton WA 76 F3
Gerang Gerung VIC 40 K4
Geranium SA 63 C8 65 K12
Gerard SA 62 B5 65 H13
German Creek Mine QLD 8 G7
Gerogery NSW 29 K12 43 A9
Gerringhap VIC 36 F2
Gerringong NSW 23 K8 30 C7
Gerroa NSW 30 C7
Getullai Island QLD 16 A2
Geurie NSW 22 D4
Gherang VIC 36 J1
Ghin-Doo-Ee Nat Park NSW 23 C11
Gibinbell QLD 7 J8 24 B7
Gibraltar Range Nat Park NSW 25 E11
Gibson Desert Nature Res WA 79 J11 83 A4
Gibson Island QLD 3 D6
Gidgegannup WA 72 E2
Gidginbung NSW 29 F13
Giffard VIC 45 F10 46 G4
Gilbert River QLD 11 F8
Gilberton SA 58 A3
Gilderoy VIC 37 D13
Gilead NSW 21 E11
Giles Meteorological Station WA 79 J13 83 A7
Gilgai NSW 25 E8
Gilgandra NSW 22 A3
Gilgooma NSW 24 H2
Gilgunnia NSW 27 K10 29 B10
Gilles Plains SA 59 E5 60 F3
Gilliat QLD 10 K6 12 A6
Gillingall VIC 43 H13 47 B8
Gilmore ACT 32 H5
Gilston QLD 5 C13
Gin Gin NSW 22 B2 27 J14
Gin Gin QLD 7 A11 9 K12
Gina SA 66 J4
Gindalbie WA 77 H11 83 F1
Gindie QLD 8 H7
Gingilup Swamps Nature Res WA 73 H14 74 H2
Gingin WA 72 G1 74 B3 76 K4
Gippsland Lakes Coastal Park VIC 45 D12 46 F6
Gipsy Point VIC 47 C13
Giralang ACT 32 B4
Girgarre VIC 41 K14 42 C2
Girilambone NSW 27 G12
Girral NSW 29 E12
Girralang Nature Res NSW 22 F5
Girraween NSW 21 E8
Girraween Nat Park QLD 7 K11 25 B10
Girrawheen WA 71 C3
Giru QLD 8 A5
Girvan NSW 23 D11
Gisborne VIC 39 E13
Gladesville NSW 19 E4
Gladfield VIC 41 J11
Gladstone NSW 25 J12
Gladstone QLD 9 H11
Gladstone SA 62 F3 65 F10
Gladstone TAS 55 D13
Gladysdale VIC 37 D12 42 K4 44 B4
Glamis NSW 23 A11
Glamorgan Vale QLD 5 J8
Glance Creek TAS 54 D5
Glandore SA 59 H3
Glass House Mountains QLD 4 F3
Glass House Mountains Nat Park QLD 4 F3 7 F12
Glastonbury QLD 7 D12
Glaziers Bay TAS 50 H2 53 H9
Glebe NSW 19 F5 21 C8
Glebe TAS 49 B2
Glen Alice NSW 22 E7
Glen Alvie VIC 37 K12 44 F4
Glen Davis NSW 22 F7
Glen Eagle WA 72 E5
Glen Elgin NSW 25 E10
Glen Forbes VIC 37 K12
Glen Gallic NSW 23 D8
Glen Helen Resort NT 90 F6
Glen Huon TAS 50 F1 53 G9
Glen Innes NSW 25 E9
Glen Morrison NSW 25 J9
Glen Osmond SA 59 H5 60 G3 61 A7
Glen Patrick VIC 39 C9
Glen Roy Con Park SA 38 D1 63 B12
Glen Valley VIC 43 F11
Glen Waverley VIC 35 E6 37 D9
Glenaire VIC 39 K9
Glenaladale VIC 43 K10 45 B11 46 D5
Glenalbyn VIC 39 A10
Glenalta SA 59 J5
Glenariff NSW 27 G12
Glenaroua VIC 39 C14 42 G2
Glenbrae VIC 39 D9
Glenbrook NSW 21 H9
Glenburn VIC 42 H3
Glenburnie SA 38 F1 63 B14
Glencairn VIC 42 J7 45 A8 46 C2
Glencoe NSW 25 F9
Glencoe SA 63 B13
Glencoe West SA 63 B13
Glendambo SA 64 A5
Glenden QLD 8 D7
Glendevie TAS 50 K1 53 H9
Glendon Brook NSW 23 D10
Gleneagle QLD 5 F12
Glenelg SA 59 J2 60 G1 61 A5 62 F7 65 J10
Glenelg North SA 59 H2
Glenfern QLD 4 J3
Glenfern TAS 50 B1 53 F9
Glenfield NSW 21 E10
Glenfyne VIC 39 H8
Glengarrie NSW 5 B14
Glengarry NSW 27 D14
Glengarry TAS 55 F9 56 F2
Glengarry VIC 45 D8 46 F2
Glengower VIC 39 D10
Glengowrie SA 59 J2
Glenhaven NSW 20 E7
Glenhope VIC 39 C13 42 G1
Glenisla VIC 38 D5
Glenlee VIC 40 K4
Glenlofty VIC 39 C8
Glenlusk TAS 50 B4 53 F10
Glenlyon VIC 39 D12
Glenmaggie VIC 43 K8 45 C9 46 E3
Glenmore NSW 21 G11
Glenmore VIC 36 C2
Glenmore Park NSW 21 G9
Glenmorgan QLD 6 F6
Glennie Group VIC 44 K7 46 K1
Glenora TAS 53 E9
Glenoran WA 73 F13
Glenorchy TAS 50 C5 53 F10
Glenorchy VIC 38 B7
Glenore QLD 10 E6
Glenore TAS 55 G9 56 J3
Glenore Grove QLD 5 K8
Glenorie NSW 19 A2 20 E6
Glenormiston North VIC 39 G8
Glenormiston South VIC 39 H8
Glenreagh NSW 25 F12
Glenrowan VIC 42 D6
Glenroy SA 38 D1
Glenside SA 59 G5
Glenstuart QLD 8 J2 13 G12
Glenthompson VIC 38 E6
Glentulloch WA 73 E12
Glenunga SA 59 H5
Glenusk QLD 8 J3 13 G12
Glenwarrin NSW 23 A12
Glenwood NSW 21 E8
Glenwood QLD 7 C12
Glossodia NSW 20 G6
Glossop SA 62 B5 65 H13
Gloucester NSW 23 C11
Gloucester Island QLD 8 B7
Gloucester Island Nat Park QLD 8 B7
Gloucester Nat Park WA 73 F14 74 J3
Gnangara WA 71 B4
Gnarpurt VIC 39 G9
Gnarwarree VIC 36 G1
Gnotuk VIC 39 H8
Gnowangerup WA 74 G6
Goangra NSW 24 F1
Goat Island SA 64 D2 68 K7
Gobarralong NSW 30 C1
Gobur VIC 42 F4
Gochin Jiny Jirra NT 87 C9
Gocup NSW 29 H14 30 D1
Godfreys Creek NSW 22 J3 30 A2
Godwin Beach QLD 4 E4
Gogango QLD 9 H9
Gogeldrie NSW 29 G11
Gol Gol NSW 28 F3 40 A5
Golconda TAS 55 E10 56 D7
Gold Coast QLD 5 A12 7 H14
Golden Bay WA 72 G5
Golden Beach QLD 4 E2
Golden Beach VIC 45 E12 46 F5
Golden Grove SA 59 C7 60 E3
Golden Ridge WA 75 A13 77 J11 83 F1
Golden Valley TAS 55 G8 56 K1
Goldsborough VIC 39 B10
Goldsmith TAS 53 B10 55 J10
Goldsmith Island QLD 9 C8
Goldsworthy WA 78 D6 82 B6
Gollan NSW 22 C4
Golspie NSW 22 J5 30 A4
Gomersal SA 60 B5
Goneaway Nat Park QLD 13 F8
Gongolgon NSW 27 E12
Goobang Nat Park NSW 22 E3
Good Hope NSW 30 C2
Goodedulla Nat Park QLD 9 G9
Goodger QLD 7 E10
Goodna QLD 3 J1 5 F9
Goodnight NSW 41 D9
Goodnight Scrub Nat Park QLD 7 B11
Goodooga NSW 6 K2 27 B13
Goodparla NT 85 E5 86 E5
Goods Island QLD 16 B1
Goodwood QLD 7 B12
Goodwood SA 59 H4
Goohi NSW 24 J5
Goold Island QLD 11 F13
Goold Island Nat Park QLD 11 F13
Goolgowi NSW 29 E10
Goolma NSW 22 C5
Goolmangar NSW 25 B13
Gooloogong NSW 22 G3
Goolwa SA 63 F8 65 K10
Goomadeer NT 87 C8
Goomalibee VIC 42 D5
Goomalling WA 74 B4 76 J6
Goombi QLD 7 E8
Goombungee QLD 7 F10
Goomeri QLD 7 D11
Goon Nure VIC 45 C12 46 E5
Goonawarra Nature Res NSW 29 E8
Goondah NSW 22 K3 30 B2
Goondiwindi QLD 7 J8 24 A6
Goonengerry Nat Park NSW 25 B14
Goongarrie WA 77 H10
Goongarrie Nat Park WA 77 G11 83 E1
Goongee VIC 40 E2
Goongerah VIC 30 K2 47 B10
Goonook Nature Res NSW 23 B12
Goonumbla NSW 22 E2 29 C14
Goonyella Mine QLD 8 E6
Goorabin NSW 29 J11
Gooram VIC 42 F4
Goorambat VIC 42 C5
Goorawin NSW 29 E10
Goornong VIC 39 A12
Gooroc VIC 39 A8 41 K8
Goose Island TAS 55 C8
Gooseberry Hill Nat Park WA 72 F3
Goovigen QLD 9 J10
Goowarra QLD 9 H8
Gorae VIC 38 H3
Gorae West VIC 38 H3
Goranba QLD 7 F8
Gordon ACT 32 K4
Gordon NSW 19 D5 20 C7
Gordon TAS 50 K4 53 H10
Gordon VIC 36 A1 39 E11
Gordon Park QLD 3 D4
Gordon Ruins SA 65 D9
Gordonvale QLD 11 D13
Gormandale VIC 45 E9 46 F3
Gormanston TAS 52 B4 54 J4
Gorokan NSW 20 B2
Goroke VIC 38 B3
Goschen VIC 28 J6 41 F9
Gosford NSW 20 B4 23 G9
Goshen TAS 55 E13
Gosnells WA 71 K6
Gosse Bore SA 66 A1 68 A6 90 K7
Gostwyck NSW 25 H9
Goughs Bay VIC 42 G6
Goulburn NSW 22 K6 30 C5
Goulburn Islands NT 86 B7
Goulburn River Nat Park NSW 22 C7
Goulburn Weir VIC 39 A14 42 E2
Goulds Country TAS 55 E13
Gourock Nat Park NSW 30 F4
Gove Peninsula NT 87 D13
Gowanford VIC 41 F8
Gowar East VIC 39 A9
Gowrie ACT 32 H4
Gowrie Park TAS 54 F6
Goyura VIC 40 H6
Grabben Gullen NSW 22 K5 30 B4
Gracefield WA 73 A13
Gracemere QLD 9 H10
Gracetown WA 73 K12 74 H1
Graceville QLD 3 F3
Gradgery NSW 27 G14
Gradule QLD 6 J5 24 A3
Grafton NSW 25 E12
Graham NSW 22 J4 30 A3
Grahamstown NSW 29 H14 30 D1
Grahamvale VIC 42 C3
Graman NSW 24 D7
Grampians Nat Park VIC 38 C6
Grandchester QLD 5 K10
Grange QLD 3 D3
Grange SA 59 F2 60 F1
Granite Flat VIC 43 D10
Granite Island SA 61 J6
Granite Island VIC 44 H7 46 J2
Granite Point Con Area TAS 55 D11 56 A7
Granite Tor Con Area TAS 52 A5 54 H5
Granny Smith Mine WA 77 F12 83 D1
Grant (site) VIC 43 H9 46 B4
Grant Island NT 86 B7
Granton TAS 50 A4 53 F10
Granton VIC 37 A13
Grantville VIC 37 K11 44 F4
Granville NSW 19 E2 21 D8
Granville Harbour TAS 52 A2 54 H2
Granya VIC 43 B10
Grass Flat VIC 38 A4
Grass Hut NSW 27 D10
Grass Patch WA 75 F13 83 J1
Grass Valley WA 72 C2 74 C4 76 K6
Grassdale VIC 38 F4
Grassmere VIC 38 H6
Grassy TAS 54 C6
Grattai NSW 22 D5
Gravelly Beach TAS 55 E9 56 E4
Gravesend NSW 24 E6
Grawin NSW 27 D14
Gray TAS 55 G14
Grays Point NSW 19 K3
Graytown VIC 39 B14 42 E2
Great Australian Bight Marine Park SA 68 K4 83 G7
Great Barrier Reef QLD 9 C11 11 C13 16 F5
Great Basalt Wall Nat Park QLD 8 B2 11 J12
Great Dog Island TAS 55 C9
Great Keppel Island QLD 9 G11
Great Lake TAS 53 A8 55 H8
Great Palm Island QLD 11 G14
Great Sandy Island Nature Res WA 78 E3
Great Sandy Nat Park QLD 7 D13
Great Victoria Desert Nature Res WA 68 F1 83 E6
Great Western VIC 38 C7
Great Western Tiers Con Park TAS 53 B10 55 J10
Gredgwin VIC 41 H10
Green Cape NSW 30 K5 47 B14
Green Fields SA 59 C4
Green Head WA 76 H3
Green Island QLD 4 C7 11 D13
Green Island TAS 50 J5
Green Island Nat Park QLD 11 D13
Green Lake VIC 38 B5
Green Pigeon NSW 25 B13
Green Point NSW 20 B4
Green Valley NSW 21 E9
Greenacre NSW 19 G3 21 C9
Greenacres SA 59 E5
Greenbank QLD 5 F10
Greenbushes WA 73 F12 74 G3
Greendale NSW 21 G10
Greendale VIC 36 A2 39 E12
Greenethorpe NSW 22 H3
Greengrove NSW 20 D4
Greenhill QLD 9 E9
Greenhill SA 59 G6 60 K4
Greenhill Island NT 85 A5 86 B5
Greenhills WA 72 B3 74 C5 76 K6
Greenmount QLD 7 G10
Greenmount VIC 45 G9 46 H3
Greenmount Nat Park WA 72 F3
Greenock SA 60 A6 62 E5 65 H10
Greenough WA 76 F3
Greenpatch SA 64 H5
Greens Beach TAS 55 D8 56 C1
Greens Creek VIC 39 C8
Greensborough VIC 35 B5 37 C8
Greenslopes QLD 3 F4
Greenvale NSW 29 H11
Greenvale QLD 11 G12
Greenvale VIC 35 A2 36 B6
Greenwald VIC 38 G3
Greenway ACT 32 J3
Greenways SA 62 D6 63 C12 65 J11
Greenwell Point NSW 30 C7
Greenwich NSW 21 C8
Greenwich Park NSW 22 K6 30 B5
Greenwith SA 59 B7
Greenwood WA 71 C2
Gregors Creek QLD 4 K3
Gregory WA 76 E2
Gregory Downs QLD 10 G3
Gregory Mine QLD 8 G7
Gregory Nat Park NT 85 K2 86 K3 88 B3
Greigs Flat NSW 30 J5 47 A14
Grenfell NSW 22 H2 29 E14
Grenville VIC 39 F10
Gresford NSW 23 D10
Greta VIC 42 D6
Greta West VIC 42 D6
Gretna TAS 53 E9
Grevillia NSW 25 A12
Grey Peaks Nat Park QLD 11 D13
Greystanes NSW 19 E1 21 E8
Griffin QLD 4 E6
Griffith ACT 32 F5
Griffith NSW 29 F11
Griffiths Island VIC 38 H6
Griffiths Nature Res WA 75 F12 83 J1
Grimwade WA 73 F11 74 G3
Gringegalgona VIC 38 E4
Grogan NSW 22 J1 29 F14
Groganville QLD 11 C11
Grong Grong NSW 29 G12
Gronos Point NSW 20 F6
Groote Eylandt NT 87 F12
Groper Creek QLD 8 A6
Grose Island NT 86 D3
Grose Vale NSW 20 H7
Grose Wold NSW 20 G7
Grove TAS 50 E3 53 G10
Grove Hill NT 85 F3 86 F4
Grovedale VIC 36 H2
Grovely QLD 3 C2
Gruyere VIC 37 C11
Guanaba QLD 5 C12
Gubbata NSW 29 D11
Gubbata Nature Res NSW 29 D12
Guilderton WA 72 H1 74 B2 76 K4
Guildford NSW 19 F2 21 D9
Guildford TAS 54 F5

Minnamurra – Murrindindi 103

Minnamurra NSW 23 K8
Minnie Water NSW 25 E13
Minnipa SA 64 E4
Minore NSW 22 C3
Mintabie SA 66 D1 68 C6
Mintaro SA 62 F4 65 G10
Minto NSW 21 E10
Minyip VIC 38 A6 40 K6
Miralie VIC 28 H5 41 E9
Miram VIC 40 K2
Miram South VIC 38 A3 40 K3
Miranda NSW 19 J4 21 C10
Mirani QLD 9 D8
Mirannie NSW 23 D10
Mirboo VIC 44 F7 46 G1
Mirboo North VIC 44 F7 46 G1
Miriam Vale QLD 9 J12
Mirikata SA 66 H5
Mirima (Hidden Valley) Nat Park WA 81 D14
Mirimbah VIC 42 G7 46 A2
Mirirrinyunga (Duck Ponds) NT 88 F4
Miriwinni QLD 11 E13
Mirrabooka QLD 15 F13
Mirrabooka WA 71 D4
Mirranatwa VIC 38 D6
Mirrindi NT 88 F4
Mirrnatja NT 87 D10
Mirrool NSW 29 F12
Missabotti NSW 25 H12
Mission Beach QLD 11 E13
Missouri Mine WA 77 H10
Mistake Creek NT 79 A14 81 G14 88 C1
Mitakooki QLD 12 A4
Mitcham SA 59 J4 60 G2 61 A6
Mitcham VIC 35 D7
Mitchell ACT 32 C5
Mitchell – Alice Rivers Nat Park QLD 10 A7 16 K2
Mitchell QLD 6 D3
Mitchell River Nat Park VIC 43 J10 45 A12 46 C5
Mitchell River Nat Park WA 81 C9
Mitchells (site) VIC 42 H7 46 B1
Mitchellville SA 62 J3 65 F8
Mitchelton QLD 3 D2
Mitiamo VIC 41 J12
Mitre VIC 38 B4
Mitta Mitta VIC 43 D10
Mittagong NSW 22 K7 30 B6
Mittyack VIC 28 H4 40 E6
Moa Island QLD 16 A2
Moama NSW 29 K8 41 J13 42 B1
Moana SA 60 K1 61 D5
Moana Sands Con Park SA 60 K1 61 D5
Mobrup WA 73 B13
Mockinya VIC 38 C5
Modbury SA 59 D6 60 E3
Modbury Heights SA 59 C6
Modbury North SA 59 D6
Modella VIC 37 G13 44 E5
Modewarre VIC 36 H1
Moe VIC 44 D7 46 F1
Moganemby VIC 42 D4
Moggill QLD 3 H1 5 F9
Mogo NSW 30 F6
Mogriguy NSW 22 C3
Mogumber WA 74 A3 76 J5
Moil NT 84 B3
Moina TAS 54 F6
Mokepilly VIC 38 C7
Mole Creek TAS 54 G7
Mole Creek Karst Nat Park TAS 54 G7
Mole River NSW 7 K10 25 C9
Molesworth TAS 50 B3 53 F10
Molesworth VIC 42 G4
Moliagul VIC 39 B10
Molka VIC 42 E3
Molle Islands Nat Park QLD 9 B8
Mollerin Nature Res WA 76 H6
Mollymook NSW 30 D6
Molong NSW 22 F4
Moltema TAS 55 F8
Molyullah VIC 42 D6
Mona Vale NSW 19 B7 20 B6 23 G9
Mona Vale TAS 53 B11 55 J11
Monadnocks Con Res WA 72 E5 74 D3
Monak NSW 28 F4 40 A5
Monarto Con Park SA 60 K7
Monash ACT 32 H4
Monash SA 62 B5 65 H13
Monbulk VIC 37 D11 42 K3 44 C3
Moncrieff ACT 32 A4
Mondrain Island WA 75 H14
Monduran Dam QLD 7 A11 9 K12
Monea VIC 42 E3
Monegeetta VIC 39 D13 42 H1
Monga NSW 30 E5
Monga Nat Park NSW 30 E5
Mongarlowe NSW 30 E5
Mongers Lake WA 76 G6
Monkerai Nature Res NSW 23 C11
Monkey Mia WA 76 B2 78 K1
Monkeycot Nature Res NSW 23 B10
Monogorilby QLD 7 D9
Monomeith VIC 37 H11
Monsildale QLD 4 K1
Montacute SA 59 F7 60 F4
Montacute Con Park SA 60 F4
Montagu TAS 54 C2
Montagu Bay TAS 49 D4
Montagu Island TAS 54 C2
Montague WA 77 D9
Montague Island NSW 30 G6
Montague Island Nature Res NSW 30 G6
Montana TAS 55 G8
Monteagle NSW 22 J2 30 A1
Montebello Islands WA 78 D3
Montebello Islands Con Park WA 78 D3
Montefiores NSW 22 D4
Monterey NSW 19 H5 21 B9
Montesquieu Islands WA 81 A9
Montgomery Islands WA 80 D6
Monto QLD 7 A9 9 K11
Montumana TAS 54 D4
Montville QLD 4 F1 7 E12
Mooball NSW 7 J14 25 A14
Mooball Nat Park NSW 7 J13 25 A14
Moockra SA 62 F1 65 D10
Moodiarrup WA 73 C10
Moodlu QLD 4 F4
Moogara TAS 53 F9
Moogerah QLD 5 J13
Moogerah Peaks Nat Park QLD 5 J13
Moojeeba QLD 16 H4
Moolap VIC 36 G3
Mooloolaba QLD 4 D1 7 E13
Mooloolah QLD 4 F2
Mooloolah River Nat Park QLD 4 E1
Moolort VIC 39 C11
Moolpa NSW 28 H6 41 D10
Moomba SA 14 H2 67 E13
Moombooldool NSW 29 F12
Moombra QLD 4 K6
Moona Plains NSW 25 J10
Moonambel VIC 39 C9
Moonan Flat NSW 23 B9
Moonaran NSW 24 H7
Moonbah NSW 30 H2 43 D14
Moonbi NSW 25 J8
Moonda Lake QLD 12 K5 14 C3 67 A13
Moondarra VIC 44 D7 46 E1
Moondarra State Park VIC 44 D7 46 E1
Moondyne Nature Res WA 72 F2 74 B3 76 K5
Moonee Beach NSW 25 G13
Mooney Mooney NSW 20 C5
Moonford QLD 7 A9 9 K11
Moongobulla QLD 11 G14
Moonie QLD 7 G8
Moonlight Flat SA 64 E4
Moonta SA 62 H5 65 G8
Moonta Bay SA 62 H4 65 G8
Moonyoonooka WA 76 F3
Moora WA 74 A3 76 J5
Moorabbin VIC 35 F5 37 E8 39 G14 42 K2 44 C2
Moorabool VIC 36 F2
Mooralla VIC 38 D5
Moore QLD 7 F11
Moore Creek NSW 24 J7
Moore Park QLD 7 A12 9 K13
Moore River Nat Park WA 74 B2 76 J4
Moorebank NSW 19 G1 21 D9
Mooreee VIC 38 D3
Mooreville TAS 54 D5
Moorilim VIC 42 D3
Moorina TAS 55 E12
Moorine Rock WA 75 B8 77 J8
Moorland NSW 23 B13
Moorlands SA 63 D8 65 K11
Moorleah TAS 54 D4
Moormbool VIC 39 B14 42 E2
Moorooduc VIC 37 H8
Moorook SA 62 B5 65 H12
Moorooka QLD 3 G4
Mooroongga Island NT 87 C10
Mooroopna VIC 42 C3
Moorrinya Nat Park QLD 8 D2 13 B11
Moorumbine WA 72 A6
Moorundie Wildlife Park SA 65 H11
Moppin NSW 24 C5
Morago NSW 29 H8 41 F13
Moranbah QLD 8 E6
Morangarell NSW 22 J1 29 F14
Morans Crossing NSW 30 H4
Morawa WA 76 G5
Morayfield QLD 4 F5
Morchard SA 62 F1 65 E10
Mordalup WA 73 C14
Mordialloc VIC 35 H5 37 F8 39 G14 44 D2
Morea (Carpolac) VIC 38 B2
Moree NSW 24 D5
Morella QLD 13 E10
Moresby QLD 11 E13
Moreton Bay QLD 3 A6 4 C6 7 F13
Moreton Island QLD 4 B5 7 F13
Moreton Island Nat Park QLD 4 B5 7 F13
Moreton Telegraph Station QLD 16 E2
Morgan SA 62 D5 65 G11
Morgan Island NT 87 E11
Moriac VIC 36 H1 39 H11
Morialpa SA 65 D12
Morialta Con Park SA 59 F7 60 F3
Moriarty TAS 54 E7
Morisset NSW 20 B1 23 F10
Morisset Park NSW 20 B1
Morkalla VIC 28 F2 40 B2
Morley WA 71 D5
Morna Point NSW 23 E11
Morningside QLD 3 E5
Mornington VIC 36 H7 39 H14 44 E2
Mornington Island QLD 10 C3
Mornington Peninsula VIC 37 J8 39 H14 44 E2
Mornington Peninsula Nat Park VIC 36 K7 39 H13 44 F1
Morongla Creek NSW 22 H3
Morphett Vale SA 60 J1 61 C5 62 F7 65 J10
Morphettville SA 59 J3
Morri Morri VIC 38 B7
Morrisons VIC 36 C1 39 F11
Morse Island NT 85 A5 86 B6
Mortchup VIC 39 E9
Mortdale NSW 21 C9
Mortlake VIC 38 G7
Morton Nat Park NSW 30 C6
Morton Plains VIC 28 K5 40 J7
Morundah NSW 29 G11
Moruya NSW 30 F5
Moruya Heads NSW 30 F6
Morven NSW 29 J13
Morven QLD 6 D2
Morwell VIC 45 E8 46 F2
Morwell Nat Park VIC 45 F8 46 G2
Moselle QLD 11 K9 13 A9
Mosman NSW 19 E6 21 B8
Mosman Park WA 71 H1
Moss Vale NSW 22 K7 30 B6
Mossgiel NSW 29 D8
Mossiface VIC 43 K12 45 B14 46 D6
Mossman QLD 11 C12
Mossy Point NSW 30 F6
Moulamein NSW 28 H7 41 E11
Moule SA 64 C2 68 K7
Mount Aberdeen Nat Park QLD 8 B6
Mount Adolphus Island QLD 16 B2
Mount Alford QLD 5 J13
Mount Annan NSW 21 E11
Mount Arapiles-Tooan State Park VIC 38 B4
Mount Archer Nat Park QLD 9 H10
Mount Augustus (Burringurrah) Nat Park WA 78 H4 82 J2
Mount Barker SA 60 H5 62 E7 65 J10
Mount Barker WA 74 J6
Mount Barker Junction SA 60 H5
Mount Barkly NT 90 B6
Mount Barney Nat Park QLD 7 J12 25 A12
Mount Bauple Nat Park QLD 7 C12
Mount Baw Baw Alpine Village VIC 42 K6 44 B7 46 D1
Mount Beauty VIC 43 E10
Mount Benson SA 63 D12
Mount Beppo QLD 4 K5
Mount Boothby Con Park SA 63 D9
Mount Bryan SA 62 E3 65 F10
Mount Buangor State Park VIC 39 D8
Mount Buffalo Chalet VIC 43 E8
Mount Buffalo Nat Park VIC 43 E8
Mount Buller Alpine Village VIC 42 G7 46 A2
Mount Burnett VIC 37 E11
Mount Burr SA 63 B13
Mount Bute VIC 39 F9
Mount Camel VIC 39 B13 42 E1
Mount Carbine QLD 11 C12
Mount Catt NT 87 F9
Mount Chapple Island TAS 55 C8
Mount Christie Corner SA 66 J2 68 H7
Mount Christie Siding SA 66 K1 68 H7
Mount Claremont WA 71 F2
Mount Clunie Nat Park NSW 7 J12 25 A11
Mount Colah NSW 19 B4 20 C7
Mount Colosseum Nat Park QLD 9 J12
Mount Compass SA 61 F6 63 F8 65 K10
Mount Cook Nat Park QLD 11 A12 16 K6
Mount Coolon QLD 8 D5
Mount Coot-tha QLD 3 E2 5 F8
Mount Cotton QLD 5 D9
Mount Cottrell VIC 36 C5 39 F13
Mount Crosby QLD 5 G8
Mount Cuthbert Mine QLD 10 J4
Mount Damper SA 64 E4
Mount Dandenong VIC 37 D10
Mount Dangar QLD 8 B7
Mount David NSW 22 H5
Mount Direction TAS 55 E9 56 E4
Mount Dowling Nature Res NSW 30 F3
Mount Druitt NSW 21 F8
Mount Drummond SA 64 H5
Mount Duneed VIC 36 H3 39 H12
Mount Dutton SA 66 E5
Mount Ebenezer NT 90 H6
Mount Eccles VIC 44 F6
Mount Eccles Nat Park VIC 38 G4
Mount Eckersley VIC 38 G4
Mount Egerton VIC 36 B1 39 E11
Mount Eliza VIC 37 G8 39 H14 44 E2
Mount Emu VIC 39 E9
Mount Ernest Island QLD 16 A2
Mount Etna Caves Nat Park QLD 9 G10
Mount Field Nat Park TAS 53 E8
Mount Fitton SA 67 J11
Mount Frankland Nat Park WA 74 J5
Mount Gambier SA 38 F1 63 B14
Mount Garnet QLD 11 E12
Mount George NSW 23 B12
Mount Gipps NSW 26 J2 28 A2
Mount Glorious QLD 4 G6
Mount Granya State Park VIC 29 K13 43 B10
Mount Gravatt QLD 3 G5 5 E8
Mount Grenfell Historic Site NSW 27 H9
Mount Gunson Mine SA 65 B8
Mount Hawthorn WA 71 E3
Mount Helen VIC 39 E10
Mount Hill SA 64 G6
Mount Hope NSW 29 C10
Mount Hope SA 64 G5
Mount Hope Res VIC 41 H11
Mount Hunter NSW 21 F11
Mount Hyland Nature Res NSW 25 F11
Mount Hypipamee Nat Park QLD 11 E12
Mount Ida WA 77 F10
Mount Imlay Nat Park NSW 30 K4 47 A13
Mount Irvine NSW 20 K6
Mount Isa QLD 10 K3 12 A3
Mount Jerusalem Nat Park NSW 7 J13 25 B14
Mount Kaputar Nat Park NSW 24 F6
Mount Keith Mine WA 77 C10
Mount Kelly Mine QLD 10 J3
Mount Kokeby WA 72 B4
Mount Kororoit VIC 36 B5
Mount Kuring-gai NSW 19 A5 20 D6
Mount Larcom QLD 9 H11
Mount Lawley WA 71 F4
Mount Lawson State Park VIC 29 K13 43 B11
Mount Leura Con Park QLD 8 H6
Mount Leyson Mine QLD 8 B4 11 J14
Mount Liebig NT 90 E4
Mount Lion NSW 25 A13
Mount Lloyd TAS 50 C1 53 F9
Mount Lonarch VIC 39 D9
Mount Macedon VIC 39 D13
Mount Magnet WA 76 E7
Mount Magnificent Con Park SA 61 F7
Mount Manning Nature Res WA 77 G9
Mount Margaret WA 77 F12 83 D1
Mount Martha VIC 36 H7 39 H14 44 E1
Mount Mary SA 62 D5 65 G11
Mount Mee QLD 4 G4
Mount Mercer VIC 39 F10
Mount Molloy QLD 11 C12
Mount Morgan QLD 9 H10
Mount Morgans WA 77 F12 83 D1
Mount Moriac VIC 36 H1
Mount Mort QLD 5 K11
Mount Napier State Park VIC 38 G5
Mount Nathan QLD 5 C12
Mount Nebo QLD 4 G7
Mount Neville Nature Res NSW 25 D12
Mount Nothofagus Nat Park NSW 25 A12
Mount O'Connell Nat Park QLD 9 G9
Mount Olive NSW 23 D9
Mount Ommaney QLD 3 G2
Mount Ossa QLD 9 D8
Mount Oxide Mine QLD 10 H3
Mount Perry QLD 7 B10
Mount Pikapene Nat Park NSW 7 K12 25 C12
Mount Pleasant QLD 4 G5
Mount Pleasant SA 60 E7 62 E6 65 J10
Mount Pleasant WA 71 H3
Mount Pritchard NSW 19 G1 21 E9
Mount Remarkable Nat Park SA 62 G2 65 E9
Mount Rescue Con Park SA 63 B9
Mount Richmond Nat Park VIC 38 H3
Mount Royal Nat Park NSW 23 C9
Mount Russell NSW 24 E7
Mount Samaria State Park VIC 42 F6
Mount Samson QLD 4 G6
Mount Scott Con Park SA 63 C11
Mount Seaview NSW 23 A11 25 K10
Mount Selwyn NSW 30 F1 43 A14
Mount Seymour TAS 53 D11
Mount Shaugh Con Park SA 28 K1 40 H1 63 A9
Mount Stirling Alpine Resort VIC 42 G7 46 A2
Mount Surprise QLD 11 F11
Mount Tamborine QLD 5 D12
Mount Tarampa QLD 5 K8
Mount Taylor VIC 43 K11 45 B13 46 D6
Mount Torrens SA 60 F6 62 E7 65 J10
Mount Vernon NSW 21 F9
Mount Victoria NSW 22 G7
Mount Walker QLD 5 J11
Mount Wallace VIC 36 C2 39 F12
Mount Walsh Nat Park QLD 7 C11
Mount Warning Nat Park NSW 7 J13 25 A13
Mount Waverley VIC 35 E6
Mount Webb Nat Park QLD 11 A12 16 J6
Mount Wedge SA 64 F5
Mount White NSW 20 D4
Mount William Nat Park TAS 55 D14
Mount Wilson NSW 20 K7 22 G7
Mount Worth State Park VIC 44 E6
Mountain Creek NSW 29 J13 43 A10
Mountain Creek QLD 4 E1
Mountain River TAS 50 E3 53 G10
Mountain View VIC 37 H14
Moura QLD 9 K9
Mourilyan QLD 11 E13
Mourilyan Harbour QLD 11 E13
Moutajup VIC 38 E5
Mowanjum WA 79 A10 80 G6
Mowbray TAS 56 G5
Mowbray Park NSW 21 G12
Mowen WA 73 J12
Moyarra VIC 37 K13
Moyhu VIC 42 D7
Moyston VIC 38 D7
Muchea WA 72 F2 74 C3 76 K5
Muckadilla QLD 6 E4
Muckatah VIC 29 K10 42 A4
Mud Island QLD 4 C7
Mud Island VIC 36 H6
Mudamuckla SA 64 D3
Mudgee NSW 22 D5
Mudgeeraba QLD 5 C13 7 H13
Mudgegonga VIC 43 D8
Mudjarn Nature Res NSW 30 D1
Mudludja WA 79 B12 81 H9
Muiron Islands WA 78 F2
Mukinbudin WA 74 A7 76 J7
Mulan WA 79 D13
Mulanggari ACT 32 B5
Mulbring NSW 23 E10
Mulcra VIC 28 H2 40 E2
Mulga Bore SA 68 B5
Mulgildie QLD 7 A9 9 K11
Mulgoa NSW 21 G9
Mulgowrie NSW 22 J4 30 A3
Mulgrave NSW 20 F7
Mulgrave VIC 37 E9
Mullaley NSW 24 J5
Mullaloo WA 71 A1 72 G2 74 C2 76 K4
Mullalyup WA 73 F11
Mullaway NSW 25 F13
Mullengandra Village NSW 29 K13 43 A10
Mullengudgery NSW 27 J13
Mullewa WA 76 F4
Mulline WA 77 G10
Mullion Creek NSW 22 F4
Mullumbimby NSW 7 J13 25 B14
Mulpata SA 62 B7 65 K12
Mulurulu Lake NSW 28 C6
Mulwala NSW 29 K11 42 A6
Mulyandry NSW 22 G2 29 D14
Mulyati NT 79 J14 83 A7
Mumballup WA 73 F10 74 G3
Mumbannar VIC 38 G2
Mumberkine WA 72 D1
Mumbil NSW 22 D4
Mumbleberry Lake QLD 12 G2
Mummel Gulf Nat Park NSW 23 A11 25 K9
Mummulgum NSW 7 K12 25 C12
Mumu QLD 13 A10
Mundaring WA 72 F3 74 C3 76 K5
Mundaring Weir WA 72 E3
Mundarlo NSW 29 H14
Munderoo NSW 29 K14 43 A12
Mundijong WA 72 F5 74 D3
Mundiwindi WA 78 H7 82 H7
Mundoona VIC 42 B3
Mundoonen Nature Res NSW 30 C3
Mundoora SA 62 G3 65 F9
Mundowey NSW 24 H7
Mundrabilla WA 83 F6
Mundrabilla Motel WA 83 G6
Mundubbera QLD 7 B9
Mundulla SA 40 K1 63 B10
Mungalawurru NT 89 G8
Mungallala QLD 6 D3
Mungana QLD 11 D11
Mungar QLD 7 C12
Mungaroona Range Nature Res WA 78 F5 82 E4
Mungerannie Roadhouse SA 67 E10
Mungeriba NSW 22 C2 29 A14
Mungeribar NSW 27 K14
Munghorn Gap Nature Res NSW 22 D6
Mungindi NSW 6 K5 24 C3
Mungkan Kandju Nat Park QLD 16 G3
Munglinup WA 75 G11
Mungo Brush NSW 23 D12
Mungo Nat Park NSW 28 E5
Mungunburra QLD 8 B3 11 K13
Mungungo QLD 7 A9 9 K11
Munjina (Auski) Roadhouse WA 78 F5 82 F5
Munmorah State Rec Area NSW 20 A1 23 F10
Munno Para SA 60 C3
Munro VIC 43 K9 45 C11 46 E4
Muntadgin WA 74 C7 77 K8
Muntz Nature Res WA 75 G14 83 J2
Munyaroo Con Park SA 62 J3 65 F8
Muogamarra Nature Res NSW 20 D6
Muradup WA 73 B12
Muralug QLD 16 B2
Murarrie QLD 3 E6
Murbko SA 62 D5 65 H11
Murcheboluc VIC 36 G1
Murchison VIC 42 D3
Murchison East VIC 42 D3
Murchison Roadhouse WA 76 C4
Murdinga SA 64 G5
Murdoch WA 71 J3
Murdunna TAS 51 E13 53 G12
Muresk WA 72 C2
Murga NSW 22 F3
Murgenella NT 85 A7 86 B6
Murgon QLD 7 D11
Murninnie SA 62 H3 65 F8
Muronbung NSW 22 C4
Murphys Creek QLD 7 G11
Murra Warra VIC 40 K5
Murrabit VIC 28 J7 41 G11
Murradoc VIC 36 G5
Murramarang Nat Park NSW 30 E6
Murrami NSW 29 F11
Murrawal NSW 22 A5 24 K4
Murray Bridge SA 62 D7 65 J11
Murray River Nat Park SA 28 F1 62 B6 65 H13
Murray – Sunset Nat Park VIC 28 G2 40 D3 62 A6 65 J14
Murray Town SA 62 G2 65 E9
Murray-Kulkyne Park VIC 28 G4 40 C6
Murrayville VIC 28 J2 40 F2 63 A8 65 K14
Murrigal QLD 11 F13
Murrin Bridge NSW 29 C11
Murrindal VIC 43 H13 47 B8
Murrindindi VIC 42 H4

Ottoway – Quarram Nature Res 105

Ottoway SA 59 D2
Otway Nat Park VIC 39 K10
Ourimbah NSW 20 B3 23 F10
Ournie NSW 29 K14 43 A12
Ouse TAS 53 D8
Outer Harbor SA 59 B2 60 E1 62 F6 65 J10
Outer Sister Island TAS 55 A9
Ouyen VIC 28 H4 40 E5
Ovens VIC 43 D8
Overland Corner SA 62 B5 65 H12
Overland Telegraph Station Reserve NT 89 G9
Overlander Roadhouse WA 76 C3 78 K2
Owen SA 62 F5 65 H10
Owens Gap NSW 23 B8
Owingup Nature Res WA 74 K4
Oxenford QLD 5 C11
Oxford Falls NSW 19 C6 20 B7
Oxley ACT 32 H3
Oxley NSW 28 F7 41 A11
Oxley QLD 3 G2 5 F9
Oxley VIC 42 D7
Oxley Island NT 86 A6
Oxley Wild Rivers Nat Park NSW 25 J10
Oyster Bay NSW 21 C10
Oyster Cove TAS 50 G4 53 H10
Ozenkadnook VIC 38 B3

P

Pacific Palms NSW 23 D12
Packsaddle NSW 26 F3
Padbury WA 71 B2
Paddington NSW 18 D3 21 B8
Paddington QLD 3 E3
Paddington Siding WA 77 H11 83 F1
Paddys Ranges State Park VIC 39 C10
Paddys River NSW 22 K7 30 B6
Padstow NSW 19 H3 21 D9
Padstow Heights NSW 19 H3
Padthaway SA 63 B11
Padthaway Con Park SA 63 B11
Page ACT 32 C3
Pagewood NSW 21 B9
Pago Mission WA 81 A11
Paignie VIC 28 H3 40 E5
Pains Island QLD 10 D3
Pakenham VIC 37 F11 44 D4
Pakenham South VIC 37 G11
Pakenham Upper VIC 37 F11
Palana TAS 55 A8
Palarang NSW 30 J3
Palgarup WA 73 E13
Pallamallawa NSW 24 D6
Pallamana SA 62 E7 65 J11
Pallara QLD 3 J3
Pallarang VIC 28 H2 40 E2
Pallarenda QLD 8 A5 11 H14
Pallarup Nature Res WA 75 F9
Palm Beach NSW 20 B5 23 G9
Palm Beach QLD 5 A13
Palm Cove QLD 11 D13
Palm Grove NSW 20 C3
Palmdale NSW 20 C3
Palmer SA 62 E7 65 J11
Palmer River Roadhouse QLD 11 C11
Palmers Oakey NSW 22 F6
Palmerston ACT 32 B5
Palmerston NT 85 C2 86 D3
Palmgrove Nat Park QLD 6 A6 9 K8
Palmview QLD 4 E1
Palmwoods QLD 4 F1
Palmyra WA 71 J2
Paloona TAS 54 E7
Paluma QLD 11 G13
Paluma Range Nat Park QLD 11 G13
Palumpa NT 86 G2
Pambula NSW 30 J5 47 A14
Pambula Beach NSW 30 J5 47 A14
Pandanus Park WA 79 B10 80 H4
Pandappa Con Park SA 62 E3 65 F11
Panitya VIC 28 H1 40 F1
Panmure VIC 38 H7
Pannawonica WA 78 F3 82 E1
Pannikin Island QLD 5 C9
Panorama SA 59 J4
Pantijan WA 81 E8
Panton Hill VIC 37 B9 42 J3 44 A3
Paper Beach TAS 55 E9 56 E4
Pappinbarra NSW 23 A12 25 K11
Papunya NT 90 E5
Para Hills SA 59 C5 60 E3
Para Vista SA 59 D6
Paraburdoo WA 78 G4 82 G3
Parachilna SA 65 B10
Paracombe SA 60 F4
Paradise SA 59 E6
Paradise TAS 54 F7
Paradise Beach VIC 45 E12 46 F5
Paradise Point QLD 5 B11
Parafield SA 59 C5 60 E2
Parafield Gardens SA 59 C4
Paralowie SA 59 B4
Parap NT 84 D2
Paraparap VIC 36 H2
Paratoo SA 62 D1 65 E11
Parattah TAS 53 D11
Parawa SA 61 J4
Pardoo Roadhouse WA 78 D6 82 D6
Parenna TAS 54 B6
Parham SA 62 G5 65 H9
Parilla SA 63 B8 65 K13
Paringa SA 28 F1 62 A5 65 H13
Paris Creek SA 60 K4
Park Holme SA 59 J3 60 G2 61 A5
Park Orchards VIC 35 C7
Park Ridge QLD 5 E10
Parkes ACT 31 C3 32 E5
Parkes NSW 22 F2 29 C14
Parkham TAS 55 F8
Parkhurst QLD 9 H10
Parkinson QLD 3 J4
Parkside SA 58 D3 59 G4 60 G2 61 A6
Parkville NSW 23 B9
Parkwood QLD 5 B12
Parkwood WA 71 J5
Parma NSW 30 C6
Parnabal QLD 9 H8
Parndana SA 63 J9
Parnngurr (Cotton Creek) WA 79 G9
Paroo Siding WA 77 C9 78 K6
Parrakie SA 63 C8 65 K12
Parramatta NSW 19 E2 21 D8 23 H9
Parrawe TAS 54 E4
Parry Lagoons Nature Res WA 81 D13
Parsons Beach SA 62 H6 65 J8
Partridge Island TAS 53 J10
Paru NT 85 A1 86 C3
Paruna SA 28 G1 62 B6 65 J13
Parwan VIC 36 C3 39 F12
Pascoe Vale VIC 36 C7
Paskeville SA 62 G4 65 G9
Pasminco Century Mine QLD 10 G2
Passage Island TAS 55 A14
Pastoria VIC 39 D13
Pata SA 62 B6 65 H13
Patchewollock VIC 28 J4 40 F5
Pateena TAS 55 G10 56 J5
Paterson NSW 23 D10
Patersonia TAS 55 F10 56 F6
Patho VIC 29 K8 41 H12
Patonga NSW 20 C5
Patterson Lakes VIC 37 F9
Paupong NSW 30 H2
Paupong Nature Res NSW 30 H2
Paw Paw SA 68 C5
Pawleena TAS 51 A9 53 F11
Pawtella TAS 53 C11 55 K11
Payne QLD 8 G1 13 E10
Payneham SA 59 F5 60 F3
Paynes Crossing NSW 23 E9
Paynes Find WA 76 G7
Paynesville VIC 45 C13 46 E6
Peachester QLD 4 F2
Peak Charles Nat Park WA 75 E12
Peak Creek Siding SA 66 E5
Peak Crossing QLD 5 H11
Peak Downs Mine QLD 8 F7
Peak Hill NSW 22 D2
Peak Hill WA 77 A8 78 J5
Peak Range Nat Park QLD 8 F6
Peak View NSW 30 F4
Peake SA 63 C8 65 K12
Peakhurst NSW 19 H3
Pearce ACT 32 G3
Pearcedale VIC 37 G9 44 E2
Pearl Beach NSW 20 B5
Pearsall WA 71 B3
Pearshape TAS 54 C6
Pearson Isles SA 64 G3
Peats Ridge NSW 20 D3 23 F9
Pebbly Beach NSW 30 E6
Pedirka SA 66 B5
Peebinga SA 28 H1 40 D1 62 A7 65 J13
Peebinga Con Park SA 28 H1 40 E1 62 A7 65 J13
Peechelba VIC 42 B6
Peel NSW 22 F5
Peel Island QLD 5 B8
Peelwood NSW 22 J5 30 A4
Peerabeelup WA 73 G14
Peery Lake NSW 26 F6
Peery Nat Park NSW 26 F6
Pegarah TAS 54 B6
Pekina SA 62 F2 65 E10
Peko Mine NT 89 H9
Pelham TAS 53 E9
Pelican Waters QLD 4 E2
Pella VIC 40 H4
Pelorus Island QLD 11 G14
Pelsaert Group WA 76 F2
Pelverata TAS 50 G3 53 G10
Pemberton WA 73 F14 74 J3
Pembroke NSW 23 A13 25 K12
Penarie NSW 28 F6 41 B9
Pencil Pine TAS 54 G5
Pender Bay WA 79 A9 80 F4
Penfield SA 60 C2
Penguin TAS 54 D6
Penguin Island WA 72 G5
Penna TAS 51 B8 53 F11
Pennant Hills NSW 19 C3 20 D7
Penneshaw SA 63 G8 65 K9
Penola SA 38 E1 63 B13
Penong SA 64 C1 68 K6
Penrice SA 60 A7
Penrith NSW 21 G8 23 H8
Penshurst VIC 38 F6
Pental Island VIC 41 F10
Pentland QLD 8 C3 11 K12 13 A12
Penwortham SA 62 F4 65 G10
Penzance TAS 51 F13
Peppermint Grove WA 71 G2
Peppers Plains VIC 40 J5
Peppimenarti NT 86 G2
Peranga QLD 7 F10
Percival Lakes WA 79 E10
Percy Isles Nat Park QLD 9 E10
Perekerten NSW 28 H7 41 D10
Perenjori WA 76 G5
Perenna VIC 40 J4
Perforated Island SA 64 H4
Pericoe NSW 30 K4 47 A13
Perisher NSW 30 G1 43 D14
Perkins Island TAS 54 C2
Pernatty Lagoon SA 65 B8
Peron Island North NT 86 E2
Peron Island South NT 86 E2
Perponda SA 62 C7 65 J12
Perth TAS 55 G10 56 J5
Perth WA 71 F4 72 G3 74 C3 76 K4
Perth CBD WA 70
Perthville NSW 22 G5
Petcheys Bay TAS 50 J2 53 H9
Peterborough SA 62 E2 65 E10
Peterborough VIC 38 J7
Peterhead SA 59 D2
Peters Island QLD 8 A6
Petersville SA 62 G5 65 H9
Petford QLD 11 E12
Petina SA 64 D3
Petrie QLD 4 F6 7 F13
Petrie Terrace QLD 2 B1
Pettavel VIC 36 H2
Pheasant Creek VIC 42 H3
Pheasants Nest NSW 23 J8 30 A7
Phegans Bay NSW 20 C5
Phillip ACT 32 F4
Phillip Bay NSW 21 B9
Phillip Island VIC 37 K9 39 J14 44 F2
Phillott QLD 15 H13
Phils Creek NSW 22 J4 30 A3
Phosphate Hill Mine QLD 12 C4
Piallamore NSW 25 J8
Piallaway NSW 24 J6
Pialligo ACT 32 E6
Piambie VIC 28 G5 41 D8
Piangil VIC 28 H5 41 E9
Piangil West VIC 41 E8
Piccadilly SA 59 J7 60 G4
Piccaninnie Ponds Con Park SA 38 G1 63 B14
Pickanjinnie QLD 6 E5
Pickering Brook WA 72 F4
Pickertaramoor NT 85 A2 86 C3
Picnic Point NSW 29 K9 41 H14 42 A2
Picola VIC 41 H14 42 A2
Picton NSW 21 F12 23 J8 30 A7
Picton WA 73 G9 74 F3
Piedmont VIC 37 E14
Piednippie SA 64 E3
Pielegia NT 88 F3
Pieman River State Res TAS 54 G3
Pier Millan VIC 28 H4 40 E7
Piesseville WA 73 A9 74 F5
Pigeon Hole NT 88 C4
Pigeon Ponds VIC 38 D4
Piggabeen NSW 5 B14
Pikedale QLD 7 J10 25 B9
Pilakatal NT 90 J2
Pilgna SA 68 C3
Pilkinga SA 68 C4
Pillar Valley NSW 25 E13
Pilliga NSW 24 G2
Pilliga Nature Res NSW 24 H4
Pimba SA 64 B7
Pimpama QLD 5 C11
Pimpinio VIC 38 A5
Pinchgut Junction VIC 36 K1
Pindar WA 76 E4
Pine Clump NSW 24 K1 27 H14
Pine Corner SA 62 K4 64 F6
Pine Creek NT 85 G4 86 F5
Pine Gap NT 91 F8
Pine Hill QLD 8 H5 13 F14
Pine Lodge VIC 42 C4
Pine Peak Island QLD 9 E10
Pine Point SA 62 G6 65 H9
Pine Ridge NSW 23 A8 24 K6
Pinery SA 62 F5 65 H10
Piney Range NSW 22 H2 29 E14
Pingaring WA 74 E7
Pingelly WA 72 B6 74 E5
Pingrup WA 74 G7
Pinjarra WA 72 G6 74 E3
Pinjarra Hills QLD 3 G1
Pinjarrega Nature Res WA 76 H4
Pink Lakes State Park VIC 65 J14
Pinkawillinie Con Park SA 64 E5
Pinkawillinie Con Res SA 64 E5
Pinkenba QLD 3 D6
Pinnacle QLD 8 D7
Pinnaroo SA 28 H1 40 F1 63 A8 65 K13
Pioneer TAS 55 D13
Pioneer WA 75 C13 77 K11 83 G1
Pioneer Bay VIC 37 J11
Pipalyatjara SA 68 A1 79 K14 83 B7 90 K1
Pipers Brook TAS 55 D10 56 C6
Pipers River TAS 55 D9 56 C4
Pipon Island QLD 16 H5
Piries VIC 42 G6 46 A1
Pirlangimpi NT 86 B3
Pirlta VIC 28 F3 40 B4
Pirrinuan QLD 7 F9
Pirron Yallock VIC 39 H9
Pirrulpakalarintja NT 90 J3
Pitalu NT 79 J14 90 J2
Pitarpunga Lake NSW 28 F6 41 B9
Pitfield VIC 39 F9
Pithara WA 76 H5
Pitt Town NSW 20 F6
Pitt Water TAS 51 D8
Pittong VIC 39 E9
Pittsworth QLD 7 G10
Plainland QLD 5 K9
Planchonella Nature Res NSW 24 C7
Platts NSW 30 J3 47 A12
Pleasant Hills NSW 29 J12
Plenty TAS 50 A1 53 F9
Plenty VIC 35 A5 37 B8 39 E14 42 J2 44 B2
Plumpton NSW 21 F8
Plumridge Lakes WA 83 E4
Plumridge Lakes Nature Res WA 83 E4
Plympton SA 59 H3 60 G1 61 A5
Plympton Park SA 59 H3
Pmara Jutunta NT 90 C7
Poatina TAS 53 A9 55 H9
Poeppel Corner NT QLD SA 12 K2 67 A9 91 K14
Point Bell Con Res SA 64 D1 68 K6
Point Clare NSW 20 C4
Point Cook VIC 36 E6 39 F13 42 K1
Point Davenport Con Park SA 62 H7 65 J8
Point Denison WA 76 G3
Point Leo VIC 37 K8 39 H14 44 F2
Point Lonsdale VIC 36 H5 39 H13
Point Lookout QLD 4 A7 7 G14
Point Pass SA 62 E5 65 G10
Point Samson WA 78 E4 82 C2
Point Souttar SA 62 J6 65 J8
Point Stuart Coastal Res NT 85 B4 86 C5
Point Turton SA 62 H7 65 J8
Pokataroo NSW 24 D2
Police Point TAS 50 K2 53 H9
Policemans Point SA 63 D9
Poltalloch SA 63 E8 65 K11
Pomborneit VIC 39 H9
Pomborneit North VIC 39 H9
Pomona QLD 7 D12
Pomonal VIC 38 D7
Pompapiel VIC 41 K11
Pontville TAS 53 E10
Poochera SA 64 E4
Pooginagoric SA 38 A1 40 K1
Pooginook Con Park SA 62 C5 65 G12
Poolaijelo VIC 38 D2
Poolawanna No. 1 Oil Well SA 67 B9
Poole TAS 55 C14
Poona QLD 7 C13
Poona Nat Park QLD 7 C12
Pooncarie NSW 28 D4
Poonindie SA 64 H6
Pooraka SA 59 D5 60 E3
Pootilla VIC 39 E11
Pootnoura SA 66 F3
Poowong VIC 37 J13 44 E5
Poowong East VIC 37 J14 44 E5
Poowong North VIC 37 J13
Popanyinning WA 72 B6 74 E5
Popiltah Lake NSW 28 C3
Popran Nat Park NSW 20 D4 23 F9
Porcupine Gorge Nat Park QLD 8 C1 11 K11
Porepunkah VIC 43 E9
Pormpuraaw QLD 10 A6 16 J1
Porongurup WA 74 J6
Porongurup Nat Park WA 74 J6
Porphyry Mine WA 77 G12 83 E1
Port Adelaide SA 59 E2 60 E1 62 F6 65 J10
Port Albert VIC 45 G9 46 H3
Port Alma QLD 9 H11
Port Arthur TAS 51 H12 53 H12
Port Augusta SA 62 H1 65 D9
Port Botany NSW 19 H6
Port Broughton SA 62 G3 65 F9
Port Campbell VIC 39 J8
Port Campbell Nat Park VIC 39 J8
Port Clinton Con Park SA 62 G5 65 G9
Port Davis SA 62 G3 65 F9
Port Douglas QLD 11 C12
Port Elliot SA 61 J7 63 F8 65 K10
Port Fairy VIC 38 H5
Port Fairy – Warrnambool Coastal Park VIC 38 H6
Port Franklin VIC 44 H7 46 H1
Port Gawler SA 60 C1 62 F6 65 J9
Port Gawler Con Park SA 60 C1
Port Germein SA 62 G2 65 E9
Port Gibbon SA 62 K4 64 G7
Port Hacking NSW 19 K4
Port Hedland WA 78 D5 82 B4
Port Hughes SA 62 H5 65 G8
Port Huon TAS 50 H1 53 H9
Port Jackson NSW 19 E7
Port Julia SA 62 G6 65 H9
Port Kembla NSW 21 C14 23 K8 30 B7
Port Kenny SA 64 E4
Port Latta TAS 54 C3
Port Lincoln SA 64 J6
Port MacDonnell SA 38 G1 63 B14
Port Macquarie NSW 23 A13 25 K12
Port Melbourne VIC 35 D3
Port Minlacowie SA 62 H6 65 J8
Port Moorowie SA 62 H7 65 J8
Port Neill SA 64 G6
Port Noarlunga SA 60 K1 61 D5 62 F7 65 J10
Port Phillip Bay VIC 36 F6 39 G13 44 D1
Port Pirie SA 62 G2 65 F9
Port Rickaby SA 62 H6 65 H8
Port Roper NT 87 H10
Port Sorell TAS 55 E8
Port Stewart QLD 16 H4
Port Victoria SA 62 H6 65 H8
Port Vincent SA 62 G6 65 J9
Port Wakefield SA 62 G5 65 H9
Port Welshpool VIC 45 H8 46 H2
Port Willunga SA 61 E5
Portarlington VIC 36 G5 39 G13
Porters Retreat NSW 22 H6
Portland NSW 22 F6
Portland VIC 38 H4
Portland Bay VIC 38 H4
Portland Roads QLD 16 E4
Portsea VIC 36 J5 39 H13
Possession Island Nat Park QLD 16 B2
Potato Point NSW 30 G5
Potts Point NSW 18 B4
Pottsville NSW 7 J14 25 A14
Pound Creek VIC 44 G5
Powelltown VIC 37 D13 42 K5 44 C5
Powers Creek VIC 38 D2
Powlathanga QLD 8 B4 11 J13
Powlett Plains VIC 41 K10
Poynter Island QLD 9 E9
Prahran VIC 35 E4 37 D8
Prairie QLD 8 C1 11 K11 13 A11
Prairie VIC 41 K12
Precipice Nat Park QLD 6 B7
Premaydena TAS 51 G11 53 G12
Premer NSW 22 A6 24 K5
Preolenna TAS 54 D4
Prescott Lakes WA 79 E11
Preservation Island TAS 55 A13
Preston TAS 54 E6
Preston VIC 35 B4 36 C7
Preston Beach WA 72 H7 74 E2
Pretty Beach NSW 20 B5
Pretty Gully NSW 25 B11
Pretty Pine NSW 29 J8 41 F13
Prevelly WA 73 K12 74 H1
Price SA 62 G5 65 H9
Priestdale QLD 3 H6
Prime Seal Island TAS 55 B8
Primrose Sands TAS 51 D10 53 G12
Prince of Wales Island QLD 16 B1
Prince Regent Nature Res WA 81 D8
Princess Charlotte Bay QLD 16 H4
Princetown VIC 39 K8
Princhester QLD 9 G9
Priors Pocket QLD 3 H1
Priory TAS 55 E14
Probable Island NT 87 C11
Propodollah VIC 40 K3
Proserpine QLD 8 C7
Prospect NSW 19 E1 21 E8
Prospect SA 59 F4 60 F2
Prospect TAS 56 H5
Proston QLD 7 D10
Prubi QLD 13 C9
Prudhoe Island QLD 9 D9
Pucawan NSW 29 F13
Puckapunyal VIC 39 C14 42 F2
Pudman Creek NSW 22 K4 30 B3
Pukatja (Ernabella) SA 90 K6
Pullabooka NSW 22 G1 29 E14
Pullen Island SA 61 J7
Pullen Island Con Park SA 61 J7
Pullenvale QLD 5 F8
Pulletop NSW 29 J13
Pulletop Nature Res NSW 29 E10
Pullut VIC 40 J5
Pumphreys Bridge WA 72 C6
Punchbowl NSW 19 G3 21 C9
Punmu WA 79 F9
Punthari SA 62 D6 65 J11
Pura Pura VIC 39 F8
Pureba Con Park SA 64 C3
Pureba Con Res SA 64 C3 68 K7
Purfleet NSW 23 B12
Purga QLD 5 H10
Purlewaugh NSW 24 K4
Purnim VIC 38 H7
Purnong SA 62 D6 65 J11
Purnululu Con Res WA 79 B14 81 H13
Purnululu Nat Park WA 79 B14 81 G13
Purrumbete South VIC 39 H8
Puta Puta NT 90 H2
Putaputa SA 68 A1 90 K2
Putty NSW 20 J1 23 E8
Pyalong VIC 39 C13 42 G1
Pyap SA 62 B6 65 H13
Pyengana TAS 55 E13
Pygery SA 64 E5
Pymble NSW 19 C5 20 C7
Pymurra QLD 10 K5 12 A5
Pyramid Hill VIC 28 K7 41 J11
Pyramul NSW 22 E5

Q

Quaama NSW 30 H5
Quail Island NT 86 D3
Quail Island QLD 9 F9
Quail Island VIC 37 H10 44 E3
Quairading WA 72 A3 74 C5 76 K6
Quakers Hill NSW 21 E8
Qualco SA 62 C5 65 G12
Qualeup WA 73 C11
Quambatook VIC 28 K6 41 H9
Quambone NSW 27 C14
Quamby QLD 10 K5
Quamby Brook TAS 55 G8 56 J1
Quanda Nature Res NSW 27 J12
Quandialla NSW 22 H1 29 E14
Quangallin WA 73 A9
Quantong VIC 38 B5
Quarram Nature Res WA 74 K4

Ventnor – William Bay Nat Park 109

Ventnor VIC 37 K9 39 J14 44 F2
Venus Bay SA 64 F4
Venus Bay VIC 44 G5
Venus Bay Con Park SA 64 F3
Venus Bay Con Res SA 64 E3
Verdun SA 60 H4
Veresdale QLD 5 F12
Vermont VIC 37 D9
Verona NSW 30 H5
Verona Sands TAS 53 H10
Verran SA 64 G6
Vervale VIC 37 G12
Victor Harbor SA 61 J6 63 F8 65 K10
Victoria Park WA 71 G4
Victoria Point QLD 5 C9
Victoria River NT 86 J4 88 A4
Victoria Rock Nature Res WA 75 B11 77 J10
Victoria Valley TAS 53 D8 55 K8
Victoria Valley VIC 38 E6
Victory Well SA 68 C5
Villawood NSW 19 F2
Villeneuve QLD 4 H3
Vincentia NSW 30 D7
Vineyard NSW 20 F7
Vinifera VIC 28 H6 41 E9
Violet Town VIC 42 D4
Virginia QLD 3 C5
Virginia SA 60 C2 62 F6 65 H10
Vista SA 59 D7
Vite Vite VIC 39 F8
Vite Vite North VIC 39 F9
Vivonne SA 63 J9
Vivonne Bay Con Park SA 63 J9
Vokes Hill Corner SA 68 E3

W

Waaia VIC 42 B3
Waarre VIC 39 J8
Wabba Wilderness Park VIC 43 C11
Wabma Kadarbu Mound Springs Con Park SA 66 H7
Wacol QLD 3 H1 5 F9
Wadbilliga NSW 30 G4
Waddamana TAS 53 C8 55 K8
Waddi NSW 29 G10
Waddikee SA 64 F6
Wadeye NT 86 G1
Waeel WA 72 B2
Wagaman NT 84 B3
Wagant VIC 28 H4 40 E6
Wagerup WA 72 F7
Wagga Wagga NSW 29 H13
Waggabundi QLD 10 H3
Waggarandall VIC 42 C5
Wagin WA 73 A9 74 F5
Wagonga NSW 30 G5
Wahgunyah VIC 42 B7
Wahgunyah Con Res SA 68 K5
Wahroonga NSW 19 C4 20 C7
Waikerie SA 62 C5 65 H12
Wail VIC 38 A5
Wairewa VIC 43 K13 47 D8
Waitchie VIC 28 J5 41 F8
Waite Creek Settlement NT 90 D3
Waitpinga SA 61 J5 63 F8 65 K10
Waitpinga Con Park SA 61 J3
Wakool NSW 29 J8 41 F12
Walalkarra SA 68 C4
Walang NSW 22 G6
Walbundrie NSW 29 J12
Walcha NSW 25 J9
Walcha Road NSW 25 J8
Waldegrave Island Con Park SA 64 F4
Walebing WA 74 A3 76 J5
Walga Gunya WA 77 C8
Walgett NSW 24 F1 27 E14
Walgoolan WA 74 B7 77 J8
Walhalla VIC 45 C8 46 E2
Walitjara SA 68 A3 90 K3
Walka NT 79 J14 83 A7 90 H1
Walkamin QLD 11 D12
Walkaway WA 76 F3
Walker VIC 37 A14
Walker Flat SA 62 D6 65 J11
Walker Island TAS 52 K7 54 B2
Walkers Crossing SA 67 D12
Walkerston QLD 9 D8
Walkerville SA 59 F4 60 F2
Walkerville North VIC 44 H6
Walkerville South VIC 44 J6
Wall SA 62 D7 65 J11
Walla Walla NSW 29 J12
Wallabadah NSW 23 A8 24 K7
Wallabadah Nature Res NSW 23 A9 24 K7
Wallabi Group WA 76 F2
Wallabrook SA 38 B1 63 B11
Wallaby Island QLD 10 A6 16 G1
Wallace VIC 39 E11
Wallace Rockhole NT 90 G7
Wallacedale North VIC 38 G4
Wallacia NSW 21 G9 23 H8
Wallaga Lake Heights NSW 30 G5
Wallaga Lake Nat Park NSW 30 G5
Wallal QLD 15 E13
Wallaloo VIC 38 B7
Wallaloo East VIC 38 B7
Wallamba Nature Res NSW 23 C12
Wallan VIC 39 D14 42 H2
Wallan East VIC 39 D14 42 H2
Wallangarra NSW 7 K10 25 C10
Wallangra NSW 24 D7
Wallany SA 68 B4 90 K4
Wallaroo NSW 32 A2
Wallaroo SA 62 H4 65 G8
Wallaroo Nature Res NSW 23 D11
Wallatinna SA 66 D2 68 C7
Wallaville QLD 7 A11
Wallendbeen NSW 22 K2 29 G14 30 B1
Wallerawang NSW 22 F7
Walleroobie NSW 29 F12
Walli NSW 22 G4
Wallinduc VIC 39 F9
Wallingat Nat Park NSW 23 C12
Wallington VIC 36 H4
Wallon QLD 5 H9
Walloway SA 62 F1 65 E10
Wallpolla Island VIC 40 A3
Walls of Jerusalem Nat Park TAS 52 A6 54 H6
Wallsend NSW 23 E10
Wallumbilla QLD 6 E6
Wallundry NSW 22 J1 29 F14
Wallup VIC 40 K5
Walmer NSW 22 D3
Walpa VIC 43 K10 45 B12 46 D5
Walpeup VIC 28 H3 40 E5
Walpole WA 74 K4
Walpole-Nornalup Nat Park WA 74 K4
Waltara NSW 20 D7
Walu NT 79 J14 90 H2
Walungurru (Kintore) NT 79 G14 90 E1
Walunuju WA 79 A9 80 F5
Walwa VIC 29 K14 43 A11
Walyahmoning Nature Res WA 77 H8
Walyinynga SA 68 A4 90 K4
Walytjatjata NT 68 A1 79 K14 90 K2
Walyunga Nat Park WA 72 F2
Wamberal NSW 20 B4
Wambool Nature Res NSW 22 G6
Wamboyne NSW 29 D13
Wammuta QLD 12 B4
Wamoon NSW 29 F11
Wamuran QLD 4 G4 7 F12
Wamuran Basin QLD 4 G4
Wanaaring NSW 26 D7
Wanagarren Nature Res WA 74 A1 76 J4
Wanbi SA 62 B6 65 J12
Wandana Nature Res WA 76 E4
Wandandian NSW 30 D6
Wandearah East SA 62 G3 65 F9
Wandearah West SA 62 G3 65 F9
Wandella NSW 30 G5
Wandering WA 72 C6 74 E4
Wandiligong VIC 43 E9
Wandilo SA 63 B13
Wandin North VIC 37 C11
Wando Bridge VIC 38 E3
Wando Vale VIC 38 E3
Wandoan QLD 6 D7
Wandong VIC 39 D14 42 H2
Wandoo Con Park WA 72 D4 74 D4 76 K5
Wandsworth NSW 25 F9
Wanganella NSW 29 H8 41 E13
Wangara WA 71 B3
Wangarabell VIC 47 C12
Wangaratta VIC 42 C6
Wangary SA 64 H5
Wangerrip VIC 39 K9
Wangetti QLD 11 C12
Wangkatjungka (Christmas Creek) WA 79 C12 81 K9
Wangoom VIC 38 H7
Wanguri NT 84 A3
Wanilla SA 64 H5
Wanjarri Nature Res WA 77 D10
Wankari NT 79 J14 83 A7 90 H1
Wanko QLD 15 E13
Wanna Lakes WA 83 D6
Wannamal WA 74 B3 76 J5
Wannarn WA 79 J13 83 A6
Wanneroo WA 71 A3 72 G2 74 C2 76 K4
Wanniassa ACT 32 H4
Wannon VIC 38 F4
Wannoo Billabong Roadhouse WA 76 C3
Wanora QLD 5 H8
Wantabadgery NSW 29 H14
Wanwin VIC 38 G2
Wapengo NSW 30 H5
Wapet Camp WA 78 E3
Wappinguy NSW 22 C7
Warakurna WA 79 J13 83 A7
Warakurna Roadhouse WA 79 J13 83 A7
Waramanga ACT 32 G3
Warana QLD 4 D1
Waranga VIC 39 A14 42 D2
Waratah TAS 54 F4
Waratah Bay VIC 44 H6
Waratah North VIC 44 H6
Warburn NSW 29 F10
Warburton VIC 37 C13 42 K4 44 B5
Warburton WA 79 K12 83 B5
Warburton East VIC 37 C13
Warby Range State Park VIC 42 C6
Ward Island SA 64 G3
Wardang Island SA 62 H6 65 H8
Wardell NSW 25 C14
Wards Mistake NSW 25 F10
Wards River NSW 23 C11
Warialda NSW 24 D7
Warianna QLD 13 B10
Warilla NSW 23 K8 30 B7
Warkton NSW 24 K3
Warkworth NSW 23 D9
Warmun WA 81 G13
Warmun (Turkey Creek) WA 79 A14
Warncoort VIC 39 H10
Warneet VIC 37 H10 44 E3
Warnertown SA 62 G3 65 F9
Warnervale NSW 20 B2
Warooka SA 62 H7 65 J8
Waroona WA 72 F7 74 E3
Warra QLD 7 E9
Warra Nat Park NSW 25 F10
Warrabah Nat Park NSW 24 G7
Warrabillinna SA 68 B5 90 K6
Warrabkook VIC 38 G5
Warracknabeal VIC 40 K6
Warradale SA 59 J2
Warraderry NSW 22 G2
Warragamba NSW 21 G10 23 H8
Warragamba VIC 41 K12
Warragoon NSW 29 K11 42 A6
Warragul VIC 37 G14 44 D6
Warrah Creek NSW 23 B8
Warrak VIC 39 D8
Warrambine VIC 39 G10
Warramboo SA 64 F5
Warrandyte VIC 35 C7 37 C9 42 K3 44 B2
Warrandyte State Park VIC 35 B7 37 C9 42 K3 44 B2
Warranmang VIC 39 C9
Warranulla NSW 23 C11
Warrapura WA 83 A7
Warrawee NSW 20 C7
Warrawenia Lake NSW 28 D3
Warrayure VIC 38 F5
Warreah QLD 8 C2 11 K11 13 A11
Warrego Mine NT 89 G8
Warrell Creek NSW 25 H12
Warren NSW 22 A1 27 J14
Warren Con Park SA 60 D5
Warren Nat Park WA 73 F14 74 J3
Warrenbayne VIC 42 E5
Warrenben Con Park SA 62 J7 64 J7
Warrentinna TAS 55 D12
Warriewood NSW 20 B6
Warrigal QLD 8 C2 11 K12 13 A12
Warrill View QLD 5 J11
Warrimoo NSW 21 H8
Warrina SA 66 E6
Warringa TAS 54 E6
Warrion VIC 39 H10
Warrnambool VIC 38 H6
Warrong VIC 38 H6
Warroo NSW 22 F1 29 D13
Warrow SA 64 H5
Warrumbungle NSW 24 J2
Warrumbungle Nat Park NSW 24 J3
Warrupura WA 79 J14 90 H1
Warruwi NT 86 B7
Wartburg QLD 9 K12
Wartook VIC 38 C6
Warup WA 73 A9
Warwick QLD 7 H11 25 A10
Warwick WA 71 C2
Warwick Farm NSW 19 G1
WA-SA Border Village SA 68 K1 83 G7
Wasaga QLD 16 B2
Washpool Nat Park NSW 25 D11
Wasleys SA 60 A3 62 F6 65 H10
Watagan NSW 20 E1
Watagans Nat Park NSW 23 E9
Watalgan QLD 9 K12
Watanobbi NSW 20 B2
Watarrka Nat Park NT 90 G5
Watarru SA 68 C2
Watchem VIC 40 J7
Watchupga VIC 28 K4 40 H7
Waterfall NSW 21 C11 23 J8
Waterfall Gully SA 59 H6
Waterford VIC 43 J10 45 A11 46 C4
Waterford WA 71 H4
Waterhouse TAS 55 D12
Waterhouse Con Area TAS 55 C11
Waterhouse Island TAS 55 C11
Waterloo SA 62 E4 65 G10
Waterloo TAS 50 J1 53 H9
Waterloo VIC 39 D9
Waterloo WA 73 G9
Waterloo Corner SA 59 A3
Waterman WA 71 C1
Watervale SA 62 F4 65 G10
Watgania VIC 38 E7
Watheroo WA 76 H5
Watheroo Nat Park WA 76 H4
Watinuna SA 68 B5
Watson ACT 32 C5
Watson SA 68 H4
Watson Island NT 87 J13 89 A13
Watsonia VIC 35 B5 37 C8
Watsons Bay NSW 19 E7 21 B8
Watsons Creek NSW 25 H8
Watsons Creek VIC 37 B9
Watsons Creek Nature Res NSW 25 H8
Wattamolla NSW 21 B11
Wattamondara NSW 22 H3
Wattle Creek VIC 39 C8
Wattle Flat NSW 22 F6
Wattle Glen VIC 37 B9
Wattle Grove NSW 21 D10
Wattle Grove TAS 50 J2 53 H9
Wattle Grove WA 71 H7
Wattle Hill TAS 51 A10 53 F11
Wattle Island VIC 44 K7 46 K1
Wattle Park SA 59 G6
Wattle Park VIC 46 E6
Wattle Point VIC 45 C13
Wattle Range SA 63 B13
Wattle Vale VIC 39 B14 42 E2
Waubra VIC 39 D10
Wauchope NSW 23 A13 25 K12
Wauchope NT 89 J9 91 A9
Waukaringa SA 62 D1 65 D11
Wauraltee SA 62 H6 65 H8
Waurn Ponds VIC 36 H2 39 H12
Wavell Heights QLD 3 C4
Waverley NSW 19 F7 21 B8
Wayatinah TAS 52 D7
Waychinicup Nat Park WA 74 J7
Waygara VIC 43 K13 47 D8
Wayville SA 58 D2 59 G4
Weabonga NSW 25 J8
Wearkata (Lower Hunter) Nat Park NSW 23 E10
Weavers SA 62 H7 65 J8
Webbs NSW 22 C2
Webbs Creek NSW 20 F4
Wedderburn NSW 21 E12
Wedderburn VIC 41 K10
Wedderburn Junction VIC 41 K10
Weddin Mountains Nat Park NSW 22 H2 29 E14
Wedge Island SA 62 K7 64 J6
Wedge Island TAS 51 H10 53 H11
Wedge Island WA 74 A1 76 J4
Wednesday Island QLD 16 B2
Wee Jasper NSW 30 D2
Wee Waa NSW 24 F4
Weegena TAS 54 F7
Weelhamby Lake WA 76 G5
Weemelah NSW 24 C3
Weemol NT 87 F9
Weerangourt VIC 38 G4
Weerite VIC 39 H9
Weetah TAS 55 F8
Weetaliba NSW 22 A5 24 K4
Weetalibah Nature Res NSW 22 B5
Weetangera ACT 32 C3
Weethalle NSW 29 E12
Weetulta SA 62 H5 65 H8
Wee-Wee-Rup VIC 41 H12
Wehla VIC 39 A10
Weilmoringle NSW 6 K1 27 C12
Weimby NSW 28 G5 41 C8
Weipa QLD 16 E1
Weismantels NSW 23 C11
Weitalaba QLD 9 J11
Weja NSW 29 D12
Welaregang NSW 29 K14 43 B12
Weldborough TAS 55 E12
Welford Lagoon QLD 13 H10 15 A9
Welford Nat Park QLD 13 H9 15 A8
Wellesley Islands QLD 10 C4
Wellingrove NSW 25 E9
Wellington NSW 22 D4
Wellington SA 63 D8 65 K11
Wellington Point QLD 5 C8
Wellsford VIC 39 A12
Wellstead WA 74 J7
Welshmans Reef VIC 39 C11
Welshpool VIC 45 G8 46 H2
Welshpool WA 71 G6
Wembley WA 71 F3
Wembley Downs WA 71 E2
Wemen VIC 28 G4 40 D6
Wentworth NSW 28 F3 40 A4
Wentworth Falls NSW 21 K9 22 G7
Weranga QLD 7 F8
Werneth VIC 39 G10
Werombi NSW 21 G11 23 H8
Werrap VIC 40 H4
Werribee VIC 36 E5 39 F13 42 K1
Werribee Gorge State Park VIC 36 B3 39 E12
Werribee South VIC 36 E5 39 G13
Werrikimbe Nat Park NSW 25 J10
Werrimull VIC 28 F2 40 B3
Werrington NSW 21 G8
Werris Creek NSW 24 K7
Wesburn VIC 37 C12
Wesley Vale TAS 54 E7
Wessel Islands NT 87 B12
West Beach SA 59 G2 60 G1 61 A5
West Bore No. 2 SA 68 B5
West Cape Howe Nat Park WA 74 K6
West End QLD 2 D1 3 E3 5 E8
West Frankford TAS 55 E8 56 F1
West Gosford NSW 20 C4
West Group WA 75 H12 83 J1
West Hill QLD 9 E8
West Hill Island QLD 9 E9
West Hill Nat Park QLD 9 E9
West Hobart TAS 49 C1
West Hoxton NSW 21 E10
West Island NT 87 J12 89 A12
West Island QLD 16 B1
West Island SA 61 K6
West Island Con Park SA 61 K6
West Kentish TAS 54 F7
West Killara NSW 21 C8
West Lakes SA 59 E1 60 F1
West MacDonnell Nat Park NT 90 F7
West Pennant Hills NSW 19 C2
West Perth WA 70 A1 71 F3
West Pine TAS 54 E6
West Pymble NSW 19 D4 20 C7
West Ridgley TAS 54 E5
West Ryde NSW 19 E4
West Scottsdale TAS 55 E11
West Swan WA 71 C6
West Wyalong NSW 29 E13
Westbourne Park SA 59 H4
Westbury TAS 55 G9 56 H2
Westby NSW 29 J13
Westby VIC 28 J7 41 G11
Westdale WA 72 D5
Western Creek TAS 54 G7
Western Flat SA 38 A1 63 B11
Western Junction TAS 55 G10 56 J6
Western Port VIC 37 H10
Western River SA 63 J8 64 K7
Western River Con Park SA 63 J8 64 K7
Westerway TAS 53 E8
Westfield WA 71 K7
Westgate QLD 15 D14
Westmar QLD 6 H6
Westmead NSW 19 E2
Westmeadows VIC 35 A2
Westmere VIC 39 F8
Westminster WA 71 D3
Weston ACT 32 F3
Weston Creek ACT 32 F2
Westonia WA 74 B7 77 J8
Westwood QLD 9 H9
Westwood TAS 55 F9 56 H4
Wetherill Park NSW 21 E9
Weymouth TAS 55 D10 56 B5
Whale Beach NSW 20 B6
Wharminda SA 64 G6
Wharparilla VIC 41 J13 42 B1
Whealbah NSW 29 E9
Wheelers Hill VIC 35 F6
Wheeo NSW 22 K5 30 B4
Wherrol Flat NSW 23 B12
Whetstone QLD 7 J9 25 A8
Whidbey Isles Con Park SA 64 J4
Whim Creek WA 78 E5 82 C3
Whiporie NSW 25 D13
Whipstick State Park VIC 39 A12
Whirily VIC 41 H8
White Beach TAS 51 H11 53 H12
White Cliffs NSW 26 G5
White Flag Lake WA 77 H11
White Flat SA 64 H6
White Gum Valley WA 71 J2
White Hills TAS 55 F10 56 H6
White Hut SA 62 J7 64 J7
White Lake WA 79 J8
White Mountains Nat Park QLD 8 C2 11 K12 13 A11
Whitefoord TAS 53 D11
Whiteheads Creek VIC 42 F3
Whiteman WA 71 C5
Whitemark TAS 55 C9
Whitemore TAS 55 G9 56 J3
Whitewood QLD 13 B9
Whitfield VIC 42 E7
Whitsunday Group QLD 9 B8
Whitsunday Island QLD 9 B8
Whitsunday Islands Nat Park QLD 9 B8
Whittlesea VIC 37 A8 39 E14 42 J2 44 A2
Whitton NSW 29 F11
Whitwarta SA 62 F5 65 G9
Whoorel VIC 39 H10
Whorouly VIC 42 D7
Whorouly South VIC 42 D7
Whroo VIC 39 A14 42 D2
Whyalla SA 62 H2 65 E8
Whyalla Con Park SA 62 H2 65 E8
Whyte Island QLD 3 D7 4 D7
Whyte-Yarcowie SA 62 E3 65 F10
Wialki WA 76 H7
Wiangaree NSW 7 J12 25 B13
Wickepin WA 74 E6
Wickham WA 78 E4 82 C2
Wickliffe VIC 38 F7
Widden NSW 22 D7
Wide Bay QLD 7 C13
Widgelli NSW 29 F11
Widgiemooltha WA 75 B12 77 K11 83 G1
Widgiewa NSW 29 H11
Wigram Island NT 87 C12
Wigton Island QLD 9 C9
Wilandspey Con Park QLD 8 E4 13 B14
Wilban WA 83 F4
Wilberforce NSW 20 F6
Wilburville TAS 53 B9 55 J9
Wilby VIC 42 B6
Wilcannia NSW 26 H5
Wild Duck Island Nat Park QLD 9 E9
Wild Horse Plains SA 62 G5 65 H9
Wildcat Bore SA 68 C6
Wilga WA 73 E11
Wilgarup WA 73 E13
Wilgena SA 64 A4 66 K4
Wilkatana SA 65 D9
Wilkawatt SA 63 B8 65 K12
Wilkie Island QLD 16 G4
Wilkinson Lakes SA 66 H1 68 F6
Willa VIC 40 F5
Willalooka SA 63 C10
Willandra Lakes World Heritage Area NSW 28 D5
Willandra Nat Park NSW 29 C8
Willangie VIC 40 G7
Willara Crossing NSW 15 K10 26 C7
Willare Bridge Roadhouse WA 79 B10 80 G5
Willatook VIC 38 H5
Willaura VIC 38 E7
Willawarrin NSW 25 J11
Willawong QLD 3 H3 5 E9
Willbriggie NSW 29 F11
Willenabrina VIC 40 J5
Willetton WA 71 J4
Willi Willi SA 68 B1 79 K14 90 K2
Willi Willi Nat Park NSW 25 J11
William Bay WA 74 K5
William Bay Nat Park WA 74 K5